INTIMATE READING

Writing American Women
Carol Kolmerten, *Series Editor*

INTIMATE
READING

The Contemporary Women's Memoir

JANET MASON ELLERBY

SYRACUSE UNIVERSITY PRESS

First Edition 2001
01 02 03 04 05 06   6 5 4 3 2 1

The names and other identifying details of some major and minor characters have been changed to protect individual privacy.

The paper used in this publication meets the minimum requirements of American National Standard for Information Sciences—Permanence of Paper for Printed Library Materials, ANSI Z39.48–1984.∞™

Library of Congress Cataloging-in-Publication Data
Ellerby, Janet Mason.
    Intimate reading : the contemporary women's memoir / Janet Mason Ellerby.—1st ed.
      p. cm—(Writing American women)
    Includes bibliographical references.
    ISBN 0-8156-2886-2 (alk. paper)—ISBN 0-8156-0685-0 (pbk.: alk. paper)
    1. American prose literature—Women authors—History and criticism. 2. Autobiography—Women authors. 3. American prose literature—20th century—History and criticism. 4. Women and literature—United States—History—20th century. 5. Women authors, American—Biography—History and criticism. I. Title. II. Series.
PS366.A88 E44 2001
810.9'492072—dc21   00-050523

For you, John

How can this be? How can any of this have really happened? And now I wonder, Should I write about this? Should I sit in the mornings and try to remember her, bring it all back, every detail. . . . Should I go over and over what shouldn't have been? Should I keep looking at what, in the end, is so unbearable?

I'm not sure. But is there really an alternative? For here was a life . . . to write her name is a painful comfort. It holds close what I can't let go, and what I can't forget.

There is nothing in this life without a marker.

—William Loizeaux

Janet Mason Ellerby has a doctorate from the University of Washington. She is an associate professor of English and women's studies at the University of North Carolina at Wilmington.

CONTENTS

ACKNOWLEDGMENTS

This book would not have been possible without the priceless, uninterrupted time that the University of North Carolina at Wilmington gave me to research and write. For that quiet semester of reflection I am extremely grateful.

I am indebted to Amy Farranto, my editor at Syracuse University Press, for her enthusiasm, encouragement, and gentleness in helping me see how this book could be better, and to Annette Wenda, whose meticulous editing added so much and whose patience and kindness were palpable all the way from Oregon. And I am grateful to Diane Freedman, whose careful reading of my manuscript and knowledge of the field of autobiographical criticism allowed me to revise more intelligently. Finally, to Nancy Venable Raines, whose book *After Silence* taught me about trauma and how to interpret it in my own life.

The book would also not have been possible without the support of my women friends who encouraged me to write not just for my own healing but also for other women who they convinced me should know this story. Thanks go to my faraway but ever faithful friends, all of whom read the memoir and then called me immediately to tell me they loved me: Karen Courington, Julie Chappell, and Moira MacDonald. Much gratitude also goes to the extraordinary women who were there for me on that first reading and have stayed by me throughout the writing process: Sally Sullivan, Barbara Waxman, Kathleen Halme, Betsy Ervin, Rebecca Lee, and Maggie Parish. My gratefulness also extends to Lindsay Aegerter, Andrea Deagon, Yael Gold, Devon White Hickey, Amy Keith, and Lu Ellen Huntley for their unswerving support. My thanks goes to my students who have served as a receptive and accepting audience as I have struggled with my own "coming out," especially Donna Packer-Kinlaw, Shannon McCreery, Helen Liseno, and Agnes MacDonald. My gratitude also extends to my sister- and brother-in-law, Mary Ellen and Bob Allen, for reading my memoir and responding with such gracious affection that I knew I was a true member of their family too. My loving thankfulness goes to my sisters and their husbands, Anne Ellerby Andreasen and Ray Andreasen and Katharine Ellerby Andrew and John Andrew, for reading my manuscript and encouraging me to tell not just my story but the family stories that belong to them as well. I also want to thank my parents and my aunts for understanding why I had to write this book even though its telling is especially saddening for them. Most important, I want to thank my husband, John Patrick Clifford, for supporting me emotionally through this long and intricate undertaking, for reading and responding to just about every word that I wrote, and for helping me to create a world of honesty for us to live in together. And finally, I want to thank my children, Todd Anthony De Puy, Helen Marie De Puy, and Kezia Anne De Puy, for reading these chapters, for coming to know their mother as well as she knows herself, and for steadfastly loving her with an unconditional love that always amazes and makes me rich in this world.

INTRODUCTION

Eight years ago, an editor who was considering my dissertation for publication suggested that I take a few weeks to write an autobiographical
introduction to the manuscript and then resubmit it. In the dissertation,
titled "Repetition and Redemption" (1989), I take three hundred pages to
elucidate creative and compulsive repetition. My abstract reads: "The
heart of the dissertation is a series of readings of a variety of texts in
which each autobiographer has lost a clear, sufficient sense of selfhood
and undertakes the task of self-narration in the belief that a repetition of
the past will reconstitute a self that will serve the present more effi-
ciently." The prescient editor wanted me to provide a personal account
of the kind of reinterpretation I was theorizing about, suggesting I use
Jane Tompkins's essay "Me and My Shadow" as a model. Suddenly embarrassed by my manuscript, which apparently hinted at significant trouble in my own past, I tucked it away in the far corner of the bottom shelf
of a bookcase that stands behind our large easy chair. I did not return the
editor's subsequent considerate phone message, and I never went back to
the dissertation, not even to mine individual chapters for conference papers or journal articles.

Unknowingly, the editor had suggested a task that I was emotionally
unprepared to tackle. To write what he wanted would have required that
I reveal what I had kept hidden for most of my life, that I narrate an event
that was fundamental to my sense of selfhood but was also a personal and
family secret.

Seven years later, different circumstances afforded me the emotional
support and motivation to attempt what had been so ingenuously suggested. I decided to try to narrate my story, using the memoir as the
genre to guide me. Determined now to tell my secret, I sought other
writers who had decided to tell their secrets. I looked for support and in-

spiration by reading memoirs by women whose experiences struck an intuitive emotional response in me. As I tentatively began the writing process, I relied on fellow memoirists in the same way I have relied on intimate women friends. I sought that corresponding puissant connection and imagined a circle of fellow women memoirists just as I have created my circle of women friends. I followed my heart, trusting the warm assurance that came unexpectedly but irrefutably when I found common threads of identity among the complex richness of our diversity.

Because I was reading specifically for psychological support, I had no interest in a balanced reading list giving equal representation to race, gender, and class differences, as I do when I create reading syllabi for the literature courses I teach. I set aside for another day culturally and artistically significant memoirs such as Toi Derricote's *Black Notebooks*, Lorene Cary's *Black Ice*, and Shirley Geok-lin Lim's *Among the White Moon Faces* that speak eloquently of racial self-division. Nor did I turn to memoirs that bear witness to poverty or racism such as Rosemary L. Bray's *Unafraid of the Dark* and bell hooks's *Bone Black*, or compelling memoirs about physical disability and stigma such as Nancy Mairs's *Waist High in the World* and Lucy Grealy's *Autobiography of a Face*. Because of my emotional disposition, because I let my heart guide my reading, the selections herein do not begin to recognize the rich diversity that can and should be found when reading a comprehensive list of women memoirists writing in America today. I had more specific goals: as I wrote, I read for private understanding and a sense of intimate comradeship as I set out on my own perilous journey of personal revelation.[1] I turned to particular women memoirists for sustenance, empathy, and guidance, for confirmation rather than expansion.

My psychological needs also determined the kind of memoirs I read.

---

1. Because I was dealing specifically with the process of revelation, I focused on memoirs that were confessional in crucial ways. However, there were other autobiographies and memoirs tied more directly to the writing life that significantly inspired me and showed me ways to proceed. For example, Alice Kaplan's *French Lessons: A Memoir* assured me that the emotional disturbance I felt throughout the writing process would make me capable of writing better than I ever had before (1993, 194). Bell hooks's *Wounds of Passion: A Writing Life* taught me the value of writing "intimately about the pleasure and the pain" in order to "document the psychological and philosophical foundations of one woman's writing life" (1997, xxiii); Jane Tompkins's *Life in School: What the Teacher Learned* prodded me once again to "let experience speak" (1996, xix).

From girlhood on, my personal reading habits have led me to novels by and about women. Because I have always used reading as a means to elude the anxieties, urgencies, and sorrows of "real life," I have also found that the longer the novel, the better. The longer I could stay in Dorothea's *Middlemarch*, for example, the more soothed and appeased were the worries and needs that had prompted me to flee the reality of my own world when I opened the book in the first place. This predilection for longer texts has not changed. Consequently, despite the current abundant array of exceptional personal essays and mixed-genre memoirs I had to choose from, I gravitated to book-length memoirs that had the novelistic girth I had sought for so long. I could still temporarily dodge my own surroundings and, at the same time, bolster myself with the ephemeral companionship of women whose life experiences had something in common with my own. Rather than assuming the guise of the rational male critical reader that I had learned to don when reading as a scholar, I allowed myself to read like a woman—emotionally, intuitively, and lovingly.[2]

As I nurtured my writing by reading, I found that, like me, many memoirists were struggling with the painful consequences of family secrets. Whether initiated by us or for us, family secrets once established become important components of our families' modi operandi. Keeping their intricate complexities hidden demands scrupulous attention. Yet, lately, our culture has encouraged us to lay our secrets down for public display. With dismay, we see them sensationalized on daily talk shows. Nevertheless, we also sense that their telling in the right forum can be an integral step to recovery. As I read, I was struck by the urgency my fellow memoirists felt to disclose truths on the way to recovering a more authentic identity. Over the months of reading and writing, writing and reading, I gathered an ensemble of American women memoirists of which I am a part. We are surprisingly close in age and education; though there are exceptions, many of us grew up with the privileges and limitations of white middle-class America. But most important, my fel-

2. In "Reading as a Woman," Jonathan Culler describes this developing theoretical position. A reader, who is reading as a woman, asserts the continuity between women's experience of social and familial structures. Experience—her own and others'—is set in a vital and productive relation to the text and becomes a firm ground for interpretation (1982, 63).

low memoirists and I were no longer willing to harbor the secrets of our pasts.[3] In a sense, I constructed a supportive writing group so that I needed not write in isolation; instead, I wrote within a compassionate assemblage of women, each of us entrusting our secrets to one another.

At a pivotal point in the writing and reading process, I realized I wanted to write not only about my past but also about the intimate reading and writing process I had created, to discuss the remarkable, recuperative influence that my fellow memoirists had on me. I was intrigued by the cultural and psychological circumstances that had elicited our revelations. In her memoir, *Vertigo,* Louise De Salvo explains that "talking about books" verified for her that the feelings she struggled with "alone in the solitary space of [her] private suffering were shared by other people" (1996, 6). Like De Salvo, I wanted to discuss the books I was reading, books by women like me, struggling but not disabled by pain. Self-understanding surely comes from self-reflection, but it also comes from reading and from writing about what we read. Taking my cue from Jane Tompkins, as that long-ago editor had suggested, I began my blend of autobiography and literary analysis, trying to capture the intimate interior confluence I was experiencing as writer, reader, and critic of the contemporary memoir. Inevitably, my scholarly training as an English professor did influence my reading. To use the literary critic Louise Rosenblatt's terminology, my "aesthetic" reading eventually evolved into "efferent" reading (1994, 24–25). In other words, emotional resonance led to intellectual complexity and subsequently the need for analysis. I found myself transacting with my growing list of memoirs like the literary critic I had worked to become.

As cultural critic, I became intrigued by the surprising popularity of the memoir in contemporary literature and the cultural conditions that have allowed for the recent attention the genre has garnered. As feminist and psychoanalytic critic, I was drawn to the psychological difficulties and the emotionally charged gender issues with which many memoirs deal. As a teacher of women's studies, I was motivated by the affirmative

---

3. If I had not been motivated to write this book exclusively in the company of women, I could easily have expanded my gathering of memoirists writing about family secrecy and its psychological costs to include contemporary men as well. The following were especially evocative for me: Mikal Gilmore's *Shot in the Heart,* Richard Rhodes's *Hole in the World,* and James Ellroy's *My Dark Places.*

significance of hearing and learning from the stories other women have to tell.

In deciding not only to write my own memoir but also to explore and analyze the relationship of my narrative to others, I join an emerging field of autobiographical scholarship and a highly regarded group of feminist critics. Esteemed writers such as Susan Griffin and Adrienne Rich have established models for this new approach that has been augmented by equally innovative feminist synthesizers of autobiography and theory such as Jane Gallop, Gloria Anzaldua, Diane P. Freedman, Brenda Daly, bell hooks, Nancy K. Miller, and, of course, Jane Tompkins.[4] In *The Intimate Critique*, editors Diane Freedman, Olivia Frey, and Frances Murphy Zauhar provided me compelling examples of criticism that resist "formal distance and conventional hierarchies of what has been termed . . . the 'male' mode of rhetoric." Instead, the editors call for the "female" mode: "open-ended, generative, and process-oriented" (1993, 2). Not only is Tompkins's influential essay included in this collection, but Shirley Nelson Garner takes a path similar to my own, discussing the ways that her great-great-grandmother's secret—her two illegitimate children—evoked her own uniquely personal response to Maxine Hong Kingston's "No-Name Woman." At the close of their introduction, the editors declare, "We deeply hope that the variety of voices and locations presented here will call forth more voices out of the void" (10). Their example has enabled me to step out of the void, join their efforts, and find encouragement in the precedent they have established for me.[5]

Intimate Reading, then, begins with my own memoir, "Bearing Sorrow."

4. These authors have guided me by their examples in the following books: Susan Griffin in *Made from This Earth, Woman and Nature: The Roaring Inside Her,* and *What Her Body Thought;* Adrienne Rich in *Of Woman Born;* Jane Gallop in *Thinking Through the Body;* Gloria Anzaldua in *Borderlands/La Frontera;* Diane Freedman in *An Alchemy of Genres;* Brenda Daly in *Authoring a Life;* bell hooks in *Talking Back;* and Nancy K. Miller in *Getting Personal: Feminist Occasions and Other Autobiographical Acts.*

5. Beyond *The Intimate Critique* are other predecessors that deserve mention. For example, in the foreword to Nancy Owen Nelson's *Private Voices, Public Lives,* Jane Tompkins encourages readers and writers to find parallels and solace in the writing of others (1995, xiv). In this collection, I found a significant compatriot in fellow autobiographical critic Melody Graulich. Graulich struggled with infertility caused by the Dalkon Shield and an insensitive, cruel doctor. She prefaces her essay with the same quote by Isak Dinesen that I use as epilogue for my own memoir. By way of Gwendolyn Brooks's poem "The Mother," Graulich discovers a "fundamental truth of feminist criticism: one cannot fully

Here I reveal and analyze my own secret as well as the long and complex processes of deception that accompanied it. Not too long ago, the cultural ideology that prescribed a commitment to superficial appearances was still firmly rooted in America. I examine that commitment, its eventual erosion, and the damaging psychological consequences of maintaining my secret for decades.

In chapter 2, I discuss the cultural shift from sanctioned secrecy in the fifties to today's clinical and social encouragement to tell all. Because secrets are complexly nested, I delve into the practice of secret keeping in my own family history, examining two events that laid the groundwork for my own required secrecy.

Chapter 3 sets the critical pattern for the rest of the book. I begin with a literary analysis of shame and explore its ramifications in Suzannah Lessard's *Architect of Desire* and Mary Karr's *Liar's Club*. At germane moments in this analysis, I blend in relevant portions of my own memoir, hoping the juxtaposition of analysis and autobiography will illuminate both. This technique is central to my idea that the memoir calls for an intimate reading, and it becomes the recurring critical motif of the book. When we agree to keep family secrets, we do so out of shame and fear of rejection. Secrecy allows families to maintain their respectability; however, the Lessard and Karr memoirs demonstrate that the habit of secrecy can be damaging. Narration can heal; telling our secrets can be transformative. These memoirs demonstrate how the revelation of family secrets can put an end to family legacies of violation and shame.

In chapter 4, I ponder the genuine risks of intimate revelation. Memoirists especially wish for reading communities that will read them with compassion. *The Kiss* by Kathryn Harrison, Dani Shapiro's *Slow Motion*, and Caroline Knapp's *Drinking: A Love Story* confront one of our culture's most compelling and problematic performances: the narrating of dysfunction and addiction. These memoirs serve as catalysts for us to interrogate ethical givens and keep open the social processes by which moral

---

claim one's own experience without seeing it—or variations of it—explored in literature" (1995, 167). Other texts important to this emerging field of autobiographical criticism include Louise De Salvo's *Writing as a Way of Healing*, Paula Marantz Cohen's *Daughter as Reader*, Suzanne Juhasz's *Reading from the Heart*, Ruth Behar's *Vulnerable Observer*, Patricia Hampl's *I Could Tell You Stories*, and my colleague Barbara Frey Waxman's *To Live in the Center of the Moment: Literary Autobiographies of Aging*.

tenets are reconstituted. Rather than feeding preconceptions, such narratives can beget the awareness, forbearance, and compassion upon which families and communities can be nourished and secured.

In chapter 5, I examine narratives of sexuality. Today we confront sexual stories in all kinds of venues, but because of their specificity and appeal, memoirs can reinforce or amend dominant cultural narratives. Mia Farrow's *What Falls Away*, Dorothy Allison's *Two or Three Things I Know for Sure*, and Claudia Bepko's *Heart's Progress* enable us to rethink sexual codes in dialectical tension rather than as pretheoretical absolutes or monolithic "rules."

In chapter 6, I explore trauma. Nancy Venable Raine's *After Silence: Rape and My Journey Back* and Linda Cutting's *Memory Slips* demonstrate the damaging consequences of personal and cultural denial. Because traumatic memories are so harrowing, discomfiting, and often unjustly degrading, survivors agree to suppress the truth of their experience. By breaking the silence, memoirs by survivors can be informative. They provide us with narratives that can foster clearer understanding of what it means to be a victim and a survivor. In so doing, they extend possibilities for more conscientious attitudes and concerned activism.

In chapter 7, I discuss memoirs that elucidate struggles with psychiatric illness. Susanna Kaysen's *Girl, Interrupted*, Kay Redfield Jamison's *Unquiet Mind*, and Lauren Slater's *Prozac Diary* help us interpret our culture's conflicted responses to the mentally ill. These memoirs give us strategies for examining our responses to disorders such as borderline personality, manic depression, anorexia, and obsessive compulsion. They contest unfeeling and uninformed prejudices against psychological debilities.

Chapter 8 asks the question, "Who can tell?" The decision to open a secret rightfully belongs to an individual when it primarily concerns her life. However, when a secret involves others, we must examine the grounds for invading their privacy and revealing what they may wish to keep concealed. Lillian Ross's *Here but Not Here*, Joyce Maynard's *At Home in the World*, and Jamaica Kincaid's *My Brother* provide instructive examples of what motivates memoirists to narrate certain stories.

In chapter 9, I conclude the book by focusing on honesty in memoirs. Although "truth" immediately raises postmodern eyebrows, I argue that it is still important to affirm its centrality, and that memoirists are working hard to get at the truer rendition of their pasts. In *The Shadow Man*, Mary Gordon pursues the truth about her father. Her effort is more than worthwhile. Integrity is a crucial dynamic for ethical energy, and the cultural appeal of the memoir is our recognition of and respect for the writer's bid for honesty.

I have lined up the memoirs that I have discussed on the shelf above my word processor. They look down on me with encouraging beneficence. These memoirists have become a circle of friends; I have spent valuable time alone with them, listening to the secrets they have confided to me. As I have followed the threads of their stories, they have shown me how to reveal my own.

The memoir wants to teach us about living through and overcoming adversity. It can demonstrate how honesty can guide us toward transformation, stability, and empowerment. But honesty does not spontaneously issue from our souls; it must be created. Adrienne Rich observes, "Truthfulness is not something which springs ablaze of itself; it has to be created between people" (1979, 193). Memoirs show us how to tell our truths.

Rather than suppress our emotions, memoirs invite us to respond with a concomitant heartfelt resonance. They call forth intimate connections. Although we may have been taught by conventional literary criticism that our personal, passionate responses need to be tempered, the memoirist reignites our ardor, sensitivity, and empathy.

Memoirists write not just for self-awareness but to confront the moral dilemmas of a dissonant culture. If we are to be rigorous interrogators of dominant ideology, we can learn from memoirs not to flatten the complexity of lived experience into fanciful bumper stickers like "Girls kick ass" or one-line axioms such as "Bloom where you are planted." American culture is far from being unilaterally conducive to women's physical and psychological well-being and empowerment. Memoirs give us morally charged individual circumstances where we cannot merely go through codified reading rituals. Zygmunt Bauman wants us to shun the predictable response by engaging in morally charged "liminal" situations, for "they are the soil in which moral subjects germinate, grow, blossom and fade" (1993, 54). The memoir offers a threshold from which we step into the dynamic, complex experience of real women's lives where we are not passive observers and from which we do not reemerge unchanged.

When ethical choices are located within the diverse narratives of real people and then subjected to open critique, the rigid criteria of right and wrong are less easily applied. The specificity of the memoir does not allow for superficial interpretation or knee-jerk censure. In exploring the ethical contradictions within a memoir, we can explore the moral contradictions within ourselves, seeing more clearly how dominant discourses have written us. Reading a memoir will not efface our deeply held convictions, but our narrative engagement can energize our ongoing scrutiny of those convictions. The memoirist does not install an alternative code of ethics, but she does ask us to examine the ethical agenda we bring to her narrative. The memoir helps us to embrace the ambiguities of the postmodern without being paralyzed by them.

As I study again my shelf of memoirs, I realize that I have dwelt on the sorrows, the horrors, and the losses within women's lives. Certainly, not all memoirs by women focus on affliction, trauma, and burden. As a unique reader propelled by my own history, I needed to find fellow travelers to support me as I bore my own sorrow and wrote my own memoir. Above me I see survivors of incest, rape, addiction, homophobia, mental illness, abandonment, and betrayal. I ask myself, "When will emotional ruthlessness and physical violation come to an end? Should I be content with my comfortable life given the horror intrinsic to too many women's lives?"

Here is the paradox: to be fully aware of the darkness in ourselves and in our culture yet continue to pursue moral and compassionate goals. The memoir offers one clear answer: seek empathy, living our lives as a worthy expression of care. By framing our stories in an ethic of candor, by detailing our situatedness, and exploring and contesting through reading and writing the moral values and cultural expectations we have inherited, we can all become more connected. Looking beyond our own needs and goals, we can come to respect and commit ourselves to those requirements and objectives of others.

Finally, if our narratives cannot always offer us the pellucid map we long for in our quest for a safer, more just, more benevolent world, if our stories do not always lead us to a clear horizon of resolution and closure, they may, we hope, lead us to a greater measure of understanding of the ineluctable past.

INTIMATE READING

1

BEARING SORROW

All sorrows can be borne if you put them into a story.—Isak Dinesen

1

The baby has been left behind. She is back on the other side of the seared, rolling hills we traversed all afternoon to get to this green valley where we have come to live. I must have forgotten to put her in the car when we gathered up all the picnic supplies and clambered in. Like the infant Oedipus, she has no shelter from the heat, since I left her lying on her back on a blanket in the middle of the hot, sunny meadow where we stopped. She is not old enough to turn over or crawl away. I begin to panic as I picture her, her tiny fists flailing and her feet kicking the air. It is still warm, but evening will be coming on, and she will soon feel the chill and be easy prey for the gaunt fox or the voracious raccoon that will come to gaze at her from the cover of the surrounding woods. Although many of us came in the car, I can find no one to drive me back to the meadow. The dust-laden, gray car has disappeared. I start running up the first long hill, but I am immediately drained of energy. My legs are dream heavy; I can barely make any progress up the scorched road, and I know there are many more hills between me and the meadow where the baby is. I try to walk fast, but I can only inch my way up the steep incline.

The next night, I put the baby down for her nap, and seeing that she is sleeping peacefully, I decide to get busy repairing the phantasmagoric disorder of the house we live in. I have many tasks to complete, and they take me hours: the other children need attention, some meals have to be prepared, and necessary errands lead me through a Dickensian maze of unknown, empty streets and shuttered shops. I suddenly realize that two days have passed, and I have not returned to the room where she is sleeping to get her out of her crib. Surely she has been wailing for someone to

3

come and get her. How could I have not heard her crying? I know she is dead; I have not been there to care for her. I approach the door that I myself closed two days ago after I had gently laid her down; everything is insufferably still. I stand in front of the door, paralyzed. I cannot make myself open the door.

My nightmares are always unsettling because they always involve a baby I have lost—a baby I can never find. I have never dreamed of the car that could take me swiftly, skimming back over the hills; I have neither reached the meadow, nor swung wide the door. When I awake, I am always gloomy—easily brought to tears and hopelessly lethargic. But I have learned over the years to adroitly reimmerse myself in my active and fortunate life, and my sullen dread of yet another vacant day gradually ebbs.

On a recent afternoon in my professional world—a university campus—I sit in a meeting with my female colleagues. We are discussing a women's conference we are planning for the spring. The theme will be "Many Women—Many Stories." I have offered to chair a panel on motherhood. I want to ask representative women to talk about their relationships with their daughters and with their mothers: a discussion of differences and similarities. Someone else, I suggest, could tell the story about her decision not to have children and another about her experience with the "empty-nest syndrome." My colleagues are enthusiastic about the idea.

One of my fellow organizers suggests two other women for the panel. One has adopted a biracial child, and another was herself adopted at six months after being abandoned by her mother. I am paralyzed for a moment. Then my heart begins to pound, and my chest clenches. My enthusiasm has evaporated, but I have to respond to her suggestion. I gather myself up and push through this anguishing intrusion.

"On the other hand," I observe with a convincing veneer of composure, "such a panel may be too unwieldy, and perhaps we would be asking women to tell stories that are too personal." I calmly promise my colleagues that I will rethink the panel's feasibility. My armpits are drenched, my hands freezing, my breathing shallow.

The next time we meet, I have an entirely different plan. "This one," I note, "can be more carefully orchestrated; it is timely; and it is necessary since we want to get funding from the medical center." Instead of motherhood, I propose a panel on women's health issues. My revamped contribution is quickly approved.

Such interludes invariably grip me, disturbing my outward façade momentarily, until I nimbly navigate the treacherous ground someone's innocent words have opened ahead. I can account for my nightmares and for such moments of anxiety that intrude upon my work, but I have been loath to tell the secrets that animate these scenes from my conscious and subconscious life.

2

I have guarded a secret for thirty-five years. I have told only a few people. Others know because they helped create its script, and a few others know because someone else told them. The secret itself is not an uncommon one, but that fact has not lessened its unique effects on me. Although the event itself happened more than three decades ago, its command over me has never diminished. Strangely, I can write the secret down with a surprising measure of calm deliberation, but I still cannot speak it without experiencing an instantaneous catch in my throat, serious trouble inhaling, and such a clenching in my chest that I have great difficulty speaking at all.

The fervent necessity to keep the secret has kept me isolated from many kind people who have wanted to know me. When I told it in the past, the repercussions were severe, even calamitous, and confirmed, I believed, the necessity for my vigilant circumspection. A long time ago, I agreed to keep the secret so that I could be free to chart my life without the entanglements of shame. But my shame became not only a wound in itself but also a far more stringent master than anyone could have envisioned. Now I need to tell.

3

On a June night, three weeks past my sixteenth birthday, I met secretly with my boyfriend, Alec, two years older than I, newly graduated, and bound for university in the fall. I had been proudly wearing his St. Christopher medal, which meant that we were "going steady," for more than a year. Our relationship had all the clamoring ardor of first love, and the sexual urgency between us had been building slowly but insistently. I was not only a diffident and unsophisticated teenager, but also trusting, submissive, and afraid of losing him to his upcoming university pursuits.

We met alone at his parents' house, and after resisting months of intensifying sexual pressure, I acquiesced. We stubbornly, if not tenderly, managed intercourse on a nubby, worn, avocado-green couch in their living room, gloomily lit by the gray light of their black-and-white TV. I have no idea how much he appreciated that experience—a first for both of us. He was completely silent throughout, and I was too mortified by the awkward difficulty to begin to gauge his emotions. I was abashed by my incapacity to feel even a glimmer of the sexual rapture I had anticipated; instead, I was acutely aware of the messiness of my blood on that atrocious couch.

I cannot reweave the scene into a romantic narrative of passionate young love finally consummated and sealed. There was no mysterious melding of two into one, no lingering kisses, no sweet murmuring, no sexual afterglow. Instead, as soon as he withdrew and I realized we had accomplished our "task," I quickly pulled up my pants. Trembling with fear rather than desire, I frantically scrubbed at the stained couch. When we said good-bye at his front door, he seemed to be admonishing me, warning, "You can't ever let me do it 'like that' again." What did he mean? I was far too shy to ask him anything about what had just happened between us. He told me to go home and take a hot bath—as hot as I could stand it.

I drove myself home, forlorn and weeping softly over the utterly unromantic turn of events, distressed already by a clear premonition of impending loss. Would the cliché prove true? Would he stop loving me because I had given in to his sexual insistence? I painstakingly took that hot bath. Only then, as I watched the thin thread of blood still weaving out of my vagina, dissipating into the scalding water, did it occur to me that he might have ejaculated inside of me. I left two days later for summer camp, carefully packing a box of sanitary pads because I knew I would menstruate during my four-week absence.

There was no need for my scrupulous packing. As I tramped up and down the steep, rugged trails of the High Sierra, I kept hoping that if I just pushed on hard enough, or got to a high-enough altitude, or carried a heavy-enough pack, or jumped into an icy-enough mountain stream, my period would start and the nightmare that was slowly taking shape would evaporate. At night, I would choose an especially rocky spot for my sleeping bag; then I would pound on my stomach and knead it roughly—nothing changed.

For years, the rituals of summer camp had been a haven for me from the anxieties of girlhood and adolescence caused by being one of the tallest girls in my class (and far taller than the boys). The vigorous camp activities in which I excelled had let me leave behind my insecurities about my body's size and, instead, appreciate my height and athleticism. But that summer, nothing could quell my anxious preoccupation with my body. Even the intensely pleasurable abandon I had felt as I smoothly cantered bareback across the camp meadows was replaced by my desperate, secret prayer that maybe riding-induced jolts would be the thing to start my bleeding. That summer, I made myself bounce along with the less experienced riders, keeping my restless horse at an awkward, impatient trot. Although I received a couple of perfunctory letters from Alec, I did not write back to him. I could not fathom what to say; it was much easier to pretend he was not a crucial player in my unfolding future. After four distressing weeks away, I threw the sanitary pads I had packed down an outhouse toilet and returned home.

I concealed my secret from everyone for the rest of that summer, even myself. I could not accept that I was pregnant, so I did not tell—not even Alec. In fact, I could no longer call him my boyfriend because when I returned from camp, I learned he was dating a girl his age named Candy. She was a wild girl, pretty and bold, and I was decisively outclassed. I was unhappy about this turn of events, but also relieved. I could remain in denial and go back to being a blameless sixteen-year-old girl, opportunely freed from his sexual persistence and capable of finding plenty of enticing distractions and uncomplicated fun.

One of my girlfriends lived with her family in Balboa Beach, and I spent as much of the remainder of that summer with her as my parents would permit. As long as I beat back panicky thoughts about the end of summer, I could be foolishly carefree, heedless of all eventualities. We rode the little ferry back and forth between Balboa and Newport Beach, strolling, idling, swimming, tanning. I refused to consider anything other than what would happen that day as I became uncharacteristically hedonistic—much more fun, my friends thought. At the same time, my healthy body was busily at work, cryptically carrying me far beyond what my conscious mind would concede.

I took to swimming far, far out, way beyond the breakers. Each time, I would increase my distance from the shore by small but perilous increments, imagining I was giving myself over, like Edna Pontellier of *The Awakening*, to a fate the ocean might decide for me. But as soon as I would begin to tire, the instinct for self-preservation would turn me around, and I would head for shore with steady, earnest strokes. These warring impulses—to surrender or persevere, to abdicate responsibility or seize my fate—have become part of the emotional tensions that from time to time still draw me out or call me home.

In mid-September, Alec was to leave for his freshman year at the University of Hawaii, assuming, I guess, that his sexual climax in June had had no profound consequences. What if he had stopped to talk to me quietly, privately, asking softly, "How are you?" What if I had then been able to tell him my terrible fear of what was happening to me, to us? Could we have made a plan for escape together? What would he have been willing to do? Very little, I suspect; still, these questions are ones I have not yet been able to stop asking myself. But my stomach still looked admirably flat, and though I often saw him at the beach, I gave him no reason to suspect. He was already moving into a future far beyond me.

When we had first met, he had been a pale, gangly boy with acne, shy and hesitant. Now, two years later, with his bleached-blond hair and deep tan, he had all the assurance that surfing competence, college plans, and sexual experience could bestow on a young man in southern California in the mid-sixties. His interest in me was minimal. When we did speak, we said little to one another of significance, though he did manage, after a chance meeting one night, to lead me away from my friends and pressure me for sex in the darkness under a Newport pier. Wounded by the audacity of the sexual proposal and baffled by a deep-seated sensation of shame, I walked away, telling him nothing. At night, alone, I kept telling myself: "It can't be. I haven't felt like throwing up once. I have no strange food cravings. I haven't gained weight. Pregnancy has got to feel like something!"

The summer ended, Alec departed, and I dejectedly prepared for school. Ultimately, my sadness and hopelessness over his unknowing desertion and my uncertain state became irrepressible. It was this conspicuous unhappiness, not any physical signs of pregnancy, that finally prompted my mother to ask me one night as I lay weeping in my bed,

"What is wrong with you?" Desperately, I confessed that I had not had my period since May.

As soon as I uttered these words, I moved from my meticulously constructed eternal present into a future where reality happened fast. The wheels of my parents' money and authority took over, and I surrendered all bids at self-control. I would not be asked to make another decision for months.

The next morning, we were at our family doctor's office door by eight o'clock, awaiting his arrival. My mother was in a rage. She started crying as soon as she began to tell him her suspicions, but her tears had nothing to do with sorrow or pity for me; I knew she was crying because she was deeply ashamed and infuriated. I realize now that from the beginning, my feelings were completely inconsequential. Nobody thought to consider them. After all, aren't the mercurial emotions of sixteen-year-old girls still dismissed as trivial, even as they are recognized as dangerous? They are to be subdued and, with luck, traversed, but they are not to be taken seriously.

As Dr. Cook and my mother talked in his office, I was silent, gutted by the night-before's revelations, by my countless apologies, by my parents' disgust, and by the monumental import of my confession. Dr. Cook calmly shrugged his shoulders, and spoke to me kindly: "Well, we'll just have to take a look." Leaving my mother to wait in his office, I followed his nurse to an examining room where she had me undress, put on a paper gown, and climb up on the examining table. Dr. Cook then came in and cheerily complimented me on my tan, then instructed me on how to place my feet in the table's stirrups and let my legs fall open. He sat down on a stool, positioning himself so that I could see his face between my bare legs, and proceeded with my first-ever pelvic exam. I was too scared to be embarrassed, too wretched to pretend bravery. Throughout the excruciating, steely prodding, I kept my eyes squeezed shut, although my tears escaped, streaming down my temples. I silently prayed as fast as I could—"Oh please, God, don't let this be true; please don't let this be true," over and over again.

Finally he removed the speculum, pushed back on the stool he had been sitting on, stood up, removed the gloves, and silently washed his hands. He grimly walked around the room, and finally circled back to the head of the table, where he looked down into my frightened eyes. "You are about three months pregnant," he sadly pronounced. It was

1964. Abortion was still illegal, and though my mother dared to ask if there was anything he could do, he insisted he could be no help. I would have agreed to an abortion instantaneously if *anyone* had offered. Had one been performed, I know I would have felt sad and guilty for becoming pregnant and disappointing my parents so completely. I would have been changed by an abortion, chastened, remorseful, careful, but I would not have suffered the irrevocable hurt the decisions of the next six months provoked. Why couldn't they take a risk, compromise for once their law-abiding principles, their middle-class proprieties? Surely, they could have found a competent doctor in Mexico, in Canada—anywhere where an "illegal" but humane abortion could have been performed.

But in 1964, San Marino was a conservative bedroom community of Los Angeles where an illegal abortion was unthinkable. The residents ranged from the upper middle class to the wealthy; all lived with privacy and comfort in single-family residences with trimmed lawns, inviting foyers, gleaming kitchens, formal dining rooms, snug dens, sparkling swimming pools. The nuclear family reigned. I knew only two school-mates from kindergarten all through high school whose parents divorced. The *San Marino Tribune* cheerily announced engagements and meticulously described weddings. There was almost no crime to report; the schools were generously supported; Lacy Park was a pristine garden. The Huntington Library was still relatively unknown and attracted scholars but not tourists. The restaurants could not serve alcohol; there were no bars, no hotels or motels, no apartment houses—just lovely homes, one after the other, on tree-lined streets frequently swept clean.

San Marino was also the national headquarters of the John Birch Society, its only extreme element. Even the few rowdy high school kids respected the city's boundaries and took their fast, loud cars to Pasadena's Colorado Blvd. High school graduates—almost all of them—went on to college, to USC, Stanford, Occidental, and the University of California branches, but not Berkeley, because it already had a reputation for being radical. If a San Marino girl wanted to subvert the norm, it was only to go to Pasadena City College rather than "away to school." Even there she would follow a well-rehearsed script and join the competition to be the rose queen for the New Year's Day Rose Parade. The one or two young men who were unwilling to yield to the college-bound script went willingly into the service (though not the Marines), even though Vietnam was already a reality. Conventionality was enforced with a vengeance, and there was absolutely no place in that manicured universe for a pregnant sixteen year old.

So, by the afternoon of the next day, my clothes had been packed and my mother and father were putting me on the airplane to my Aunt Jo and Uncle Neil's in Youngstown, Ohio. I remember my mother was nervous, hurried, and her voice was clipped. I could tell she was still very angry with me, but her anger helped me say good-bye. I wanted to get myself out of her sight so she would not have to be so disturbed, so tense, so furious. But my father seemed defeated and unsure. I was amazed when I noticed him crying at the gate. I had never seen my confident, controlled father, a celebrated Los Angeles attorney, in distress. I have never seen him cry again. I know that despite his great disappointment in me, he was suffering from the decision to send me away—a necessary, humane banishment, he imagined, but exile just the same.

The narrative my parents constructed was that I was being sent to live with my aunt and uncle because I had fallen in with a bold, unruly crowd at San Marino High School. That part had a semblance of truth— I had been running with a raucous group of girls, heavily under the influence of the Beatles whose music had managed to infiltrate our San Marino confines. We would smoke together, dress up in miniskirts over black fishnet stockings, and then apply lots of black eyeliner and white lipstick. My mother and I had been arguing for months over how long I could grow my hair. I wanted it parted down the middle and straight down my back; she liked "the pixie" with carefully trimmed bangs. My girlfriends and I were trying to look like the Beats, but to our parents and our teachers the look we were cultivating must have seemed shockingly slutty. We would sneak out by making fake baby-sitting arrangements, shoplift some liquor, get drunk, and go dancing at the Pasadena Civic Auditorium, where one time we saw Bob Dylan perform. My parents had caught and punished me twice for these escapades.

Given those temptations, the account for my abrupt departure probably seemed reasonable. They feared, they told their friends and mine, that the peer pressure would be too great, and that I would again be drawn to that crowd and their antics no matter how closely I was supervised. Besides, I needed to study harder because my junior year grades would be crucial for college, and the distractions in Youngstown would be minimal compared to the diversions Pasadena and L.A. had to offer a yielding, reckless girl. Within the borders of my world, these reasons for relocation could be legitimate.

Youngstown proved an unexpected haven for me. I fell in love with my new relatives. I am the youngest child in my family, and by the time I was a teenager both my sisters had left home. My parents were caring, but they each had flourishing, satisfying careers. We often clashed over my adolescent need for attention and affirmation, and like many busy parents, they were often irritated that my privileged life did not translate into perpetual cheerfulness. I had been lonely in our large, quiet house, and had eagerly escaped its emptiness by seeking the reckless frivolity of my friends and the passionate attention of my boyfriend.

But in this homey, bustling Youngstown house, I had come to live not only with my Aunt Jo and Uncle Neil but also with my two prudent, well-behaved teenage cousins. Suddenly, I had a new brother my age and a younger sister, and now, having learned the heavy price for disobeying rules, I wanted to be good. My cousins were smart; they studied; they enjoyed their parents, and their parents enjoyed them. I was in a place where I could both have fun and be well behaved, where pleasure was not rebellion that required deception and guile. My new life felt, for a brief but enchanting time, like a fresh start. But, in fact, my life was still mostly wizardry; my status depended completely on duplicity—on not letting anyone suspect I was pregnant.

I started my junior year at the local public high school. Had the school officials known of my pregnancy, I would not have been allowed to enroll. I suppose I appeared to my fellow students and teachers like a shy, studious, though not atypical sixteen year old. I spent all my free time with my cousins: movies, horseback riding, shopping, sledding. I fell in love with the snow; I read hungrily; I pushed myself academically for the first time ever and received A's for my efforts. I ignored my slightly distended stomach, the strange interior flutterings, and finally the vigorous kicks against the thick, tight girdle my Aunt Jo bought for me. Although she conscientiously took me to speak to a psychologist about how I was feeling, all I could do in her office was cry and cry. It was so upsetting that I asked my aunt not to take me back again, and she agreed. I stayed in school until Christmas break. With my Aunt Jo's help, I had kept the secret secure.

Inevitably, of course, I became visibly pregnant, and for reasons that seemed unarguable to me then, my secret had to be kept in Youngstown too. So on New Year's Day, my aunt took me to the Florence Crittendon Home for Unwed Mothers in Akron, fifty circumspect miles from Youngstown and two thousand obliterating miles from San Marino. Surprisingly, the home was a good place for me to be—at first. It was a ponderous and vast old house with heavy, dark wood paneling and ornate fixtures that impressed me greatly after the relatively unadorned stucco homes of California. Like the young Jane Eyre, I would sit for hours in the library, reading in the window seat, or I would pump away furiously on the battered player piano in the solarium.

There were many such "homes" for unwed mothers at that time. It was a place where privileged, not poor, girls were sent. Approximately thirty girls lived at the home at a time, and the ones I made friends with were very much like me; their parents, like mine, had sent them there to protect everyone from the shame of their pregnancies and to facilitate the adoption process. It was a rule that every girl who came to live at Florence Crittendon would without question give her baby up for adoption. While I was there, I heard about only one girl who had not had to abide by that rule—because her baby was born with such severe birth defects that it could not be adopted. Then the secret could no longer be kept, and she got to go home with her marred baby boy. The Florence Crittendon Homes have not all stopped operating, but their numbers have greatly diminished. The Akron home no longer exists. The Victorian values that fed its business finally lost their grip on middle-class America. Abortion became legal; ideology shifted so that girls could decide to keep their babies; the pill became readily available—all these progressive social changes have erased much of the need for such "homes."

But it was still 1965, and I had no choice but to settle in, continuing high school in the basement of the house with other girls who did not want to fall behind academically. The teachers were retired women, and the classes were small; I was a stellar student in that setting. My favorite subject was French. I had an ancient and peculiar teacher who came in to teach only me because I was the only girl at the time who wanted to study French. She was very much like my own lovable grandmother, whom I missed but who also had to be protected from the truth about me. I was drawn to her, and she clearly liked me and was eager to teach me *even though* I was seven, eight, nine months pregnant! Her kind regard for me was one small but treasured instance of validation in that winter of sweeping adult disapproval. I was also able to keep up with English, history, and biology. I read as much as I could: *Marjorie Morningstar, Gone with the Wind, Doctor Zhivago,* and finally *Tess of the d'Urbervilles.* Although my aunt forbade me to choose a name for my baby, I secretly chose the name Sorrow, as had my fictional heroine, Tess. The consoling identification, the peace, and the escape these long novels offered me turned into a life-long personal means of comfort and a professional commitment to the healing power of narrative.

I was frequently cheerful among these girls who were just like me; after all, I was not alone, was I? We could leave the home during the day, and a group of us would go for long walks into downtown Akron where we would do the kinds of things most teenage girls were doing—buying candy, shopping for makeup and nail polish, listening to 45s in the record store sound booths. Sometimes we would see "real" high school girls also pouring over the makeup counters at Woolworth's or examining scarves and mittens at the J. C. Penny's, but then we would hurriedly leave, fiercely aware of our jutting stomachs. Though I had companions at Florence Crittendon, I felt keenly detached, severed from my family, far from the familiar, and acutely, though secretly, homesick. Was this place a safe haven for lonely girls or a necessary banishment for the disgraceful? I could not tell.

We shared very little of ourselves with one another, for we were all too full of secrecy and guilt. And so many subjects could not be broached: we could not talk about home because we were not to tell where we were from. We could not make lasting friendships because we could not tell each other our real names. I was not "Janet Ellerby" at the Florence Crittendon Home; I was "Jan Mason." I had two roommates—Tina and Bernadette—but the only thing we could actually tell each other was why we had chosen our particular aliases. Mine seemed plain and flat—my aunt had decided on it for me—especially compared to Bernadette, who had chosen the name of the Catholic saint to whom the Virgin Mary had revealed herself with the words, "I am the Immaculate Conception." Now her choice seems incredible to me, but at the time I found it wonderfully dramatic and perfectly fitting. Immaculate conception seemed as feasible as intercourse to me, for we never talked of the particular circumstances that brought about our pregnancies, nor did we mention boyfriends, past or present. The girls who were from Akron were allowed visits from only their parents, and they never accompanied us on our walking forays.

We might have talked about our futures, but the prospect was so befogged by the real event looming ahead of us that such dreaminess seemed senseless and strangely out of place. This period was a secret time to be gotten through, a shameful present that would become a forgotten past. We all thought we would emerge from it untarnished and free. We believed in the adult world and that if we followed these elaborate, ritualistic procedures, we would be purged. Why become attached? None of us wanted to know anybody later on who was a player in our scrupulous and defensive charade.

When girls would go into labor at the home, they would sit in a special rocking chair in the TV room, and when their contractions got to be about fifteen minutes apart, they would be whisked off to the hospital. They would return in two or three days, pale and quiet. I assumed the tired cheerlessness I saw in their faces was the natural aftermath of giving birth, and that I too would be sick for a while after my delivery. I imagined it as something akin to having the flu. My aunt took care of all the arrangements concerning the adoption procedures and my medical care. Although all the girls at Florence Crittendon were required to attend classes to prepare us for childbirth, I still could hardly believe I was pregnant with a baby. Aunt Jo encouraged me to think of "my condition" as a kind of temporary setback—like a broken leg or a serious bout of pneumonia. When I did think of giving birth, I pictured a bright day with my aunt, in complete control of the situation, by my side, taking me to the hospital and handing me over to my doctor's superior care. I imagined myself sleeping peacefully while he carefully monitored my contractions because, you see, I would be unconscious. Aunt Jo told me, and I believed her, that I would feel very little pain and would later be unable to recall the ordeal because she and my doctor had agreed to have me as heavily sedated as was safe throughout the entire ordeal. It was a nice way to anticipate the event, but as often happens in life, these plans would go terribly awry.

Around seven o'clock, the evening of March 19, 1965, I began noticing a tightening of my stomach—no pain but definite contractions. I got to sit in the special rocking chair, and other girls sat cheerfully around me, timing the irregular intervals. It was exciting until we all had to go to bed at eleven. It was expected that the girls at Florence Crittendon would be in labor for at least twenty-four hours, if not longer, so everyone, especially me, assumed that I would spend an uncomfortable night but that the next morning I would still be there. Either it would have been "false labor" or I would be back in the rocking chair, conscientiously timing my contractions as my aunt drove down from Youngstown to take charge. We were very wrong, and a long, forsaken night of intolerable fear, loneliness, and finally panic ensued.

Alone in my bed, I kept checking my watch with the flashlight my aunt had given me so I could read after the lights had to be out. At one in the morning, my pains were ten minutes apart; at two, eight minutes; at three I decided to stop counting the minutes and to will my body to put a halt to this process that was escalating all too rapidly. At four, in the middle of an intense contraction, my water broke, seeping into the mattress, warm, plentiful, and alarming. According to the rules of the house, given that development, I had to wake the housekeeper. I reluctantly knocked on her door, apologizing for getting her up. She was clearly tired and annoyed by the disturbance; this part of her job must have been one of the most unpleasant. However, she called and awakened an on-call nurse, for our regular nurse, who lived in a garage apartment behind the home, was off duty that night. The housekeeper could not take me to the hospital because she could not leave the house unattended, and again rules forbade that she just call for a cab and direct the driver to deliver me to the hospital. Instead, a nurse I was unfamiliar with had to come from across town to fetch me. As if to deepen the melodrama, it was snowing hard outside; the nurse called back to say she had decided to call a cab and come for me that way rather than try to drive herself. I was to wait for her in the downstairs hall with my coat and overnight case ready. The housekeeper went back to bed.

I waited for her alone for almost an hour, wondering how I would live through this nightmare unaccompanied. The pains were shocking; I could not help but cry out every time one gripped me, so I kept stuffing my mittens in my mouth. The house was cold, dark, profoundly still. Above me on the second and third floors, everyone slept. My muffled cries and subsequent whimpering awakened no one. I kept looking at the phone. I imagined calling my parents. I needed them then more than any other time in my life; this was my hardest thing, and I was completely alone. Early on my aunt had told me that it was too upsetting to my parents to hear about the details of the pregnancy. I did not dare call them now in the middle of this Dickensian night and draw them into my panic and pain. I just sat there and imagined dialing the phone, and then I could hear their phone ringing next to their bed in San Marino and my mother's concerned "Hello," and then my inexcusable begging to please, please help me.

Finally, a little after five A.M., a woman I had never seen before but had to assume was the on-call nurse walked in the big front door and hustled me out to the cab waiting in the snow. She seemed inexplicably angry with me and entirely unsympathetic. She was exasperated by my tears and moans. When the cab driver showed concern, she irately dismissed him, snapping that there was plenty of time and that I was just acting like a baby myself. My labor pains were by now coming one on top of the other, yet I was unable to convince her that they were valid, that I was in actual, desperate pain. Completely distraught, I frantically begged the cab driver to help me—which infuriated her; she shouted at me, "Shut up!" and slapped me hard across the face. I was dumbfounded by her malice and utterly helpless. When we finally arrived, she shrilly cursed me when I told her I did not think I could walk and hauled me out of the cab. More afraid of her than of the pain, I hobbled across the entryway, through the doors, and into a brightly lit hall. After yanking off my snow-covered coat, she gripped my arm like a vise. Later, I would watch her fingertips, four little purple bruises each with a small cut at the top from her fingernails, slowly disappear from the inside of my arm. But at that moment, with the white hall still ahead of me, that kind cab driver did help me; he had run ahead and found an orderly who now moved quickly to guide me into a wheelchair. I was admitted at five-thirty and taken to a labor room where a nurse gently helped me undress. A young doctor, probably an intern, examined me quickly and asked, "Why did you wait so long?" I had no idea how to answer his question.

I still cannot fathom why I was fated to meet the cruelest person of my life on that portentous night. I would see her only one more time. When I returned to the "home," I told Tina what had happened. Apparently, she told an adult who must have questioned the on-call nurse's conduct. A few days later, she slammed into my room, livid, hissing at me to keep my mouth shut. I was terrified. This lesson was my first that the details of that night were best left to my dreams. As I write it down, I am confounded by how much the cab ride itself sounds like an overdone, theatrical nightmare. It also astounds me that my parents, my aunt, and my baby's father were all sleeping peacefully while I was being mistreated by a stranger. They had wanted to protect me so I would not be traumatized, so they sent me to Akron, made complicated and expensive arrangements, but I still ended up alone at five A.M.—helpless, terrified, abandoned. It remains a paradox that this thing my parents did because they wanted to safeguard me from the cruelty of people did just the opposite. Instead, despite good intentions, they sent me defenselessly into a night from which I have never completely recovered.

I gave birth a little after six A.M., March 20, to my six-pound, four-ounce daughter in a very cold delivery room. I was told to curl up and then given a shot in my lower back; immediately I was numb from my waist down. I did not see or feel my daughter being born, but I heard her crying, and the young intern, forgetting for a minute my circumstances, proclaimed jubilantly, "You have a beautiful baby girl!" I asked and was allowed to look at her for about a minute and to touch her face, her wet, dark hair, her tiny, perfect hand. Her crying was infectious, and my crying resumed, this time much like hers, those same big, gulping wails. Somehow I knew that this chance was my only one to claim her, and I begged the nurse to let me hold her. It is an image I will always carry, a terrible burden and at the same time a treasured memory because it is all I have: the resolute nurse shakes her head: "No. I'm sorry; we can't let you hold her"; the baby is crying so hard, her fists and legs are furiously beating the air— her high, shrill command to comfort and suckle—my arms are outstretched, they extend before me, and then she is taken out of my line of vision. I push up, trying to get off the table, but I cannot move my legs; I seem to be tied down. A male voice, perhaps the intern, says, "We're going to let you sleep now." I feel the puncture of the shot; the room warms; my sobs ebb, though my body continues to shudder uncontrollably.

I knew that I was finally being granted that promised unconsciousness that was supposed to have shielded me from the blunt pain and harsh separation, and exhausted, I welcomed the warm drift away from that night, yet I knew that a door was closing that I would not be able to reopen. I would not see my daughter again.

I learned later that I was never to have seen the baby; she was to have been whisked away while I was still unconscious, but because there was not enough time for my regular doctor to get to the hospital to deliver the baby and because I was fully conscious, at least some of Aunt Jo's instructions were ignored. How grateful I am to the people in the delivery room for giving me that minute with my baby, no matter how much anguish, no matter how many nightmares that moment has evoked. Sorrow's tiny image still abides with me. It has clarified rather than faded over these thirty-five years, and though I might now have difficulty picturing my mother's face even though I have only just visited her, my wailing baby remains crystalline in my memory. She torments me, yet I cherish my enduring Sorrow.

I stayed in the hospital for two days. The baby was placed in a nursery on a different floor from mine, so when I faintheartedly walked down to the nursery to look at the babies, none of them was mine. I was given a shot so my milk would dry up, and my chest was bound with long lengths of white flannel. I had a roommate too—an enormous woman who had just lost her premature baby. She was already the mother of five, and she was kind to me. Although she too must have been feeling her own grief, she seemed resigned to the loss of her baby. She told me something important: that I would someday have my own babies, and they would make up for this loss that now seemed so unbearable. Her assurance gave me a glimmer of hope, if not solace. Her priest came to see her and gave her the Host to eat, and they whispered together about arrangements. She kindly asked me to pray with them, and we prayed for our lost babies. Her husband was large and astoundingly cheerful. I remember him telling the doctor confidently, "It won't be long 'til we're back here again!" The doctor grumbled to him to be sure his wife take off some weight first, but I had no doubt that they would be back, and I could picture their chubby, angelic babies waiting to be born. Her husband was adept at sneaking milk shakes for both of us into the hospital. Today, they are still my comfort food.

When my aunt arrived on the second day, delayed by the same blizzard that had made my journey to the hospital so frightful, I felt guilty for my inconsolable weeping. Aunt Jo repeated what I already knew: I should feel relieved that "it" was over and thankful for all my mother and father were doing to get me out of this secret trouble. I believed her and felt guilty for what seemed like thanklessness, yet I could not garner relief or gratitude. Neither emotion was available to me then, no matter how sensible my aunt's remonstrances sounded.

I had to return to the Florence Crittendon Home for ten days—another part of the home's procedures. There was a special room for girls who had given birth, with four beds lined up against a gray wall like a dismal ward. For some odd, unaccountable reason, no other girl gave birth during those ten days. What may have been to others welcome privacy was for me bitter loneliness. I had no roommate, no confidante. I know now that I was in desperate need of gentle commiseration, but there was no one to ask it of. All the other girls, all of whom were still pregnant, avoided me as I had avoided the downcast girls who had preceded me in this special room. I lost the will to wash or eat, and sleep was almost entirely elusive.

After ten days of listless despondency, I was asked to bathe, dress, and come downstairs. In the company of the housekeeper, a social worker, and a representative from the adoption agency, I signed the requisite adoption papers. The formality was ominous, and again I was overwhelmed by complete loneliness and utter helplessness. I knew then that this ritual was not one that would bring me closure to a trial well endured, and I realize now that I had been coerced by well-meaning people into doing something that for me was unnatural, aberrant. But then, at sixteen with no sense of self-reliance, no means of self-support, for me there was simply no other option. I had never been encouraged to be decisive or to think independently, and any previous tries at independence had gotten me into only deeper trouble.

My signature allowed my baby to become the daughter of a professional couple who could not have children of their own. I was told that her adoptive parents were stable, smart people in their thirties. Their professions would ensure that she would be raised in a home free from financial worries; in fact, she would have the same kind of upbringing that I had had. Her adoptive mother was going to stop working, and they planned to adopt at least one more child. At some point in her life, she would be told that she was adopted.

I remember the housekeeper searched for me after the signing—and again I found myself apologizing to her, this time for worrying her by hiding in a remote part of the house where I could mourn undetected. It never once occurred to me that I did not have to give up my baby. I did not know that I had a right to her. If she was anyone's, she was my parents', and they did not want her. What I wanted was so irrelevant that I did not even hazard asking it of myself. I was shattered even though I was told over and over that I should feel relieved, fortunate—the worst was over.

4

One day, when I was still at the Florence Crittendon Home, Aunt Jo came down to visit, and I remember telling her that I felt I would some-day be obliged to tell the man who wanted to marry me that I had had a baby. She replied instantly and forcefully with complete self-assurance, "Absolutely not! Everyone has secrets, and you have a right to yours." I accepted her pronouncement as correct; secrets were not only protective but evidently also a way to exercise my free will, something I did not have then but was beginning to realize I wanted. I also remember listening trustingly to an older girl at the home who told me that if I did not have sex for seven years, my hymen would grow back. "Then," she said, "you can get married and your husband will find you a virgin." I thought I had been saved! He, whoever he was, would never know I had ever had sex, much less a baby! That I eagerly believed both these assertions is indicative of how naïve I was. I adhered fervently to a world constructed in the fifties, and for years remained unequipped to critically examine the vilifying assumptions about women that stood behind my necessary secrecy and required virginity.

Looking back now at those incomprehensible, lonely gray days at Florence Crittendon after giving birth, I respect the new, forlorn girl I was, pacing around that bleak room. Now I can appreciate and account for my confusion and dejection. Now I can take the word *trauma* and apply it to that night of solitary physical pain, which I had been in no way prepared for, and to my unanticipated and inescapable agony in that cold delivery room. I know now I was feeling the torment a new mother feels who loses her baby. When a woman loses her child after carrying it for nine months, when her baby dies, we feel intense sympathy for her. It seems the worst possible misfortune. We wonder how she will cope with her grief; we hope she will become pregnant again soon so that her loss can somehow begin to heal. Yet, I was expected to feel happy, relieved, unburdened. No wonder I was baffled. I had been told what to anticipate—unconsciousness—but my actual experience had invalidated all predictions. Furthermore, I had to keep my grief deep beneath the surface because if I showed it, such indulgence would be perceived as ungrateful and unreasonable. After all, I had been saved from lifelong humiliation, hadn't I?

Perhaps my life has been easier; perhaps I did have more choices because I gave my child away. Returning to California at sixteen with a newborn to care for would have dramatically changed the direction of my life—at least for a few years. But instead of the putatively burdensome responsibilities of motherhood, I was permitted to return to a presumably carefree adolescence, a seemingly untroubled university education, as well as adventurous trips to Europe, Hong Kong, and Japan. My daughter's adoption into a safe and stable home is surely testimony to the well-meant intentions and the sensible decisions of the adults around me. For my parents, it was the best possible outcome for an onerous obstacle; for her adoptive parents, it was a long-desired wish finally granted; for my daughter, it was a dependable future: a reliable mother and father.

I am the one who could not, cannot, will not find release from my sacrifice; my remaining adolescence was careworn, my university education discordant, my world travels lonesome. I was a mystery to myself, confused by waves of solitary brooding and a recurring sense of difference and separation. I was and remain haunted by my tiny daughter and prone to an inconsolable anguish over her loss. Yet, I want it this way. By writing this story down, my purpose is not to remove my loss or mitigate my grief—they are all I have of her. I would not surrender them.

However, I do write for a crucial purpose: to relinquish the secret. Rather than safeguarding me, the secret has worked to sabotage me. Rather than free me from disapprobation, the secret has shackled me with guilt. My hope is that by finally telling the secret, renarrating the story, I can reinterpret the characters and in so doing reexamine myself and my fellow players on that faraway stage. Could it be that I was not the bad girl who did the unpardonable? Could I regard my parents with more benevolent eyes? Were they not driven by something other than a heartless commitment to superficial appearances? Will it help to examine us all as pawns to a cultural ideology in which the stigma of bearing an illegitimate child robbed us of our chance to make a different choice?

Whether by us or for us, the choice was made, and once the secret was ensconced, it became the substructure of what I was. Keeping its intricate complexities has demanded my scrupulous attention for most of my life. I am ready to lay it down.

5

A few days after the adoption signing was concluded, I numbly returned to southern California for what was to be perceived as my "spring break." I was ostensibly out of school in Ohio for the week and home for a visit. I was actually thinner on my return home than was normal, and no one could have guessed from my appearance that two weeks earlier I had given birth. It was important to my parents that I be noticed so that those people who might be counting on their fingers could see me—this slim girl—and dismiss any suspicions about my absence since fall. I was not only allowed to see my girlfriends, but also encouraged to—even the wild ones. Still feeling depleted and blue, I did not want to join up with these girls, who now seemed to me both mindless and dangerous. But my parents pressed me on cheerily: "Get out; have fun; come on now—smile!" Compliantly, I went with friends for hamburgers, to the movies. Dutifully, I even spent a wary day at Newport Beach, the beacon of my girlhood, feeling completely dissociated from the lighthearted child I had been there the previous September, and hyperaware of the profundity of my difference.

But my pensive, cheerless disposition was benignly interpreted as the newfound maturity my parents had hoped I would acquire in Ohio. My friends believed the subterfuge. When they asked questions about my life in Youngstown, I adroitly lied, embellishing the counterlife I had been creating for them in my letters home. Openness and honesty were revoked; they no longer felt like options in a relationship.

The secret was launched, and we began to orchestrate its many facets. I could not, for example, just stay home after the "spring break"; people in California expected me to finish the school year in Ohio. Nor could I return to my Aunt Jo and Uncle Neil's and reenroll in the public high school I had attended in the fall; people in Youngstown had been told I had returned to California after Christmas for back surgery. (This lie had nicely coincided with my aunt's excuse to the school I had attended that I had injured my back and, therefore, could not participate in P.E.) Apparently, a return to Youngstown in April would have been too suspicious, so, instead, it was off to another aunt's home, this time in Des Moines. Here, the excuse for my unexpected visit was that my mother was ill; only my Aunt May and Uncle Lewis knew the actual circumstances. Once again I was enrolled in a public high school where I completed my junior year.

This phase of the secret had its unique challenges. When I would write to my girlfriends in San Marino, my letters could not have a Des Moines postmark, so I had to send the letters to my Aunt Jo in Youngstown, and she would mail them from there so they would have the appropriate postmark. My frame of mind throughout these maneuvers? I was dazed, bashful, contrite, and at the same time as restless as most sixteen-year-old girls. In Aunt May's house, Uncle Lewis and my new set of cousins were kind to me, but Aunt May seemed suspicious. She made it clear to me that she was doing an extraordinary favor for my parents in letting a troublesome, "easy" girl like me into her home. And I seemed to confirm her suspicions. Though not one high school boy had approached me for "a date" when I was at school in Youngstown, in Des Moines I was immediately and inexplicably desirable. The phone rang a lot, and she was extremely dubious as to why. I was as surprised as she and could give her no explanation for this puzzling popularity, but I wanted to get out of that house whenever I could. The day she allowed me to drive her car alone, I was so full of giddy delight that I went speeding around a corner, ran over the curb into a large rock, and flattened her tire, bending the rim in the process. Needless to say, I did not drive again during my two-month stay, and the dates I was allowed to accept were sternly supervised.

I diffidently returned to San Marino at the end of the school year with excellent grades, and no mention of the Florence Crittendon Home for Unwed Mothers on my school transcript. Though I was hesitant and wary, the secret had been an outward success. My reasons for leaving and returning were so plausible that when I started my senior year at San Marino High School, no one questioned the veracity of my successful year away. To everyone it seemed I had returned with my priorities straight, better equipped to study hard, apply to college, and follow the path my parents expected of me. I understood the insatiability of high school gossip and knew that no matter how lonely the secret might leave me, I could tell no one. Furthermore, I felt culpable for the significant financial sacrifice my parents had made to construct the secret; I dared not risk squandering their money, and they required protection from my shame as well. I had come to accept that my secrets were an inextricable part of my integrity; not only that, but they were also my duty.

I had adopted my parents' worldview almost entirely; only my extreme grief contradicted their expectations, which was another secret. I could not let them know how sad I was. I could not tell them I had seen my baby, that I longed for her desperately, that I thought about her obsessively. Confessing my sorrow would break the truce we had made. They would forgive me if I would behave like the happily reformed teenage daughter I was supposed to be—not a mother distraught over the loss of her baby girl. The abyss between these two selves was so vast that I could not manage both at once. To cope, I had to relinquish my truer, grieving self, denying her existence so that the imposter might succeed.

My parents and I had an unwritten pact. I had to do my part. And I believed I had done something absolutely egregious. I accepted the necessity to keep the secret then, and I have carried that need all the way into the present. Yet, with the secret came the belief that ultimately underneath my cheerful, appropriate mask, I was incontrovertibly bad and, because I kept the secret, irrefutably untrustworthy.

And, of course, as secrets will, this one has multiplied, like cancerous cells, invading every part of my life. The trauma itself was never forgotten and never examined. Instead, it was internalized, implanted. It was the seed that became an unfathomable array of behaviors in my relationships with my parents, with my ex-husbands, my children, my sisters, my friends, my colleagues. The seed has always carried guilt with it, but the guilt shifts, depending on the context of the secret's current existence. With my parents, the guilt for that "difficulty" I put them through as a teenager still remains; I still feel the need to apologize to them for my ineptitudes even as I have gone on to build an admirable career and raise three loving and capable children. Yet, the guilt my parents unknowingly kindle in me has never abated; instead, it has been compounded by the disappointment I have seen register in their faces when I have had to tell them again and yet again that I have failed at marriage. No matter what, I have been unable to cast off my essential impropriety.

For them, keeping the secret of the pregnancy was the only requisite. They had no idea of its power—that it would splinter into a myriad of other secrets, each concealed in uniquely cryptic ways. First it was my grief, invariably prodding me into disconsolate moods that my family and friends found irritating and uncalled-for. Later, while away at college, I came to know more progressive people who thought having sex at sixteen was not only natural but perhaps even healthy—yet still the secret split again. Having sex as a teenager was natural, but I suspected that giving up one's baby would be read as unnatural, coldhearted, and, therefore, unpardonable. Fear of condemnation and rejection was succeeded by yet another offshoot—an urgent yearning to have another baby. I had to keep this secret assiduously, especially from men.

My first husband, Allen, and I met while I was attending the University of Oregon. I was twenty-one when Allen told me he loved me. Understandably fearful of becoming pregnant, I went to the student health center, got the pill, and we began to have sex. He wanted to know about past lovers; how had I lost my virginity? He wanted details. So, hoping for understanding and compassion, I defied my Aunt Jo's advice to keep the secret and confessed—misery ensued. He made me feel despicable, not (at first) for having had sex, but for willingly giving away my baby. To him this flaw was unforgivable; he believed that when he told his father, a Christian minister, his father would forbid him to see me again. He was shocked when his father advised him not to judge me so uncharitably.

For unhealthy reasons of his own, Allen proposed to me after our graduation. His parents and mine urged us to marry, because for both it was still unthinkable that we live together. My parents may have discouraged the marriage had they known of his mean-spirited reproach, but I concealed his sporadic animosity as best I could, believing that it was deserved given my shameful past. For harmful, impenetrable reasons, I accepted his proposal, despite his continued chastisement. We had an impeccable wedding, performed by his beaming father in my parents' resplendent garden: the (tarnished) bride in white lace with flowers in her hair. The *San Marino Tribune* reported the fortuitous event in detail; the façade of propriety prevailed.

The marriage was a fiasco, short and explosive. We immediately moved across the country to Washington, D.C., and I submitted myself to Allen's castigation for six months. Throughout those hurtful months, he kept insisting that I had been stretched inside by giving birth, and, therefore, I was not giving him sexual pleasure. Believing him, I humbly made a visit to a gynecologist. Once again, another crucial moment of my life occurs in a gynecologist's office with me on the examining table: As the doctor is giving me the pelvic exam, I tell him about my husband's complaint and ask him if I can be repaired by an operation—stitched up tighter. He stops the exam and stands, looking at me intently over my propped legs. I am surprised to see that he is disturbed by my request. Very slowly and very earnestly he tells me that there is nothing wrong with the size or shape of my anatomy—interiorly or exteriorly; in fact, he says he would not have known I had had a baby had I not told him. He says several times, "This is your husband's problem, not yours." He explains carefully that he is not a psychologist, but to him my husband's complaint sounds like a psychological problem because, he reiterates, there is nothing abnormal about me. He urges me to see a marriage counselor.

I bounded out of that office, happier than I had been in years. What a release! I was not damaged goods! One week later I threw propriety, protocol, and social graces all out the door, and ran away to New York with the man I thought was my rescuing knight, my Lancelot—a seemingly wondrous Latino man who was managing the restaurant where I had gotten a temporary job. I had known him for about two weeks.

I quickly confided my secret to my new lover, Ricardo, sensing the revelation would be the litmus test for whether he would keep me. But as a broad-minded man raised in the sixties, Ricardo had learned to scoff at the idea that virginity was even desirable, and he was also relieved that I did not have a child to complicate our madcap escape. I read his acceptance of the secret as proof of his unconditional love and married him without hesitation as soon as I could get a divorce, paying no mind to the early hints that we were altogether unsuited for one another.

We moved back to Los Angeles, and he became quickly frustrated by the empty desolation to which I would often unaccountably succumb. He wanted that lighthearted, sexy California girl for his wife—one he thought would explore the L.A. club scene with him, drinking and dancing, the one who had spontaneously decided in an hour to leave her husband of six months, defy her parents' expectations, and embark on a life of high adventure. Instead, I became pregnant only two months after our "escape" and immersed myself in my pregnancy. He explored the club scene on his own with my blessing. I had a much more important task to which to attend—growing my baby. Yet, when my beautiful, healthy son was born, I wept for three days. How could this be? I was shocked that his birth had not "cured" me; I loved my new baby with a startling passion, but still I longed for my baby girl.

Ricardo reluctantly agreed to a second child, and the night of my daughter's birth, I was joyously triumphant. I could not sleep the entire night. I kept trying to awaken her, to nurse her—finally, I thought, she has arrived. Yet, even this—my exquisite baby girl—did not mend me. Still there was this yearning, an inextinguishable desire. When I became pregnant with our third child, Ricardo made it clear that he had had enough. I gave birth to my second—no, my third—daughter, and divorce followed shortly thereafter. For a while, I reveled in that tumultuous life, always with a baby on my hip—bottles, diapers, Cream of Wheat, the stroller, the park. Always they were there with me. If the vacancy opened up in the middle of the night, I could go and watch them sleeping, breathing in deeply the soothing, sensual smell at the napes of their necks. Who needed a husband when I had finally gotten what I wanted? I have tried since to become pregnant, driven by that fruitless search for the baby that would supplant the memory, but I have never again conceived. I could ask myself how many babies would it have taken to restore what I lost, but I know the answer.

Yet, my children have been the key to my abiding coherence, preserving my focus, compelling me to maneuver up out of despair and isolation, furnishing me with ways to exhaust my irresolvable disquietude. I have loved them with a fierceness that is by all means excessive. That they could never really heal me was beside the point. Having them was and is healing; they saved me. Although I married again and then yet again, those relationships were always secondary, peripheral to the real relationship I was committed to, for only through my beautiful, growing-too-fast children was there a means to temporarily forget my lost baby girl.

I had kept on the move, having left San Marino for Ohio, for Iowa, then for Oregon, for Washington, D.C., New York, back to California and the San Fernando Valley; then to Coeur d'Alene, Idaho, then Seattle, finally North Carolina. Me and the kids—we were the team, and the man that might join us for a while at one stop or another was ultimately extraneous to my real needs and desire. Along the way, the secret multiplied into a profusion of secrets. I had to keep the secret from my husbands that I was not using birth control; I have had to keep secret from my family why my husbands walked out, trying to make it look like they were guilty philanderers when, in fact, they left because my love for them was shallow, incomplete, and finally unsatisfying. I have had to keep all kinds of secrets from friends and colleagues about my baby and about all those husbands—my sullied past that at a glance surely makes me look like a fickle libertine! What a plight! So much shame; so much to hide.

My secrets become even more disgraceful to me when I make friends with women with young children. I cannot fault women for their passionate involvement with their babies; I have felt that way too. Yet, that ardent intensity makes it easy for me to imagine how quickly they will damn me: "How could you give your own baby away? How could you? How could you?" The secrets continue to multiply. Shame surfaces when I imagine my best friends learning about everything—friends who think they know me well and who have unguardedly and courageously confided in me their own secrets. I have never told them; somehow it has always become too late in the friendship to tell, so the guilt has propagated into culpability for not telling, for keeping from them this immense and crucial part of me.

Once Ricardo took it upon himself to tell my secret. It was years after our divorce, but my children's father, angry with me for moving them to Idaho, was in need of some unscrupulous revenge, so one day while they were visiting him, he told my children that I had given away a baby girl before they were born. He did so because he knew it would be the surefire cruelest way to hurt me. I believe now that his motive was also a hateful attempt to undermine my children's love for me. It is testimony of their compassionate and generous hearts that they came to me gently, lovingly, asking softly, tentatively about what had happened and understanding immediately my great loss. Since then, they have been my protectors, never my judges.

Still, the secret endures. In any discussion of love, it surfaces only to be restrained. In any discussion of motherhood, childbirth, adoption, nature, nurture, it materializes only to be suppressed. In any talk of honesty and authenticity, duplicity and dissembling, it torments me. Paradoxically, I have been a reliable fake. I have never disturbed my parents by discussing what happened, never my Aunt Jo—not once. They do not know this story.

But, finally I must disturb surfaces. I apologize to those loved ones I intrude upon because of these revelations. Life has moved me to a place where self-examination can no longer be put off. My children are in separate cities, pursuing their own desires. I have had to let them go, for they have insisted, as they should, on their own independence despite me. Now I find I need to confront the secret self, to explore her, to see her not as shameful and sullied, but perhaps as much more interesting and certainly more vivid than the version I have been offering.

By telling the secrets, I want to risk the depths rather than linger on the surface of selfhood, reveal the intricacies, examine the conflicts, and, finally, extend this more complete self into my world and my work. I want a candid representation; I want to join the carefully constructed counterlife with the authentic life. I am no longer on the run. I believe I am strong enough to take the chance that many people take daily—living in the world forthrightly, drawing on their experience without fear of censure or rejection. With my own flawed humanity revealed, I dare to ask for tender forgiveness, uncritical acceptance, genuine intimacy.

My baby girl is lost forever. Even if the adult woman should find me someday or if I find her, the infant I touched but could not hold will never be placed in my arms. What was denied then is denied forever; that which was lost is irretrievable. Still, I have been fortunate. Losing my daughter has turned out to be the greatest loss I have had to suffer. Sometimes, I try to think of the adoption more generously, as my unselfish gift rather than my deprivation, but this thinking is not the truth and does not assuage my sorrow. My first daughter and me. We met for a moment on a frigid Ohio morning. Judged unfit for one another, we were placed on separate paths. Two girls alone, yet indelibly connected. I have never lost sight of her. I dream she is even now approaching.

2

MEMORY WAS THE ENEMY
Two Family Secrets

> *Nothing is absolutely dead: every meaning will have its homecoming festival.*—
> M. M. Bahktin, *Speech Genres and Other Late Essays*

Our current moral universe posits remembrance as an unalloyed good thing. Our culture agrees that we must never forget the abominations of the Holocaust, the atrocities of slavery, the savagery of My Lai, the butchery of the Khmer Rouge. The popular media relentlessly reinforce the positive value of remembering, revelation, and disclosure. We are living under a powerful zeitgeist of unrestrained candor, what Maureen Dowd calls the "if-its-about-me-it's-interesting view of life" (1998, A31), an era when Oprah and Montel reign and thousands line up for public confession on television. As cultural critic James Atlas notes, this urgency to bare our souls to all has deep roots: "It reflects our historic American longing to discover who we are. The literature of the self has a long tradition. . . . The Emersonian 'I,' declaring the primacy of subjective consciousness, was a vigorous 19th-century theme" (1996, 26).

As a consequence, the memoir is thriving. Henry Louis Gates Jr., the chair of African American studies at Harvard, regards the memoir as a means to "free [not only] personal secrets but family and race secrets too. In the business of testifying," he maintains, there should be no "rules or limitations" (qtd. in Boxer 1998, B6). Memoirs have the potential to do important cultural work, liberating secrets, revitalizing memory, and encouraging more intimate and probing responses. They also make for satisfying reading, challenging the memoirist to write with a dexterity and aesthetic imaginativeness more akin to fiction than autobiography. Probably because the need for authenticity is greater, Susan Suleiman observes, "If a memoir is felt to be fraudulent, there are shock waves" of disapproval among readers, especially if the events described are traumatic. Unlike fiction, "the category of memoir implies a kind of contract" (ibid.). Serious readers take memoirists at their word, trusting the reliability of their renditions. Readers expect an unflinchingly accurate and discerning portrayal of the actual events of their lives. Implicitly charged with veracity, the memoir stands as a psychologically meaningful and culturally salubrious literary enterprise. It serves as an intellectual site where intimate narratives of socially significant memories can publicly resonate.

Elie Wiesel concurs: "Memories, even painful memories, are all we have. In fact, they are the only thing we are. So we must take very good care of them" (ibid.). Yet, benefits of a truthful and reflective remembering have not always been as respected as they are today. As a young Jewish boy in Europe at the beginning of World War II, novelist Aharon Appelfeld tried to forget that he came from a Jewish home. He changed his appearance so he would not look Jewish and washed his tongue so that Jewish words would not slip from his mouth. "Memory was our enemy," he recalls (ibid.). After liberation, when his memory was restored, it was, for him, like a religious awakening.

There is a significant difference between today's professional and popular encouragement to remember and reveal and the guarded secrecy of both my great-grandparents' lives in the 1890s and my parents' in the 1940s. My ancestors unknowingly followed Nietzsche's concerted practice of "active forgetfulness": the willful and purposeful erasure of scars that repeated remembering would turn into open wounds (Casey 1987, 7). My family wanted to, indeed needed to, forget its traumas, to obliterate its catastrophes. Because memory was seen as a betrayer, secrets became de rigueur. The secrets my ancestors began to keep in 1892, the secrets my parents began to keep in 1946, and the secrets I began to keep in 1965 are the strands of a collective web of family forgetfulness.

Because I have been steeped in the cultural resurgence of candor and its aversion to denial, I have decided differently. Responding to my culture's emphasis on sincerity, I have felt obligated to revisit a key narrative of my life and to examine its repercussions. I have done so to discover a more authentic self, to reconstruct a healthier subjectivity, as well as an occasion for cultural critique. As a consequence, the quest has led me back beyond my own into other secret histories that paved the way for losing Sorrow.

I come from a family that loves to talk, relishes the occasion to tell jokes and anecdotes, and cherishes certain family memories; nevertheless, for generations a proclivity for secrecy was an implicit dynamic of their memory practices. Evan Imber-Black notes, "no family wakes up one morning and says, 'Let's make a secret' " (1998, 56). When they discovered my pregnancy, it seemed to me that my parents decided spontaneously, "Let's keep this a secret." But for them, the path of secrecy was more instinctive, more customary, and finally the only permissible option. This new secret would be nested in a well-established edifice of secrecy. Remaining at home in plain sight, gawked at by friends and neighbors as my pregnancy progressed, was an unfathomable alternative.

I was always puzzled at my parents' alacrity upon learning of my condition. How did they know instantly that I had to be spirited off? How could my Aunt Jo and Uncle Neil be approached and persuaded so rapidly to temporarily adopt me and my condition? How could arrangements have been made so rapidly that I was on an airplane for Youngstown two days after the discovery? How did they know how to concoct such plausible excuses for my sudden departure? By unlocking secrets in my family's past, I have come to understand and accept how an already well-established family practice could ensure that my pregnancy was adeptly camouflaged though, of course, not immutably erased.

The first event—my great-grandfather's suicide—occurred more than a century ago and was kept a family secret for two generations. It was disclosed recently not because of the gravity of the secret itself, but because of the fame of one of his granddaughters, Katharine Hepburn. Nevertheless, because the incident happened so long ago, and because it was hidden away as shameful, the details that might have helped to explain my great-grandfather's ultimate hopelessness were lost to succeeding generations. And so instead of understanding, the family is left only with mysterious gaps, enigmatic lacunae.

However, there is a second story of unendurable affliction in my family's past, another haunting narrative of what Thoreau called our "quiet desperation": people suffering in silence because the heartache itself is so shameful. The second secret is particularly bitter, especially for my parents, but I open it in the heartfelt belief that our most painful memories are inextricably part of what we are. I take great care in this telling, not only to repair the historical connections that were broken by grief and shame, but also to reinscribe the secret into the public space of memory. I also do so with the belief that my family's secrecy was not unique. The cultural mores of the time sanctioned this kind of repression. Now, however, my family secrets serve as representative anecdotes of an amnesia of shame we can no longer abide. How else can families or a nation make sense of who we are and why we have become so?

Alfred

> The fact that a situation is ubiquitous does not absolve us from examining it. On the contrary, we must examine it for the very reason that it is or can be the fate of each and every one of us.—Alice Miller, Drama of the Gifted Child: The Replace for the True Self

My mother had always been told that her grandparents died quite young; no cause was given. She assumed natural causes; there was no reason to think otherwise, as pneumonia, consumption, and a host of other infectious diseases took the lives of so many in the late nineteenth century. It was not from her mother that she learned of her grandfather's suicide but from a biography about her famous cousin and childhood playmate, Katharine Hepburn. My mother had purchased Young Kate to see how their shared past had been depicted.

Because Hepburn and her family history has garnered so much public interest, this family secret has been uncovered and documented by several biographers, though not without inaccuracies. Here is the story as best I can tell. My great-grandfather Alfred Houghton lost his first wife and was left with a year-old daughter, Mary. He was married again to the beautiful and accomplished Caroline Garlinghouse. They had three daughters: Katharine, Edith, and Marion, my grandmother. Alfred and Caroline died in their early forties, and the girls were raised under the guardianship of their uncle, Amory Houghton, the owner of Corning Glassworks.

In the Hepburn biography Young Kate, Christopher Andersen states that Caroline Houghton was diagnosed with cancer in 1892. Alfred, Andersen asserts, took "the doctor's diagnosis of Caroline's cancer hard; it seemed nothing short of incredible to him that at the age of forty-one he should have to endure watching a second wife's slow, painful death" (1988, 43). After collapsing from nervous exhaustion, he left Caroline in Buffalo, New York, for his older brother Amory's home in Corning, where he could recuperate. He rested in Corning for two weeks; then looking fitter than he had in months, he went out one evening for a carriage ride. His body was found, a pistol shot through his temple, a revolver still clenched in his hand (44).

The *Corning Daily Democrat* reported Alfred had been "a sufferer of nervous prostration" and that the magnitude of his responsibility for the management of the Buffalo Scale Works had "proved too great a strain for him"; the *Corning Weekly Journal* reported that he was a man of "uncommon business ability, and of spotless integrity"; a local paper in Buffalo reported: "A. A. HOUGHTON SHOOTS HIMSELF—One of the Owners of the Buffalo Scale Works Kills Himself in a Fit of Despondency" (qtd. in ibid., 45–46). According to Andersen, Caroline died only five days after her husband's suicide (46).

Andersen's biography leads us to infer that the motivation behind my great-grandfather's suicide came from his despondency over Caroline's illness, and this deduction is reinforced by Caroline's reported prompt death. But Andersen has the date of her death wrong. Caroline actually lived on for two more years, not dying until 1894 after making arrangements for all her daughters to attend Bryn Mawr when they came of age.

In her autobiography, *Me: Stories of My Life,* Katharine Hepburn sheds more light on Alfred and Amory: "His relationship with his older brother Amory was complicated. Amory had fired him from the glassworks because he was always late. Then Alfred became the head of the Buffalo Scale Works. He was a moody fellow by nature and a victim of severe depressions. During one of these episodes, he was visiting Amory in Corning and he disappeared. He was found, dead of a self-inflicted gun wound in the head, on the railway tracks. No note—nothing" (1991, 10). Hepburn leaves the circumstances that led to the suicide murky, and the "moody" Amory remains a puzzle. Furthermore, Hepburn's report of Caroline's illness explicitly contradicts Andersen's. According to Hepburn, Caroline was not diagnosed with stomach cancer until *after* Alfred's death.

The psychological reasons behind Alfred's suicide will always remain enigmatic because in burying the narrative surrounding his death, the family buried the actual history that would have let us know this intense, desperate man. He was visiting Amory when he went to the rail yards and shot himself. What transpired to spark such a rash result? How had death become the only option for a beloved husband, father, and respected businessman? The answers to those questions are buried behind the stigma and shame that obscured the tragedy. The origins of the decision to conceal Alfred's suicide from his daughters came from a complex mix of history and culture. This larger context, in which suicide is viewed as a desecration and judged with scorn, established the family protocol that the details about this man be blurred and ultimately hidden. Ironically, although we now know how he died, my great-grandfather himself remains unknowable, a significant and consequential loss.

Richard

> *He had two lives: one, open, seen and known by all who cared to know . . . and another life running its course in secret.* —Anton Chekov, "Lady with Lapdog"

I am looking at a face taped to the wall above my desk. It is the face of my father, my aunt, my grandfather, and my grandmother converging and merging. It is the smiling face of my uncle. It is a face to whom reparation can be made.

Not until I was fourteen did I happen to catch the first slip. One night, a fleeting reference to a man I had never heard of danced across our dinner table. My father was telling a fishing story to several guests, and as he narrated, he inserted a detail that astounded me. He said, "My brother was in the front of the canoe." What a jolt! A brother? I was already schooled in the narrative rules that pertained to my parents' storytelling, and I knew that it was entirely impermissible to interrupt at that moment and ask, "What brother?" So I kept quiet and retreated to my room to ponder this cryptic revelation.

I knew there was a secret lurking. I pictured my grandparents' living room and the pictures of my father and aunt in two rich leather-edged frames connected by tiny gold hinges. There was no third section to the lavish frame; nothing had been detached from either smooth leather border. There were no pictures and never any mention of another child, a boy, anywhere.

There was something shameful about this brother. He could not have died from illness or in war, for I would have heard that story. My mother had a beloved brother who had died tragically of pneumonia in his twenties, shortly before his wedding. He was a promising, handsome young man with a knack for the comical, so he figured large in my mother's humorous stories. After his death, my mother said she was not sure how she could live with such a great sorrow in her heart. Only by immersing herself in the care of my newborn sister could she make her way through the long, sorrowful months that followed his death. If she told me about her brother with such loving words, what could possibly have happened to this other brother?

Eventually, I got my sisters alone and quizzed them about our father's slip. They knew a little, and between the three of us, we have found out more from our mother over the years. Today, however, we still have only the sketchiest of details; the secret has been well kept. Last Christmas, thirty-five years after I heard the first slip, I heard another. Again my father was telling a story of when he was a boy: "My brother and I crawled out of our beds, down the stairs, and under the dining room table so that we might catch Santa Claus delivering our presents, only to fall asleep as we waited." I was transfixed, but again, the narrative protocol of our family prevented me from saying, "Dad, tell me more about your brother."

What I do know is that Richard was born one and one-half years after my father. My sister tells me that my grandparents favored my father, the eldest, and did not hide their partiality. While my father was a model student and gifted athlete, Richard was a disappointment. Though he was at one time also an athletic star at the University of Michigan as a hurdler on the track team, he apparently did not do well academically at the university. While the older brother, my father, was gloriously surpassing all expectations, the younger brother was often a frustrating failure. Cast thus, how did he manage emotionally? When he needed the unqualified approbation of his parents, he was, I sense, dismissed for such neediness.

My father seemed to succeed at everything he attempted. He graduated from the university, married above his social standing to my beautiful and educated mother, joined her prominent Grosse Point family, put himself through law school despite the depression, had two bright and bonny daughters, and bought a new home. With the advent of World War II, he did the honorable thing and enlisted.

Richard also married and had two children. Though he too tried to enlist in the war, he was rejected because of a testicular hernia. My mother says this blow was crushing to Richard; the fervor to serve was at an impassioned pitch, and a young man out of uniform must have felt disgraced. Apparently, Richard could find no constructive means to compensate for what must have seemed to him a vilifying flaw tied in complex ways to his masculinity, self-esteem, and sense of honor.

After the war, my family moved from Michigan to southern California, the promising new frontier, the land of plenty, where fresh starts were waiting for anyone with energy and tenacity. My father quickly found a job with a respectable law firm, immediately passed the California bar exam, and bought a house for my mother and sisters in the Los Angeles suburb of South Pasadena. Richard soon followed in my father's steps. He came to this postwar boomtown in June 1946 with the money he had received from the sale of his house in Michigan. He expected to find a job and buy a home so that he too could bring his wife, Betty, and their two young children, Richard Jr., six, and Carolyn Jean, three, out west. But something went terribly wrong. He either could not find a job or did not look for one. My Aunt Betty and the children still came, but when they arrived in Pasadena, it was discovered that all the money was inexplicably gone. But Richard still managed to rent them a cabin in Big Tujunga Canyon, Pasadena.

Betty's parents came to visit from her hometown, Pleasant Ridge, Michigan. When Richard complained to his father-in-law that he worried about security in what felt like a large, perilous city, his father-in-law bought him a .25-caliber Belgian automatic. When Betty's parents were about to leave, my mother says she and my father tried to convince them that they should take Betty, Richard Jr., and Carolyn Jean with them. My mother says of that time, "We knew something was terribly wrong, but we didn't know what." But Betty's parents did not want to interfere in their daughter's life. Betty did not want to leave Richard, so her parents returned to Michigan alone.

Shortly thereafter, however, it became clear that Richard and Betty were not going to make it in California. Their money had vanished, and Richard had still not found work. They were given money by someone in the family for train tickets to return to Michigan, and they packed up to leave. On November 14, my mother and father were full of foreboding and wanted to be sure that the family got safely on the train. My father went to the Los Angeles train station in search of them, my mother to the Pasadena station. It was my mother who found them at the

Pasadena station, but when she asked Richard to let her see the train tickets, he confessed they were gone. Apparently, my uncle was so disturbed, perhaps so delusional by then, that he had packed up his family and taken them to the train station even though he had sold their tickets.

I can imagine how desperate my mother must have been. What had Richard expected to happen? How could she have begun to conceive of the extent of Richard's mental crisis? Anxiously, she took Betty into the station bathroom and asked her to put the kids into her car and come home to South Pasadena with her; Richard could follow. My mother pleaded, "At least let me take the kids with me." Betty refused. She agreed to return to my parents' house, but insisted that they would all come with Richard.

My mother and father waited for hours, but the only person to come to their door was a police officer, knocking politely but with cataclysmic news. Richard had driven his family to a secluded ravine near the Rose Bowl, parked under a bridge, and shot his children, his wife, and himself. Richard was dead; Carolyn Jean, shot through the head, died almost immediately as she lay in her father's lap; Richard Jr. was found also shot but alive in the rear seat of the car but died at the hospital a few hours later; although Betty had also been shot through the head, she would survive—her injuries would leave her blinded for life.

My mother remembers the headlines screaming the words "MAN SHOOTS WIFE, KILLS TWO CHILDREN AND SELF" (1946, 1: 1). My parents were horrified by the crime, devastated by the loss, and mortified by the exposure. Here was our name, ELLERBY, printed on the front pages of the *Pasadena Star News* and the *Los Angeles Times*. Would my father, identified in the articles as Richard's brother and just starting out in his respected law firm, suddenly be suspected of a similar homicidal predisposition? Would my oldest sister be teased mercilessly by her classmates? How could their new community welcome the Ellerbys given such a scandalous introduction?

In her book *Trauma and Recovery*, Judith Herman observes: "The ordinary response to atrocities is to banish them from consciousness. Certain violations of the social compact are too terrible to utter aloud: this is the meaning of the word *unspeakable*" (1992, 1). When my parents called my grandparents to tell them that Richard, Richard Jr., and Carolyn Jean were dead, that Betty was critically injured, their response was immediate and unequivocal: "Never speak of Richard again." From that time on,

Richard, Betty, Carolyn Jean, and Richard Jr. were all obliterated from the family narrative.

Betty's parents flew back out to Los Angeles, and when their daughter was physically stable enough, they told her news I cannot imagine having to process. They shortly thereafter took her home to Michigan where somehow she slowly recovered. My mother has told me that she eventually remarried and had more children. There is great consolation in knowing that fact. My sisters, only eight and four at the time, were not told what happened, although my oldest sister recalls sneaking into the neighbor's garage and reading their old newspapers to find out what she could. The distractions of childhood allowed their memories of their aunt, uncle, and cousins to fade quickly. The secret was established. Only my mother has been willing to break the edict, though never within earshot of my father, and never in any detail.

Indeed, she never told any of us one of the strangest details of the scandal. On November 16, the *Los Angeles Times* reported that the Pasadena police had revealed evidence of a mystery woman, known only as "Mary E." Her picture and a cryptic note that referred to the promise of "tomorrow night" and signed "Nite, darlin" were found among my uncle's effects ("Mystery Woman Linked to Suicide-Murder Case" 1946, 1: 1). Perhaps this hint of adultery seemed insignificant to my parents given the enormity of the violent loss of life. Still, its stain must have added even more to their overwhelming sense of horror and shame. I know nothing more about the mysterious "Mary E." On November 18, the *Pasadena Star News* reported that the police had closed their investigation and that no coroner's inquest would be held into the deaths of the father and two children ("Murder-Suicide Probe Closed" 1946, 2: 9).

I try to put myself in my parents' place. What would I do if a policeman arrived on my doorstep with such horrifying news? How to endure it? They chose to continue on the path they had started on, to build their family with devotion and determination. My mother had learned from her own brother's death that absorbing herself in the needs and love of a newborn could ease the loss of death. And so they conceived a baby— me—a symbol of their steadfastness and optimism. And they erected a secret, a secret to enable them to live on in the world, a secret to protect us from the shame of such a stunning transgression. The shameful skeleton of Richard established a family obligation: conceal the negative, bury the shameful.

In Richard's own internalized narrative, he must have harbored an unforgivingly shameful self-concept that grew into a tormented inadequacy. Did he think of himself as irrevocably cursed? Why else would he not only commit suicide, but also take the lives of his wife and children? Carol Gilligan seems close to answering these questions with her description of the savage violence of male depression: "Like an autoimmune disease in which the body turns on itself, the depressed [male] psyche attacks itself, rejecting itself as worthless, incapable and morally despicable" (1997, 24). Richard's narrative of self-loathing must have been so commanding that it extended beyond the confines of his self, on into his descendants.

The biological predisposition to depression seems clearly established, and given the significance of my genetic inheritance, the suicides of my despondent great-grandfather and my deeply disturbed uncle could raise fears in me for my own mental health. Certainly, my shame has been tenacious and unhealthy, but it has not been an annihilating master. I am neither Alfred nor Richard, though perhaps, like them, I too have suffered from a disease of sorrow and, like them, tried unsuccessfully to swallow my grief. Our possible affinities give me even more cause to resist their abandonment, especially Richard and his family. There is a Yiddish proverb: "The son wishes to remember what the father wishes to forget." This daughter wishes not only to remember but also to record what her parents and grandparents have wanted to forget forever. I understand their wish, but in my quest to break with the family practice of secrecy and the resultant, unavoidable shame, I cannot observe it. My psychological endeavor is to untangle my life history and to comprehend my multiple inhibitions. Our cultural commitment to honesty compels me.

We can live better by acknowledging what we know. Releasing the secret unbinds the shame. Indeed, instead of shame, I feel measureless regret for Richard, deep sorrow for the loss of Richard Jr. and Carolyn Jean, and great tenderness for my Aunt Betty. How acutely she must have suffered. I cannot pretend to know what this family was actually like, because I was not born until two years after the tragedy, but like Mary Gordon, in speaking of an aunt she never knew, "I feel the responsibility to bear witness to the loss, the wreckage . . . to bear witness to the darkness that . . . became the only refuge. The place to hide the shameful wreckage from shining America" (1996, 151). I also feel immeasurable sympathy for my mother and father, for they have had to live their lives with the painful memories of Richard, Betty, Richard Jr., and Carolyn Jean in silence, with no consoling words for their loss, with no healing words for their needless shame. I know so little of my lost uncle, aunt, and cousins because of my parents' concern, their desire to protect us.

I do not follow their example; their need to forget is not mine. Nancy Miller declares, "We don't choose our families, but we get to revise their myths" (1996, x). Like Maxine Hong Kingston, who breaks an imposed familial silence by writing about No-Name Woman (1977, 18), her banished aunt who committed suicide after giving birth to an illegitimate baby, I too refuse to participate in the decreed silence. After more than fifty years of deliberate forgetting, I get to revise my family's tradition that silence is obligatory, binding, and better. I do not want my Uncle Richard and his family to be lost in my family's obsession to conceal all that is shameful. I turn to fiction for guidance, to Toni Morrison's *Song of Solomon:* Pilate mourns her greatest loss—the suicide of her granddaughter, Hagar—by proclaiming to all who will hear her and to the sky itself, "She was *loved!*" (1987, 319). So too were my great-grandfather, my uncle, my aunt, my cousins. They were loved, and I will care for their memories. I will acknowledge and honor them, as I will now always acknowledge and honor Sorrow, as members of our family, not with shame, but with enduring love.

3

SECRET HISTORIES OF SHAME

This can be said about shame: those who experience it feel that anything can happen to them, that the shame will never cease and that it will only be followed by more shame.—Annie Ernaux, *Shame*

Living without Sorrow required that I find a place to lodge her memory not only within the lonely hours of guilt-ridden despondency but also within the ordinary events of my everyday life. My pregnancy, her birth, and her adoption were such oppressive secrets that the shame they generated became the regulator of my emotional life. I took the accusation "You ought to be ashamed of yourself" to heart, allowing it to overshadow any real accomplishments. Sorrow and shame were always there. Amid the most ordinary daily tasks lay traps that could transform my perception of myself as decent, responsible, and self-possessed into someone with a contemptible past, an imposter hiding behind a mask of respectability. Negative charges lay in wait for me, their jarring intensity capable of leaving my identity in baffling disarray.

Narrative

How to theorize the most personal part of myself? Could I be both witness and critic, turning my analytical skills on my own psyche? Apprehensively but unwaveringly, I started to write. For the first time, I recorded my secrets, steadfastly narrating the key events. Besides the editor who had once urged me to begin with the personal, I received encouragement from other writers, such as Robert Karen, who maintains, "Putting shame into words appears to be a critical first step in freeing oneself of its damning logic" (1992, 46). Natalie Goldberg coaxed me to abandon the rigorous but guarded confines of theoretical discipline, to relinquish control, to write on waves of emotion (1991b, 3). I placed her words over my word processor and let them guide me as I sat down to write. She counsels: "The deepest secret in our heart of hearts is that we are writing because we love the world, and why not finally carry that secret out with our bodies into the living rooms and porches, backyards and grocery stores? Let the whole thing flower: the poem and the person writing the poem" (120).

Missing their suggestiveness for serious narrative work, academics regularly dismiss New Age texts such as Goldberg's as clichéd, oversimplified, and solipsistic. Yet, in *Street Smarts and Critical Theory*, Thomas McLaughlin observes that New Age literature promotes "narrative as a way to gain a deeper and more authentic selfhood" (1996, 80). Although postmodernism has made me too skeptical to fully embrace utopian New Age philosophy and believe in the possibility of transcendence and a new "self," authenticity has been part of my narrative quest. As a postmodern critic, however, I realize that the "authentic" is often a mirage. With that understanding, I have made the mirage my goal. When I draw close enough to the hard, clear horizon of self-awareness for the illusion to disappear, I savor momentarily my newfound clarity, knowing full well a new mirage, a new glimpse at an authentic core, will inevitably find me in disciplined pursuit. Like Sisyphus, all I can do is persevere in the journey of the examined life, acknowledging the interplay of blindness and insight as I strive for reflexivity, perhaps even wisdom—the most genuine subjectivity I can construct.

Ideology

Looking back, I realize that for decades I was in what psychologists David Feinstein and Stanley Krippner in their book *Personal Mythology* call a "consensus trance," which "embodies the hidden assumptions that are at the basis of our understanding of the world, and it programs much of our behavior. . . . Members of a social group usually do not realize the limitations of the group's world view because it is all they have known, and those around them operate within a similar structure" (1988, 191). Without reflection, I had accepted almost all of the rules and limits of my family and of the dominant paradigms of my gender, race, class, locality, and age. I had submissively consented to a definition of the real within

which there was no room for illegitimacy—only shame. Although growing up in the sixties was supposed to be a time when young people my
age subverted paradigms, my shame was too great for me to freely fall
into the joyously heady liberation of the Age of Aquarius. I lived my life
dissembling, trying to fit into the cultural norms I had inherited from my
parents and, at the same time, uncomfortably pretending that I too had
been infected with the giddy recklessness of the late sixties and early
seventies. That the two cultures unavoidably and consistently clashed
worked to make me feel only more and more shameful in my parents'
world and like a misfit in the world of my contemporaries.

Another way to conceive of the dominant paradigms of a culture is
suggested by Sam Keene's *Fire in the Belly.* Concerned with the social construction of masculinity, Keene coins the term *consensus realities,* which, he
suggests, are composed of myths. Keene's authoritative myths are analo-
gous to what postmodern critics refer to as ideology: the largely invisible
and unconscious assumptions that inform our minds, emotions, and actions. According to Keene, these myths must be dismantled:

> The task of any individual who wants to be free is to demythologize
> and demystify the authority or myth that has unconsciously informed
> his or her life. We gain personal authority and find our unique sense of
> self only when we learn to distinguish between our own story—our au-
> tobiographical truths—and the official myths that have previously
> governed our minds, feelings, and actions. This begins when we ask:
> "What story have I been living? What myth has captivated me?" (1991,
> 33–34)

I inherited the cultural norms and the authoritative myths of my family,
the strongest of which was my psychological propensity for shame that
unconsciously informed my life, governing my feelings and actions. In a
kind of twisted logic, behavior that would beget shame seemed almost
expected, inevitable. I was captivated by the myth that my most authentic self would most surely disappoint and, thus, needed to be hidden
from those people I would have love me.

Emotion

Thomas Scheff and Suzanne Retzinger, authors of *Emotions and Violence*, argue that if a culture is to be stable, it must provide people with means for discharging their emotions. However, this design becomes complicated if we are deeply ashamed of certain emotions, as we often are of our fears, grief, anger, and even shame itself. Scheff and Retzinger maintain that when we inhibit the discharge of emotion, we do so to the detriment of our psychological well-being (1991, xix).

In my own family culture, which placed propriety and composure above all else, there was no conceivable place for the discharge of agitated emotions other than perhaps surreptitiously, alone in our bedrooms, doors shut, heads under the pillows. In our home, my sisters and I learned early on to hide or camouflage our moody, needy, inconsistent selves. A performance of propriety became our habitual way of being with one another. Our "consensus trance" was one of feigned well-being no matter what emotions were roiling underneath. Other than in isolation, there simply were no allowable means for dealing with our emotions, though we had, of course, our share of anger, jealousy, sadness, fear, even jubilation—but all were too demonstrative. Although emotional tension and grief are unavoidable in the process of living for both children and adults, my sisters and I were expected to be placid, positive, and unemotional. No matter what, we were to comport ourselves with good manners and tempered optimism.

For me, this social contract was arduous, for I was an unusually apprehensive child and insecure adolescent. Filled with anxiety about my flaws and shortcomings, unsure about the legitimacy of my feelings, and, at the same time, highly sensitive, I grew up startlingly submissive and unaccountably lonely. But I was surprisingly adept at stifling this highly emotional temperament. The headstrong part of me, the turbulent crusader that might have audaciously strode beyond the family into the world, was continually flattened in my attempt to be emotionally acceptable. How to construct a self when so many facets of my personality had to be suppressed, thwarted?

At the core of the fabric of our family was a kind of emotional quarantine. From a matrix of preceding generations, we inherited shame as the authoritative family superego that regulated our minds, feelings, and actions. Given that we were required to keep emotions secreted away and made to feel shameful if they surfaced, it is no wonder that a hasty, passionate decision had to be reigned in and then buried.

Secrecy

My secret was yoked to the other family secrets. Although the suicides and murders were "successful" secrets, meaning they were properly entombed deep within the family's consciousness, their aftermath—shame—continued as a powerful, ongoing engine, reinforcing the habit of secrecy, giving it weight and energy. Shame and secrecy became family patterns for dealing with breaches of discipline, with the unsavory and unexpected, and with the inevitable intrusions from the outside world.

For a long time, it appears that the capacity to experience shame was functional rather than debilitating for my forebears. Their great shame made them politic, vigilant. Concealment was discretion, a crucial ingredient in their culture's narrative of middle-class respectability. It allowed them to maintain appearances and achieve acceptable success. On the surface, it appears that the initial pacts to keep the secrets were judicious. Better to suppress disturbing events and move into a healthy future without the grim shadows they would surely cast. Denial was pragmatic; consequently, restraint, suppression, and repression became the tenets of our lives.

In contemporary culture, however, denial seems more the mark of the unauthentic, the fettered. Surely, part of my motivation for this inquiry is the insistent belief of contemporary culture that disclosure, not discretion, is a more reliable path to mental health. Clinical and social encouragement to tell all is a crucial difference between the vigilant secrecy of my parents' and grandparents' lives and the tentative candidness of my own. From sophisticated feminist theory to the crude sensationalism of talk shows, we are encouraged to disclose, to reveal, to admit, to confess. I am predisposed to give credence to these cultural winds, because I believe that all of our family secrets have had interconnected and painful consequences. Preserving their secrets must have dearly cost my grandparents and parents. They repressed the truth not only because they feared it would forever tarnish our otherwise morally sound family, but also because to acknowledge the events would have brought back acute feelings of frustration, loss, guilt, horror, shame. Like me, the truth must have filled them with a dreadful fear of being stigmatized and spurned. Like me, behind their fear of rejection must have lurked an ineradicable sense of self-loathing.

Life experience has taught me that my family is not unique. Secrets and families go together, so intimately intertwined that I begin to wonder if secrets are not a vital thread in the fabric of all family unity. When I idealize what a family might be, I think of a dinner table where members can reveal themselves to one another in all their conflicted and compelling complexity without fear of censure or rejection. But when I look at the real families I know, I often find just the opposite. Instead of gathering with unrestrained forthrightness, families assembled at dinner tables judge with almost uncanny perspicacity what can and cannot be revealed, what can and cannot be said. New family members, a son-in-law or daughter-in-law perhaps, are at sea for a while until they catch on to the subtle nuances of permissible topics, emotions, and revelations.

I find myself the offspring of a family that has chosen design over authenticity because the real is too shameful. I have inherited both a belief in an irredeemable secret self and the narrative impulse to organize the intricacies of my life so that nothing will reveal my shameful center. Just as I was bequeathed a verbal acuity, I too received the cunning to deceive and the tenacity to maintain the mental vigilance that is required to avoid self-disclosure. I often wonder what we could have been had we not had to expend the rigorous psychological energy that was required to conceal our secrets. Would the consequences of honesty have been so dire if we had cast off our shame and risked living forthrightly?

Shame

I hold shame responsible for many of the distortions and anxieties of my life. Why shame and not guilt? We cannot go through life without a certain amount of guilt. If we are to be moral, we must feel troubling self-reproach when we transgress social norms. However, unlike shame, guilt is triggered by improper conduct; guilt "generates confession and the goal of forgiveness" (A. Morrison 1996, 14). Shame, on the other hand, generates secrecy, an unabated need for acceptance, and an irresolvable fear of rejection. In his book *Shame and the Origins of Self-Esteem*, Mario Jacoby argues that shame "is felt as a deeper injury than guilt" (1994, 2). Scheff and Retzinger describe it as "the most social of all emotions, since it functions as a signal of threat to the social bond" (1991, 5). Shame is about membership in a certain race or family; it is about not being pure enough, or pretty enough, or thin enough, or smart enough; it is about the self. Although shame can be triggered by behavior, it is not the behavior that is wrong; it is the self that is wrong. According to Robert Karen: "[S]hame itself is less clearly about morality than about conformity, acceptability, or character. To be ashamed is to expect rejection, not so much because of what one has done as because of what one is" (1992, 47). Andrew Morrison, in his book *The Culture of Shame*, refers to shame as a core unworthiness: "a sense, a conviction, a belief about the self that we find intolerable and that we try to manage by turning away in one way or another" (1996, 12). No other emotion, says Morrison, prompts concealment as does shame. Anxiety and depression may cause us to withdraw, but that retreat is because we are ashamed of the state we are in. Shame, a fundamental feeling of loathing against the self, insistently induces deep-seated feelings of unlovability that permeate all aspects of one's life.

In her memoir, *Shame*, Annie Ernaux also attests to shame's pervasiveness, claiming, "My shame was followed by more shame, only to be followed by more shame. Now everything in our life is synonymous with shame. . . . It was normal to feel ashamed . . . it had become part of my own body" (1998, 108–9).[1] For women especially, shame is tied to their bodies. Although I have felt shame for not being intelligent enough or articulate enough, the intense locus of my shame has always emanated from my body that has not been slender enough, appealing enough,

---

1. Ernaux's autobiographical volumes have captivated French audiences for years. *Shame* has been heralded as an example of her "scrupulous self-awareness and precision" as it offers "a searing authenticity." In the memoir, Ernaux states she will carry out an "ethnological study" of herself, and in so doing, she provides impeccable detail of her town, its social geography, her family, and her private Roman Catholic school. Reviewer Claire Messud says that "the careful, unflinching specificities of *Shame* give voice to a resonant and universal truth; and Ernaux's particular discomfort is most profoundly, that of being human" (1998, 16). Review Richard Bernstein compares Ernaux to Joyce: "Ms. Ernaux's delicate, mystical exploration is stylistically very different from anything Joyce ever wrote, but it contains much the same sense of wonderment at the silently watching child that never really leaves us" (1998, E8). In her review, Nancy K. Miller maintains that "even the most jaded reader of contemporary memoirs trafficking in extreme situations will be rattled by the violence that emanates" from Ernaux's precise language and "the remarkable surface" of her writing (1999, 35).

graceful enough, and, especially, pure enough. Leon Wurmser notes, "[The] tendency for shame anxiety to spread from one situation to all situations makes it akin, even if not causally related, to paranoid ideas" (1981, 53). My own shame anxiety about my teenage pregnancy spread from the loss of my virginity and the impurity that implied to a paranoid sense of contamination and deformity caused by childbirth. I was so suffused with shame that I immediately and wholeheartedly believed my first husband's perverse suggestion that I needed reconstructive surgery in order to satisfy him sexually. Although a discerning doctor rescued me from that ordeal, I have continued to discover how the ubiquitous and distorting effects of shame can impoverish us by blocking our capacity for relationships built on trusting disclosure. The primary fear of rejection and the concomitant need for secrecy prevents us from that other compelling desire—to be loved absolutely, beyond our shameful transgressions and inadequacies.

In Joseph Adamson and Hilary Clark's recent collection, *Scenes of Shame: Psychoanalysis, Shame, and Writing*, Donald Nathanson notes that every tale of scientific, political, romantic, or economic courage and accomplishment "is about effort that was carried along on a wave of enthusiasm sufficient to wash away potentially stultifying shame" (1999, vii). The abundance of recent memoirs and their popularity represent a cultural wave of supportive attention sufficient enough to give those of us with painful, shame-laden pasts the courage to challenge the stifling impediments that have heretofore checked our forthrightness and threatened our well-being. The best of contemporary memoirists have taken as their humane project the washing away of stultifying shame and have thereby reinfused the genre with an aesthetic intensity capable of narrating the deepest of human emotions. Readers have responded by identifying intimately and avidly with the compelling authenticity of their stories.

Telling

My parents still live comfortably, quietly, and peacefully in their southern California haven. There seem to be no ghosts in their sunny home, surrounded as they are by their beloved orchids and the leafy avocado groves beyond. Why have I intruded even indirectly upon their privacy by telling our secrets? Frederick Buechner, author of *Telling Secrets*, suggests that the human family has secrets that are not only important to tell but also tellingly important: "They are telling in the sense that they tell what is perhaps the central paradox of our condition—that what we hunger for perhaps more than anything else is to be known in our full humanness, and yet that is often just what we also fear more than anything else" (1991, 2–3). Like Buechner, I have learned that I do not just harbor the secret of Sorrow; I am that secret. Having her and losing her gave birth to some of the most integral parts of my being, blending both positive attributes and unhealthy compulsions. I hope that by telling the story, I may finally be known more fully, may overcome much of the fear that has kept me secretive, helping me to discover a healthier identity.

Constructing a narrative can engender personal transformation. If we are to subvert Freud's conclusion that "we are lived by unknown and uncontrollable force" (qtd. in Roemer 1995, 99), if the past is destiny, then narrating the past can give us a way of liberating ourselves from it. Narrative theorist Michael Roemer maintains that "the storyteller attains a measure of freedom, separateness, and identity in the telling" (100). Philosopher Jonathan Lear sees the therapeutic narrative process as the means to "free us from the grip of various illusions about who we are, how we go on, what we mean" (1998, 272). For McLaughlin, creating the narrative artifact "can be the agent of healing, the springboard up into a new consciousness" (1996, 83). For Louise De Salvo, this "creative searching" allows us to "symbolically resolve" the "harmful events into something meaningful" (1999, 42). Our writing, our work of art, "permits us to pass from numbness to feeling, from denial to acceptance, from conflict and chaos to order and resolution, from rage and loss to profound growth, from grief to joy" (ibid., 57). In other words, telling can be a means of healing and propitious transformation, for me and indeed for all serious memoirists. I have written, therefore, in hope that by putting the origins of my shame into words, I will have taken the critical first step in extracting myself from its damning logic.

We cannot assume, however, that we can necessarily forecast sunny outcomes for those writers who tell their stories or that, by telling, we will emerge restored. Such auspicious expectations are jejune. Psychoanalysts know that the excruciatingly painful stories that have caused shame and self-loathing require protracted narration, renarration, and intense analysis. We cannot expect to emerge heroically—vanquishers of family skeletons, saviors of integrity and truth—simply by telling.

Memoirist Tracy Thompson, author of *In the Beast: A Reckoning with Depression*, says that although her writing was "a pleasure, because things made sense for the first time," once she turned in her manuscript, she "was laid low by self-loathing. I had this voice in my head saying, people are going to laugh at you" (qtd. in Michener and Sachs 1995, 95). In the catch-22 logic that follows in shame's wake, not only do memoirists risk ridicule and still more shame for their revelations, but they also risk punishment and rejection by those people who still want their secrets to be kept. At times memoirists of shame see only a cul-de-sac, not a liberating exit.

In her memoir, Ernaux recounts the momentous, shame-laden afternoon of her childhood, an afternoon when her father tried to kill her mother. At fifty-seven, forty-five years after the event, Ernaux admits, "This is the first time I am writing about what happened. Until now, I found it impossible to do so, even in my diary. I considered writing about it to be a forbidden act that would call for punishment" (1998, 15). Like Ernaux, I too fear the punishment I may incur for confiding the forbidden and defying my family's edict for secrecy. I risk profound disapproval or even, yet again, another banishment from the family enclave.

After publishing her memoir, *The Liar's Club*, Mary Karr began to wonder about the "psychic penalties" levied on confessional memoirists. She found them to be significant. One memoirist, Frank Conroy, who wrote *Stop-Time*, stayed drunk for three weeks between each chapter. Carolyn See collapsed with severe viral meningitis two hours after finishing the first draft of her memoir, *Dreaming*. See maintains, "It was my brain's way of saying, 'You've been looking where you shouldn't.' " Scott Peck was disowned by his maternal grandparents after his memoir, *All-American Boy*, revealed his homosexuality (qtd. in Karr 1995b, 78). As I myself have been finishing up this manuscript, I have been plagued by nightmares of ghastly lesions crusted over my back. These swollen, mossy gray scales are, I assume, a creepy sign of my anxiety about exposure.

Not only do I risk much by writing, but I also understand that relating reliable accounts of the events of my past will not everlastingly overturn my inherited narrative strategies for convolution, concealment, and deception. I will not achieve transparent authenticity by way of this narrative. I know too much about psychoanalysis to presume that I can vanquish shame and sorrow simply because I have given accurate and sincere testimony to particular occurrences during this crucial time in my life. Ritualistic transformation is too quixotic.

In their book *Testimony: Crises of Witnessing in Literature, Psychoanalysis, and History*, Shoshana Felman and Dori Laub explain that testimony does not offer a completed statement or a totalizing account of events. Instead, testimony is a process: "It does not possess itself as a conclusion, as the constatation of a verdict or the self-transparency of knowledge" (1992, 5). Like testimony, narrating my memories does not bring me to a definitive sense of closure and acceptance. The memories have not settled into undisturbed awareness. The emotions they elicit remain in excess of the details; there is no verdict that can as yet contain what occurred. Narrating has been set in motion by the memoir. Completion has not yet been accomplished.

Ernaux observes that although she has put the sequence of events of that horrifying Sunday into writing, the abstraction of speech fails to reduce the magnitude of the event itself: "It remains what it has always been since 1952—something akin to madness and death, to which I have never ceased to compare the other events in my life in order to assess their degree of painfulness, without finding anything that could measure up to it. . . . I have taken the risk of revealing it all straight away. Yet nothing is revealed, only the stark facts. The day is like an icon immured within me all these years" (1998, 26). Although the night of Sorrow's birth will always persist as the arresting icon of my memory against which I too compare all other suffering, much more than stark facts emanate from its center. Many possible narratives issue from Sorrow's story. All must be open to revision. The emerging needs of the present will require that I keep the story in process, unfinished, that I recognize its facets as discrete accounts, as unexpected repetitions, that I continue to dissect and reassemble, reinterpret and rewrite the text of the world surrounding that night in Akron when I lost my child and the self I thought I was meant to be.

Nevertheless, along with other memoirists, by way of this initial telling, I do establish a much more cognizant subjectivity, one in which I have more self-command because I comprehend more, appreciate more, acknowledge more. My shame and sorrow are now situated, grounded, parts of a real history. Ernaux, like me, accomplishes a valuable narrative task by grounding the iconic memory in a specific history. She records

not only the details of her father's murder attempt but also the ideological context within which the act occurred:

> I have brought to light the codes and conventions of the circles in
> which I lived. I have listed the different languages that enveloped me,
> forging the vision I had of myself and the outside world. . . . I would
> never be like the other girls again. I had seen the unseeable. I knew
> something that . . . [my] sheltered environment should have guarded
> me against, something that implicitly bracketed me. . . . I began living
> in shame. (91–92)

Like Ernaux, I find that by bringing to light the social codes and conventions of San Marino in 1965, by forging a vision of myself in that world,
I can forgive myself for never being like other girls again. I understand
how I came to feel bracketed by difference. The events of my past still
evoke feelings of sorrow and embarrassment; I am still living in shame.
However, by reconstructing and revisioning this past, its effects are
quite different from the psychic turmoil its secrets once produced when
they were too shameful to be articulated. McLaughlin maintains: "Stories can heal. Creating stories, telling and sharing stories, reading and
hearing stories are seen to be catalysts for healing change, ways of overcoming physical disease, spiritual emptiness, personal disintegration,
and loss of meaning" (1996, 87). Telling is not a cure, but it can be reha-
bilitative. I am not new but evolving, becoming, in process.

For my ancestors, the keeping of secrets became a way not to confront what was going on privately and publicly. They would not risk revelation, yet had they told their secrets, people may have been able to
help them reimagine what became, ironically, in silence, a crippling, destructive repetition of shame. I can trust my audience in ways my parents
could not. If I reveal the roots of my shame, the response I receive may
be empathetic and corrective. If the secret goes untold, if the narrative
stays repressed and reified in the past, it cannot be influenced by the vi-
cissitudes of historical change. Having an incoherent family narrative,
with pieces missing and false images, has meant for my family that our
lives have not truly been our own. Shame has distorted coherence and
has forced us to submit to another narrator. We learned to create alternate stories to hide in. From that perspective, unpacking the concealed

has been transformative. It has been conscious work that has allowed me to gain control over the thematics of shame in my life.

I narrate, therefore, on the presumption that my re-creation of my narrative can impose a new kind of coherence. By telling my story in my limited way, I can see better the strictures that caused my family to impose secrecy and shame. I wish to relinquish a way of living in the world that has proved wanting, ineffectual, sorrowful. My story is cathartic not only because I can refigure the real, but also because it informs the sense of shame I still carry with me. Even as the story continues to unsettle me, it unfolds new perspectives of open, forthright daily living.

The Architect of Desire:
Beauty and Danger in the Stanford White Family

One of the memoirs that has most encouraged and supported me as I have worked through and articulated my own past is Suzannah Lessard's *Architect of Desire: Beauty and Danger in the Stanford White Family.*[2] Lessard confirms that family trees are much more than diagrammed history. They are emotionally entangling legacies that furnish us with ways of being in the world, some sound and some lamentably unhealthy. Like me, Lessard learned "how close the generations are, how powerfully lives reverberate down through the structure of family, deeply affecting each other" (1996, 5). She goes back through the generations of "The Family," her family, to examine the violent men who preceded her in order to put an end to an unwanted, harmful heritage.

Lessard grew up on the Place, the magnificent estate designed by her great-grandfather, the famous beaux-arts architect Stanford White. She was encompassed by a large extended family, many of whose members

2. Many reviewers named *The Architect of Desire* as one of the best books of 1996. Ruth Conniff praises Lessard for unfolding an overworked topic—stories of sexual abuse— with "depth and power." Conniff observes, "Lessard brings together not just the personal and political, but the social, moral, mythic, and architectural elements in our culture" to create "a beautiful book" (1997, 31). Christopher Lehmann-Haupt found the memoir "emotionally transporting," one that gives "meaning to the cyclone" by "telling of the damage it wreaks" (1996a, C19). Paul Goldberger praises the book, concluding: "In the end this book is about the loss of innocence, innocence about art as much as life, and while its memories are sad and painful, it is a paean to passion" (1996, 7).

lived on the Place. With a beautiful and talented mother and a musically gifted father, a loving great-grandmother, attentive grandparents, aunts, uncles, sisters, and cousins, we might assume that Lessard led a blessed, even blissful childhood; however, because of an insistent need for decorum and, therefore, secrecy, the Place was unsafe for children.

The principal family secret was the disastrous scandal in her great-grandmother's life: Stanford White's seamy and excessive womanizing that led to his murder by Harry K. Thaw. Of course, White's hedonism is not a secret at all. There have been books written and movies made about his dramatic depravity, particularly his seduction of Evelyn Nesbit (Thaw's wife) when she was only sixteen. But on the Place, any talk of that public history was forbidden. To the family and neighbors, Stanford was remembered as someone with terrible manners; the family rose above the misfortune "with the aid of character and good breeding" (48), or what I would more candidly call oppressive restraint and repression.

Nevertheless, there are cracks in the surface of the family decorum. Although Lessard describes that surface as "halcyon" and "bright," she also observes: "It is in the nature of this kind of surface, that, like reflections on water, it is automatically self-sealing: the challenge is not so much to pierce the slick of reflections as to maintain the break" (72). In so speaking, Lessard is describing the vital yet difficult task of the memoir: to articulate the forbidden, to disturb the placid surface of good breeding. Her resolution is bold and unnerving, for ruling family paradigms quickly reimpose boundaries and reseal surfaces when breaches are noticed and breaks detected.

On the Place, harmony and charm disguised a violent subtext of perversity and male violence. Because those people who might have curbed such abuse would not acknowledge its existence, egregious behavior was unfailingly overlooked. Halcyon surfaces were maintained, but at tremendous cost:

> [W]hile [a] message [of dynasty, wealth, power] told me I belonged to a dominant family and in so belonging was, surely, supremely safe, I was in fact unprotected there, for unaccountable, destructive forces continued to exist unacknowledged within the family sanctuary. And while the covert, unaccountable power all around was dangerous to me, especially as a little girl, it was really dangerous to all members of

the family since it was, as a force, almost by definition blind. . . . [V]io-
lence was an independent force that savaged the family, making of an
individual a victim or perpetrator according to its whim. (117)

Lessard not only retells the violent past of Stanford White but also
traces and names the violence that the extended family encountered
through intricately intertwined generations before and after Stanford,
including her own father's abuse of her and her sisters. How could such
degenerate behavior have gone unchecked for so long? How could generations of indulged men escape accountability for their sexual violation
of young girls, including their daughters?

One answer lies in history—in her great-grandmother's and grandparents' endeavor to deny the pain and shame of Stanford's murder and
the lurid surrounding circumstances. Lessard is struck by the indiffer-
ence, even numbness, of the family to that violent ending. "That Stanford had been murdered did not seem to rate as a story in the family.
Certainly there was no resolution of this terrible incident—none at all"
(198).

How familiar Lessard's observations sound to me. The course of silence about the suicides and murders in my own family was decided on
well before my time, and it became the course we were to adhere to for
life. Because of the shameful discomfort they would provoke, certain
traumatizing events were forbidden to be recounted in Lessard's family
as they were in mine. However, without allowing such stories to be told,
retold, and reworked, without allowing each family member to try on
the stories and examine their relevance, the stories are locked into grisly,
nightmarish reifications. More important, the custom of secreting away
the shameful and not acknowledging the perverse becomes habitual and
expands to distort the present and future. And so warped discretion
overlooks the shameful acts of current players on the familial stage.

Within Lessard's extended family on the Place, the capacity to ignore the preoccupation with sex that many of the uncles, nephews, and
fathers demonstrated finally led to the rape of one of the younger
cousins, Pamela, by William, an older cousin, during a family barn
dance. Pamela's first priority was that no one in the family should know.
She told only some school friends who helped her get tested for pregnancy; the results were negative. Six months after the rape, she finally

did tell her mother, but when her mother mentioned it in passing to other family members, their reaction was remarkable—they did nothing. Lessard continues:

> Certainly, I [Lessard] had no thought of confronting William, or bringing him to account, either within a family forum or a court of law. Indeed I hardly thought of it at all. I would not think of the rape when I encountered William, or even when I saw William and Pamela in the same room at a family event. It's not that it disappeared from consciousness altogether, but, like a fox killing rabbits in the woods, it was somehow not a part of history. My knowledge of it disappeared into the old family silence, in which the world appeared unchanged in a nitroglycerine air. (308)

Unthinkable, yet conceivable given the family's customary course of silence, Pamela's rape was filed away in the unmentionable history of sexual crimes. The only family member to speak of the rape with impunity was William, who continued to flirt and taunt Pamela with words such as "Don't worry, I won't rape you again" (309). Rather than confront the sexual violence handed down through generations, the adults of the family, male and female, ignored signs of what seems almost inherited male sexual deviance. Unintentionally, thoughtlessly, and perhaps malevolently, the family left its young girls vulnerable as sexual prey.

When Lessard describes herself as "marooned in family history" (236), she is also depicting my experience. Marooned in a history of family secrecy and isolated from others—even other family members—because of my pregnancy, I reentered life after Akron repudiating a critical part of myself because my most intense and demanding emotions had to be buried. Such fragmentation left me unable to effectively negotiate relationships. Famished for approval and highly vulnerable to any demonstration of kindness, I had no trustworthy foundation from which to measure other people. Even today I find that whether individuals merit my esteem or not, I want their admiration. Acquiring the approval of others temporarily masks a self I still see as faulty, flawed.

Although not as physically vulnerable as the female children of the Place, I was for years so emotionally needy that I would ingenuously and repeatedly acquiesce to the desires of others. Men had to show me only a modicum of attention, tenderness, and approval, and I invited them wholeheartedly into my life without pausing to consider the price that could be exacted for their passing consolation. When these hasty alliances floundered, the emotional aftermath left me feeling more desperate, more needy, more alone. Although outwardly I espoused independence and autonomy, inwardly I craved intimacy and protection. My failure to attain either of these ideals led me inevitably back to shame.

Lessard is able to move out of her own advanced stage of estrangement and isolation and break through to connection by way of what she calls "revolutionary grace." Her family, like mine, had ritualized for generations "the grace of the quotidian . . . a conservative kind of grace that enriches and thus reinforces the texture of the status quo. It says nothing need be changed" (309). When revolutionary grace strikes, it breaks through the unconscious, automatic stance—the consensus trance—of the habitual. It can reverse the chronology of a hundred years. However, unlike the Aristotelian reversal or the Joycean epiphany, such grace does not fit neatly into our classic narrative structures. It originates neither in a particular individual, nor out of precipitating events, nor within a manifest, causal chronology. "A story that turns on [revolutionary] grace turns on an unprecedented factor that is inherently lawless and unpredictable, an unconditional transforming force that flashes suddenly like lightning" (314).

The moment of revolutionary grace for Lessard comes unexpectedly when one of her sisters, Madeleine, asks for a meeting of all the sisters one afternoon on the Place. Madeleine has been undergoing psychoanalysis in France, and in one of her sessions, she has mentioned to her psychoanalyst that her father had sexually fondled her when she was a child. The occurrences seem insignificant to her, but her doctor urges her to discuss her memories with her sisters. So she calls them together and relates this disregarded part of her childhood. Lessard describes the scene: "Her plain words were spoken calmly. But as she spoke I had a sense of something like a sound barrier breaking, a psychic reverberation that reached to the edge of the cosmos and down to the subcellular level at the same time. With it, the world cracked open. And inside was the world" (315). At the gathering, each of the sisters in her turn, Suzannah included, relates memories of sexual violation by their father during their childhood and adolescence. The real history of the family is finally spoken. The sisters are no longer left alone with memories that seemed "bloodless and irrelevant and easy to downplay." Instead, they are connected—"a *true* familial connectedness" (316–17). The Rosetta stone to this connection is finally telling their stories to one another. Only then do they see clearly. Only then do they recognize the violent sexual whirlwind that has been raging beneath the calm landscapes of the Place. Only then do they break the habit of looking for protection in silence, discretion, and the façade of harmony.

One of the obstacles in revealing a serious family secret is that the revelation affects not only the teller, but also all who fostered the secret. In telling mine, I am involving my mother and father, aunts and uncles, cousins, ex-husbands, husband, children. The telling affects them all, and I often find myself feeling guilty that I am compelled to tell such a sad story. Even though I do not tell to cast blame or release anger, the people I love and wish to protect are implicated in negative ways in the telling. They deserve a better story, for they are good and kind people.

Like many memoirists, Lessard faces a similar problem, because both her father, who violated his daughters, and her mother, who did not protect them, are still living. As readers we cannot help but wonder how each must feel about the accusations leveled here. In Lessard's acknowledgments, she enigmatically thanks her father for their "long discussions of aesthetics" and concludes by thanking both parents "because," she says, "in the end I owe everything to them" (330). Although she reveals that because he was apparently drinking heavily throughout their childhood, her father has no recollection of what his daughters remember (321), he is explicitly accused in this book, as are other men in the extended family.

As could be expected, her revelations have caused considerable controversy inside the family. According to reviewer Paul Goldberger, some family members have denied Lessard's accusations altogether, while others have taken issue with her "airing of family laundry" (1996, 7). I can appreciate why family members are so irritated, for like my own family, they have, observes Goldberger, "tried so hard through the 20th century to live down the scandal of White's reputation, only to have it portrayed by a new generation as worse than we had thought, and not as an anomaly but as part of a continuing pattern of White family values—no wonder Ms. Lessard is unlikely to be a sought-after guest at her relatives' Thanksgiving tables" (7). But my and, I believe, Lessard's reasons for telling our secrets are not to accuse or reproach irresolute family members but to come to grips with our elusive and sometimes destructive family alliances and to get a purchase on a selfhood that is no longer fractured by an inordinate need for discretion. Lessard makes clear her intentions in telling: "We try to see these things not to demolish but to strive toward a whole world, because an unwhole world is ghostly: no matter how beautiful it might be, no connection is possible there. We do this not to place blame but to make connection possible. We do this to live" (325). Lessard tells her story so that her son and all future children on the Place will not have to live in an unwittingly dangerous family context. I tell my story to bring an end to my destructive habits of deviousness and to offer a warning, to women especially, about the treacherous nature of shame.

My own moment of revolutionary grace came about when I was cornered by a lie and had to admit to the truth. Getting caught was misery, but because of it, I was finally able to fathom that I had never truly been able to present myself honestly within any of my most intimate relationships. Always, beneath my customary effervescence, I was hiding secrets—not just the cryptic despondency that evolved out of the secret of Sorrow, but many secrets. Because I was so burdened with shame and a consequent high-strung fearfulness, I could never dare relinquish myself to the truly intimate connection I craved because I had no faith that the acceptance that would ground such a connection was possible. I had married and remarried, each time ignoring the nagging fear that my husband would be sorely disappointed as soon as he figured out who I really was. To me, securing commitment depended on fakery, and when the charade failed, divorce followed. This eventuality was not necessarily painful for me because I was so exhausted by my dissembling that the chance to be truer to my own personality, history, and wants was a relief.

This pattern was clearly deleterious for all, but to make matters worse, I imagined I had to maintain other intimate relationships on the side to bolster me, just in case my marriage failed and I was once again left alone. For a long time my most trustworthy intimate relationship was socially acceptable (though most likely psychologically unhealthy), for it involved my thorough infatuation with and commitment to my children. They came first no matter what. But as they got older and insisted on their own independence and autonomy, my escape route from predetermined rejection had to shift to another venue.

The last time I built the intricate substructure of a secret alliance, the hidden compact was an intense, highly sexualized friendship with another man thousands of miles away. While deeply in love with my future husband, John, whom I profoundly respected and longed to marry, I felt compelled to keep the other less desirable man waiting secretly in the distance, for surely, eventually, John would recognize my irredeemable flaws and leave. I needed a backup. Perhaps unconsciously, I allowed John to discover my secret correspondent, and the results were psychologically cataclysmic. I had to admit my duplicity. I had lied; I was a liar; I had been taught early on to lie. I was destroying what was noble and full of promise in my life because the feeling that I was personally unworthy of love cut much deeper than my ability to commit to emotional intimacy based on trust and confidence. My fear of rejection would not let me stop undergirding my relationships with unstable foundations of deceit.

But this time something different transpired. The pattern of falling back on someone else unraveled. I could not fall back on my children for comforting distraction; they were all away at college. I would not fall back on my secret "friend" because I was angry and exasperated with this man whose clandestine presence had sabotaged my life while he surreptitiously carried on his own duplicity with impunity. My women friends could offer no surcease, for I was so profoundly ashamed of myself that, once again, I could admit to no one the strange narrative I had been secretly writing. For the first time, I alone had to face my tired, desperate, deceitful self. Alcoholics call this place hitting bottom. I hit bottom because of an unappeasable need for acceptance and a corresponding disbelief in its possibility.

My own moment of revolutionary grace came on the day I realized that I had to start telling the truth. Connection requires truth. So simple, yet for so long inconceivable. For years I had been playing over and over in my mind E. M. Forster's words, "Connect . . . only connect." But how? Much like the crack of lightning that awakened me one night by momentarily igniting the intricate boughs of the magnolia tree outside my window, grace awakened me with a shock, giving me a startling clarity of perception, a newfound self-consciousness, a whole new way of being in the world. There could be candor, and there could be connection.

John did not leave me in disillusionment and distrust. Instead, he compassionately heard me out, not just once but for, to me, agonizing weeks. Brimming with anguish, we followed the crooked narrative—all that had happened to me, the silent weight of the past that seeped into

every interaction of the present. Together we analyzed the psychological compulsions that had kept me marooned on my island of subterfuge.
As I told him the story, I realized that it was time to write it down. Honesty could not exist between just him and me; it had to be my way of
being in the world.

Gerald Goodman, a professor of psychology at UCLA and longtime
student of self-disclosure, is dubious about our recent cultural propensity
to confess and then to publish these confessions. Quoted in a *Time* article
on memoirs, Goodman maintains that "writing confessions can be easier
than talking confessions. There's nobody to interrupt, ask questions,
give advice, make interpretations." Furthermore, he cautions: "Book disclosures allow people to edit out the most shameful parts of their lives. I
call this 'decoy disclosure.' I'm not persuaded that these writers are authentically repairing their lives. They're doing something that usually
requires vulnerability to another person. But in this case, there's no other
person—rather the whole world" (qtd. in Michener and Sachs 1995, 95).
But surely this is not always the case. In my own attempt to improve if
not repair my life through disclosure, I am making myself vulnerable not
only to the world, a daunting audience for confession, but also to the
people I love and to whom I yearn to be truthful. In fact, there is an entire cast of real individuals within my memoir, many with whom I share
kinship, who will hold me accountable to the most truthful version I can
compose. If Lessard's cryptic acknowledgments are to be credited, I am
not the only memoirist to feel an acute responsibility to be reliable. Why
write the memoir if not to be honest? Fidelity must be at the heart of any
authentic and serious urge to reveal.

The Liar's Club

Another supportive memoir throughout the process of my truth telling
(for the fear that had made me a liar did not immediately dissipate in that
moment of grace) was Mary Karr's *Liar's Club*.[3] The title alone attracted

3. The reviews of *The Liar's Club* have been resoundingly positive. Molly Ivins says,
"This book is so good I thought about sending it out for a backup opinion. . . . It's like
finding Beethoven in Hoboken" (1995, 21). Catherine Bowman compares Karr to Virginia Woolf: "Karr sees the past as a series of occasions that explode into lucid 'moments
of being' " (1995, 6). Reviewer Karen Schoemer observes that Karr's anecdotal style is so

me, because I already considered myself a clandestine dues-paying member. As she described her own childhood, Karr articulated many of the feelings I had about my own evolution.

I know what she means when she recounts how she intuitively knew that something was "Not Right" about her family and herself: "The fact that my house was Not Right metastasized into the notion that I myself was somehow Not Right" (1995a, 10). As a child and adolescent, I was shy and insecure because I felt deviant. Conversely, as a child Karr is gutsy, quick with the verbal comeback, almost always ready to fight kids who insult her or her unconventional family. The examples set by her feisty mother and her brawny, pugnacious father make her someone to be reckoned with on the block.

Nevertheless, because she is "thirsty for liking" (64), she is also highly vulnerable. One evening when she is only seven, she follows a teenage boy, who had kindly doctored her bee sting with spit and mud, into a garage where he rapes her. Though quite young, she already senses the whirlpool of consequences if she should she tell. "He didn't even have to threaten me to keep quiet. I knew what I would be if I told" (68). She knows that her father will gut the boy like a fish, her mother will burst into tears, and her grandmother will not be surprised. She knows intuitively that she will be labeled as sexualized in some grotesque way if she tells the truth. Also, through silence, the rape seems less real. Reality can be denied—just as Lessard and her sisters deny that their father sexually violated them for years, just as Pamela refrains for months from telling her mother that William raped her.

Sadly, even seven-year-old girls know that silence is a talisman against the horror of rape. But denial is a malevolent charm. It can be a crutch, but it also cripples, as is clearly the case for the extended family on the Place. In her memoir, Karr finds a liberating space for the revelation that must come. In so doing, she addresses her rapist directly and forcefully:

---

captivating that by the time Karr "works her way around to the book's centerpieces, horrifying incidents of abuse and sexual molestation, you're so completely in her corner that you feel just as trapped as she is" (1995, 61). Karr herself says that so many of the memoir's readers identified with her experience that she had to "gin up" a working definition for a dysfunctional family: "any family with more than one person in it" (1996, 70).

Hey, bucko. . . . Where will you be when the news of this paragraph floats back to you? For some reason, I picture you changing your wife's tire. She'll mention that in some book I wrote, somebody from the neighborhood is accused of diddling me at seven. Maybe your head will click back a notch as this registers. . . . Probably you thought I forgot what you did, or you figured it was no big deal. I say this now across decades and thousands of miles solely to remind you of the long memory my daddy always said I had. (66)

Karr's testimony is not only powerful, but also jubilant. She justly refuses to carry her shame into her future. She places it where it belongs—on her rapist. Shame has found its rightful owner and, we can only hope, has taken up residence in the heart of the true perpetrator.

I love Karr's splendid anger; in my anger, I too long to reach out beyond these pages with my own emphatic testimony. I often find myself imagining Sorrow's father in my audience. Maybe someone from our high school will see my name and read this book. Maybe she will realize just who he is and decide he should know about the lives that he, in a moment of heedless gratification, changed profoundly. Then, I dream, he will finally have to confront what happened while he went off to a sunny life at the University of Hawaii with his surfboard and his bottle of peroxide. The irresponsibility granted his gender and the thoughtlessness his privilege encouraged allowed him to dally in an Oahu wonderland, while I was secreted away at the Florence Crittendon Home for Unwed Mothers. And one night, while he slept peacefully, I was left to bear alone the inconceivable, splitting birth contractions that preceded the birth of our daughter and severed me forever from the girl I thought I would be. While he made college friends, I was harassed by my own Nurse Ratchett. When I saw him again some years later and tentatively told him he had a daughter in this world, he had the luxury of time, distance, and utterly unruffled male detachment to tell me he did not believe me.

Reading Karr's memoir gave me the heady permission to acknowledge my anger while also setting an example for how to direct it imaginatively to its rightful recipient. However, it is not Karr, herself, with whom I most closely identify in *The Liar's Club*; it is her mother, Charlie. As Mary and her older sister, Lecia, grow up, they find their mother more and more unstable, more and more drawn to the blinding oblivion of alcohol, so psychologically damaged that she once had to be hospitalized after burning the contents of the girls' room in a huge bonfire and then coming after them with a butcher knife. But Charlie's past remains a mystery to Karr until, one day, grown-up and living on her own, she returns to her mother's house. While rummaging through the attic, she finds a neat lineup of four tiny jewelry boxes, each containing a different wedding ring, each ring an emblem of Charlie's four previous and until now hidden marriages.

Karr maintains that "few born liars ever intentionally embark in truth's direction, even those who believe that such a journey might axiomatically set them free" (311). Charlie has no intention of telling Mary about those rings, and Lecia has no intention of helping Mary solve their mysterious origins. According to Lecia, "people who whined about their childhood were woosies, ne'er-do-well liberals seeking to defraud the insurance industry out of dollars for worthless therapies." Her advice? "Unconscious mind, my ass. . . . Get over it" (311).

Lecia's attitude about mining the past is more typical than not. The great backlash against the confessional memoir is exemplary of the impatience many reviewers feel with those of us who wish to explore our pasts in public writing and exorcise our demons along the way. When we write in the confessional mode, made popular more than two hundred years ago by Rousseau's *Confessions*, we become especially vulnerable to patriarchal disapprobation no matter what the genre. Confessional poets, essayists, and memoirists tilt the balance within the conventions of autobiography away from abstracted intellect and toward "feminine" emotion; they tend to privilege "unmanly" divulgence over levelheaded discretion. Some critics attack this discursive shift primarily because it makes hitherto private anguish public. However, for cultural critic bell hooks, our fidelity to privacy is really a way of saying, "I don't want to have to attend to something outside of myself," and is, in fact, a screen for a profound narcissism (1994, 224).

The confessional memoir is also maligned for smudging the lines between erudite culture and the odiousness of the *Jerry Springer Show*. In the *New Criterion*, Alan Brooke lambastes *The Architect of Desire* as "another example of the current trend for taking a nasty little family story, which would far better have remained decently buried and trying to gussie it up with pretensions of mythic, universal import." Indicative of the contradictions within the memoir backlash itself, Brooke declares in the same review that *The Liar's Club* is "an honorable piece of work," even though it does not "gloss over the grimmer aspects of family life" (1997, 64).

Are currently popular memoirs no more than highbrow versions of *Sally Jesse Raphael* or *Montel?* For many the disclosures on these shows are simulations of the catharsis possible in serious revelation. I myself have watched transfixed as Montel reunites nervous adopted children with their joyous biological parents, weeping with them, identifying intimately with their stories of the lonely, incomplete years they have waited for these dramatic reunions. I have been gripped by revelations of injustice, abuse, terror. In her book *Private Matters*, Janna Malamud Smith sternly critiques talk shows and their hosts, but at the same time, she maintains that the issues these programs raise are complex; they cannot be dismissed as merely cheap, prurient, and debasing: "Side by side with the lode of fool's gold sits a nugget of the real thing: important revelations and people who have good reasons for making them. By doing so they attack hypocrisy, challenge social distance, and reveal the way misuses of power corrupt and abuse privacy" (1997, 18–19). Nevertheless, the quiet thoughtfulness, the continuity, the supportive attention that healthy revelation requires are glaringly missing ingredients in the talk-show format. Horrible and forbidden stories are mesmerizing spectacles for TV viewers, but they have the capability of becoming psychological bombshells in the lives of the tellers. Oprah, Montel, and Sally, who are really sensationalist journalists and not psychiatrists, appear fiercely supportive and authentically compassionate for the duration of their airtime, but they quickly disappear from the lives of these troubled people into the hermetic security of their beyond-affluent lives. Once the highly vulnerable and commodified guests have exposed their most private selves to millions, they are left to cope with the potentially calamitous aftermath of their honesty without the kind of caring sustenance that should accompany their risky undertaking.

Some of these arguments surrounding the ethics of public confession are taken up in a recent issue of the *New Yorker* that focuses on private lives. Daphne Merkin, a reviewer of Joyce Maynard's *At Home in the World*, complains with the tedious refrain that "ours is a culture addicted to exposure, to 'outing' ourselves and others" and says that Maynard's only excuse "for breaking a code of silence . . . is the usual one offered in such memoirs: the quest for self-knowledge" (1998, 154). Merkin casts May-

nard as well as other memoirists as solipsistic, indiscrete, and psychoti-
cally attention grabbing. Collectively, we are still highly ambivalent
about breaking codes of silence, especially when it comes to the privacy
of the family where, as Karr's and Lessard's memoirs demonstrate, harmful and abusive practices most often endure unobserved. As a culture, we
no longer want total silence, yet we still tout the virtues of restraint and
reticence and denigrate solipsism as a vice rather than an advantageous
catalyst to psychological well-being.

Despite Merkin's cavalier dismissal of the need and desirability of
pursuing publicly the hard truths of our private lives, most reviewers find
The Architect of Desire and *The Liar's Club* exceedingly worthwhile. Molly
Ivins praises Karr for her "poet's precision of language, . . .gift for understanding, . . .[and] insight into people," and the "wealth" of a story that
stirred up her own memories of childhood and family (1995, 21). In the
opening essay, "Show and Tell: When Did Privacy Go Public?" of the
"Private Lives" issue of the *New Yorker*, Nancy Franklin perceptively discusses the cultural phenomena with which we are now grappling: "The
fact is, we are not sure where we want to draw the line when it comes to
knowing about other people's lives. There is the appeal of the forbidden,
the lure of the closed door, the pleasure of—to use the appropriately
Peeping Tom-ish lingo of the Internet—lurking." Our culture is asking
that we open forbidden doors: "More than ever, we seem to need to hear
the stories of other people's lives and to share our own" (1998, 11, 12).

Sensing that something desperately needs to be uncovered in
Charlie's life, Karr ignores her sister's admonishment to forget the past
and resolves to persuade her mother to give up her secrets. Karr also
mentions "grace" when she describes the chain of events that led to her
mother's revelations. Her depiction of grace is quite different from
Lessard's, though no less engaging: "Truth was conspiring to assemble itself before me. Call it fate or grace or pure shithouse chance. I was being
guided somehow into the chute that led down the dark corridor at the
end of which truth's door would fly open" (311).

Like Madeleine, Lessard's sister, Karr is also encouraged by a therapist to ask her mother a list of questions she has drawn up. Reluctant to
ask, Karr knows that in her "family lingo" such questions could prove
lethal (312), but her therapist insists they are legitimate, not cruel. Karr
poses the questions to her mother for days, persisting even when Charlie
locks herself in the bathroom for hours. Karr's perseverance is so annoy-

ing that her mother finally agrees to answer. Over several pitchers of margaritas, she reveals a painfully hidden and unresolved past, a history that has left her plagued by an unbearably heavy burden of shame and loss.

Married at fifteen, Charlie gave birth to a boy and a girl, Tex and Belinda. The marriage deteriorated. Returning from work one day, she found her husband had vanished with the babies. It took a long time to locate them, and by the time Charlie showed up with a court order assigning her custody of the children, they ran from her crying. "Then," Karr says, "Mother did what seemed at the time the Right Thing, though had she Thought, she may have Thought Twice about how Right the Right Thing would wind up being, for surely it drove her mad" (317). Instead of claiming her children, she was overwhelmed by the sense of unworthiness relentlessly instilled in her by her ex-husband. Watching them cower behind her ex-mother-in-law, she felt powerless to provide for them and persuaded herself that they were better off with their father and his new wife, so she tore up the papers, gave up her custody, and left.

She then remarried, and then remarried again and yet again, hoping each time that the next man would be the one who would be able to get her kids back. Each marriage failed, and sadly enough, having Lecia and Mary Karr with her fifth husband also failed to fill "the big black hole" that Charlie explains "just swallowed me up. . . . I just collapsed into it" (318). Her mother descended into years of alcoholism, mental illness, and two more marriages (one a remarriage to Lecia and Mary's father).

Sitting at the bar with her mother amid the drained pitchers and shredded napkins, Karr asks Charlie why she never told them what had happened to her—the earlier marriages, the lost children. Charlie's answer is one that those of us who have kept closely guarded, shame-laden secrets understand all too well. Karr explains: "Her exact sentence stays lodged in my head, for it's one of the more pathetic sentences a sixty-year-old woman can be caught uttering: 'I thought you wouldn't like me anymore' " (318).

Charlie's fearful response reveals the tremendous cost of shame and the quandary it poses. Shame makes us mentally unhealthy because it is so difficult to vanquish. There is no redoing the past. Charlie did give up her children; her marriages did fail. I gave up my daughter; my marriages also failed. The causes of shame remain ever present within our history. Although the only possible way to reconsider the validity of shame and lessen the weight of a burdensome past is to reveal and then to observe

the effect on those people we tell, such a confession is unbearably perilous. If the truth was known, Charlie believed that she would lose not
only Tex and Belinda, but also Lecia and Mary. They would no longer
love her, and she would lose them as well. So she lived as best she could
with her shame, temporarily drowning it in the oblivion of alcohol, the
attentions of men, the escapades of moving, and the indulgence of
money, but never really escaping its tenacious hold until, finally, her
daughter's pure determination convinced her that she could tell.

The consequences were nothing like the rejection she had feared for
so long. In fact, the very next day Lecia hired a detective to find the lost
kids, who were now adults in their forties and "damn eager to be found"
(316). Rather than disownment, the consequence of telling was the reunion Charlie had long ago given up on, and, Karr recounts, "it marked a
time when our house began to fill with uncharacteristic light" (317). As
happens, Karr had inherited Charlie's sense of shame without even
knowing its actual locus. But after she learned about the two lost children, she found that by telling, Charlie had absolved them both. "All the
black crimes we believed ourselves guilty of were myths, stories we'd
cobbled together out of fear. We expected no good news interspersed
with the bad. Only the dark aspect of any story sank in. I never knew despair could lie" (320).

Shame does lie. It teaches us that to tell the truth will lead only to rejection, pain, and even more isolation. However, by reading the stories
of people such as Charlie, the grip of shame can lose some of its hold on
our psyches. By hearing the stories of Suzannah Lessard and her sisters,
who finally and intrepidly tell their stories and put an end to a family
legacy of sexual violence, we can understand the fuller implications of
the psychological and emotional damage that shame and secrecy can do.
By letting these narratives set an example of the virtue of forthrightness,
we can find the courage to tell our own stories. Only then can we recast
our myths of shame and fear into stories that rightfully deserve compassion and beneficence. Only in telling can we begin to make right the
wrongs of the past.

4

LIVING IN PLAIN SIGHT
Audience and Memoir

I have come to believe over and over again that what is most important to me must be spoken, made verbal and shared, even at the risk of having it bruised or misunderstood. That speaking profits me, beyond any other effect.—Audre Lorde, Sister Outsider

Although writing my memoir has proved cathartic, I am like Charlie, Mary Karr's mother: I too am afraid of the responses of people who will now know all my secrets. I dread what most who guard secrets fear when it comes to revelation—rejection, condemnation, or offense. I worry that my personal writing will be considered sentimental or juvenile or that telling the secret will sound self-indulgently maudlin. I fear disapproval for having jumped on the memoir bandwagon, for commodifying my life, or, as one of my more insensitive male colleagues put it, for "spilling my guts" in order to publish. I have had threatening audiences in mind from the start, the same kind of powerfully inhibiting audiences that led me to agree to keep the secret in the first place.

In order to begin writing at all, I had to take the rhetorician Peter Elbow's advice and write my initial drafts in what he calls "the desert island mode." Repressing my awareness of that hostile audience, I "unleash[ed] language for its own sake . . . without much *intention* and without much need for *communication*" (1994, 264, 271). Although I surely intended my memoir to convey meaning, I alone functioned as the audience, composing primarily for my own understanding, continuously switching back and forth between writer and reader, thinker and rememberer.

The next step was to shape the text for an intended audience. My purpose was to share the narrative with my husband, close friends, sisters, and children. That was an intimidating and demanding stage, one I took with caution and doubt, but one I knew I had to take if I was going to allow the memoir to fulfill its possibilities. Although the initial writing-to-understand was crucial, the real purpose of the project was to narrate the secret that had kept me psychologically isolated while also destabilizing a substructure of my moral character. I hoped not only to peel away the secret's intricacies for this initial audience but also to create a more integrated and honest persona that would enhance, not diminish, my inner life.

My carefully chosen group of first readers, all of whom I knew cared about me (even though I felt they had never fully known me), was supportive and encouraging. They did not feel misled, fooled, tricked, or betrayed; instead, they expressed sadness for my loss, frustration with the social mores of 1965 that encouraged repression and denial, and outrage for the harrowing night of Sorrow's birth. Their empathic responses were crucial to my project and me. I could now continue.

Next came the move into a more public forum and an audience of colleagues, students, and strangers. Philosopher Jorge Gracia refers to this grouping as the writer's contemporaneous audience: "members of his and similar social groups who have the basic educational and cultural tools to be in principle capable of understanding the text in question and who are roughly contemporaneous with the author" (1996, 146). I knew I had to risk disclosure before peers who did not know me personally. Nervously, I read the memoir to strangers for the first time at a woman's retreat, seated in a circle with thirty women. As a member of a panel at a scholarly conference, I read it again, this time with even greater agitation, but I felt sure this kind of exposure was a necessary ingredient in my struggle to put my secrets to rest. Without telling my story to contemporaneous audiences, I could not begin to draw forthrightly on my actual experience in both my personal and my professional lives. So tentatively, I reached out publicly to these two audiences, and their compassionate responses were confirming and inspiring. When I ask myself why these audiences are necessary at all for the memoirist, I find the answer by recalling these early audiences. Their affirming reactions served as both acceptance and impetus: acceptance of my truer self and an impetus to continue the difficult work of composing that self.

Of theoretical interest for the memoir is the way those of us with ostensibly shameful secrets so cautiously seek our audience. As the psychological stakes rise, the relationship between the memoirist and her audience becomes more acute and nuanced. Whether it be a coming-out story, an account of sexual abuse, or a confession of addiction, intimate revelation is such a genuine risk that an understanding of rhetorical context is crucial. When we publicly reveal our personal experiences, we are making them available to all kinds of listeners. As the rhetorical theorist Susan Wells points out, the reading "public is not simply a neutral container for historical events: it has a history, its own vexed construction, its own possibilities of growth and decay" (1996, 328). Because we cannot count on a sympathetic public, memoirists try to weave into their narratives the intricate contextual strands their audience needs to be receptive and benevolent. Fearing a damning reception, I endeavored to chronicle in my memoir some of the texture of the social and familial fabric that led to losing Sorrow. My readers needed the specificity that would help them grasp why the plot unfolds as it does. I also wanted to be an agent of change, hoping that by disclosing how I became a pawn to conservative mores, readers might come to think of pregnant teenagers more charitably, might regard regretful birth mothers more sympathetically.

Memoirs have to make their own way in the world, of course, but memoirists do hope that their narratives will invoke collective empathy. Nevertheless, we can never fully control the role our audiences might take. Given the fluid, shifting stances available to readers, they may indeed decline the engaged, empathic role we hope to invoke and become, instead, detached and dispassionate, unforgiving and judgmental. But finally, memoirists must proceed as best they can. After all, we need readers; they are crucial collaborators in completing the writing transaction. The readers of my memoir are evaluators not just of my writing, but also of the most vulnerable facets of my subjectivity. Like most memoirists, I have risked much, opening long-barricaded, shame-laden parts of myself for scrutiny. Readers may reject the compassionate role I ask them to adopt, but regardless of the role they take, they become, as they read, intertwined with my emotional well-being in ways that differ qualitatively from reading fiction.

Narrative has a healing power, and memoirs such as Lessard's and Karr's are good examples of this emotionally medicinal process, but memoirs also ask probing questions about the ethical and political functions that narrative can perform. Indeed, the ultimate goal of a memoirist may be to transform her audience and so change society. Beyond personal redemption, the telling of shameful stories has the possibility to kindle an audience's awareness, forbearance, and compassion so that democratic communities can be nourished and strengthened. On the other hand, the intent of the memoirist might be to provoke consternation and contention and thereby to unsettle an indifferent community or to bind it together by fueling disapprobation and protest. By attempting to invoke empathic audiences, memoirs can serve as catalysts, asking us to interrogate ethical givens, helping us to keep open the social processes through which we reconstitute our social tenets.

I publish my memoir, then, convinced that social good can come from honest revelation. Furthermore, I suggest that by writing, reading, and analyzing the memoirs that are now part of our contemporary literary landscape, by telling stories and invoking audiences to listen compassionately, we can see better our true similarities, understand better our authentic differences. The contemporary memoir is such a radical form of narrative because it describes real sorrow, suffering, shame, trauma, and violence from the victim's point of view, from the outsider's perspective, the one who has kept silent for fear of unmasking the secrets that render her most vulnerable.

In *Sister Outsider*, Audre Lorde observes that for most women, the transformation of our silences into language seems dangerous, "for we have been socialized to respect fear more than our own needs for language and definition." Nevertheless, "we fear the visibility without which we cannot truly live" (1984, 44, 42). Ironically, the intricate webs of dissembling are stifling, even enslaving, traps that, in fact, do nothing to temper our fears. Lorde alerts us of the futility of our silence: "We can sit in our corners mute forever while our sisters and our selves are wasted, while our children are distorted and destroyed, while our earth is poisoned; we can sit in our safe corners mute as bottles, and we will still be no less afraid" (42). Not only will our silence do nothing to bring about social change, but it also does little to assuage our suffering or allay our fears. Furthermore, "While we wait in silence for that final luxury of fearlessness, the weight of that silence will choke us" (44).

The memoir is, then, emblematic of a larger social practice: casting off the albatross of silence. And so, the memoirist's attempt at authenticity is hollow without audience. The liberating outcomes of self-revelation are simply unattainable outside the embrace of communities able to hear the voices of its members. Defining, naming, and speaking for ourselves is not only psychologically beneficial for memoirists as members of communities, but also salubrious for communities themselves. By authorizing memoirlike procedure, responsibly intimate disclosure in locations where we gather together as friends and acquaintances, colleagues and peers, caretakers and caregivers, fellow learners and fellow citizens, we can learn what needs attending to, what requires our concern. By allowing time for the personal in our classrooms, our churches and synagogues, our workplaces, our civic groups, our shelters, our prisons, our hospitals, and our homes, we can better create the stage for meaningful collective work. A community will best serve its members when there are fluid and reciprocal channels of revelation and understanding, when the community can behave compassionately, generating trust, openness, connection, and mutual responsibility.

My parents and their community taught me to internalize a disapproving audience. I accepted the necessity for secrecy as a way to protect myself from the opprobrium of that reified audience. Fearing such an adversarial audience, I adopted a distorted narrative, one that was written for me and my parents by a culturally authoritative, condemning discourse. Over time, I have come to realize that the key to finding release from that falsified narrative is to *retell* the story to audiences that can respond out of another value system, one that promotes tolerance, compassion, and understanding. In a kind of cathartic ritual—a discursive purgation—memoirists finally need audiences who will through empathy release them from the shame of their secrets. By invoking such sympathetic audiences, memoirs democratically foster communal circles of writers and readers that can enrich us all.

The Kiss: A Memoir

> We're taught to expect unconditional love from our parents, but I think it is more the gift our children give us. It's they who love us helplessly, no matter what or who we are.—Kathryn Harrison

One of the most controversial of recent confessional memoirs has been *The Kiss: A Memoir*, by Kathryn Harrison.[1] Even before its release, an an-

---

1. Although I cover a great deal of the combustible reception *The Kiss: A Memoir* received, there was much more, most of which continues the argument: should Harrison

ticipatory buzz was stirring among its first audience—the New York publishing world. Copies sent out for prepublication endorsements were photocopied and eagerly passed around. The reviews illustrate the varied emotional ways audiences receive controversial sexual stories. Reviewers were significantly divided: the disapproving were pugnaciously hostile; the approving were earnestly sympathetic.

Phillip Lopate, a respected critic of autobiography and editor of *The Art of the Personal Essay*, liked *The Kiss*, remarking on its lyrical and analytical quality, comparing it favorably to Marguerite Duras's *Lover* (qtd. in Shnayerson 1997, 56). But in the *Village Voice*, Rhonda Lieberman finds it a much hyped "J. Crew version of Marguerite Duras, . . . oedipal soft-porn-fest with the craftsmanship and virtuosic lack of irony of Martha Stewart arranging a casual country brunch that just happens to be ready when her TV guests drop by" (1997, 10). Jonathan Yardley of the *Washington Post* dismisses it as "trash . . . [with] not an artful word in it" (qtd. in Alther 1997, 33). In the *New Republic*, James Wolcott is so repelled by the memoir that he feels obligated to comment on all of Harrison's writings, claiming they "constitute a narcissistic act intended to invite misery and humiliation upon her children, especially her daughter" (qtd. in Wolff 1997, 19E). The antagonistic audience cannot seem to get past an explicit admission in the memoir: Harrison *agreed* to have sex with her father not when she was a defenseless child but when she was twenty. Harrison's complicity is apparently more disturbing than her father's se-

---

have used the memoir genre in order, asks Suzanne Moore, "to exonerate herself? Is she not culpable?" Moore, impatient with "the mountains of self-obsession and self-deception that pass for heavily marketed 'honesty' these days," observes that feminist writing "may well do the author good but inflicting it upon others is an act of sadism by committed masochists" (1997, 44). In her essay "Doing Daddy Down," Elizabeth Powers is critical of Harrison's "postmodernist style—pastiche, sentence fragments, backtracking, fast-forwarding, a general lack of narrative momentum." To Powers, Harrison does not appear to be very well or deeply read: "It is hard to tell from this memoir whether she is even familiar with the Oedipus story. And without cultural freight, without history, although there may be self-invention, there is no connection" (1997, 39). Mim Udovitch also objects to Harrison's failure "to bring any sense of rigorous engagement with her material . . . because of the remote, almost somnambulant tone." For Udovitch, the book has "all the facility, in both its positive and negative connotations, of (to cop a line from Joan Didion) a story you tell yourself in order to live" (1997, 57, 58).

duction and has transformed some usually thoughtful readers into damning, obdurate judges.

A supportive audience would read the memoir more intimately.
Rather than immediately condemning Harrison, intimate readers and reviewers take the time to discover how it could happen that a bright but
inexperienced young woman could be so disturbed and needy as to
assent to such a taboo alliance. Susan Cheever, a memoirist who has
written about her own troubled father, comments that Harrison demonstrates how "with enough skill and courage we can look back on [the
past] and mourn, and rejoice, and understand" (1997, 11). Tobias Wolff,
a memoirist who has also written about his abusive stepfather, finds it
"remarkably courageous and well-told" and adds an insightful admoni-
tion that the critics raging against Harrison are "using her as a target of
convenience for their animus against the genre she's working in—the
memoir" (1997, 19E). Insights gained from bitter experience often help
us to be more sympathetic with our fellow sufferers.

Reviews of memoirs that confront such transgressive behavior can
sometimes tell us more about the psychology of the reviewers than
about the literary merit of the memoir they are reviewing. In her review
for the *Women's Review of Books*, Lisa Alther suggests that the outraged
male reviewers who are so intent on demolishing or suppressing *The Kiss*
are, in fact, demonstrating the well-known psychological phenomenon
of reacting most fiercely against that to which we are most drawn. Were
they "titillated by its incest? . . . Why not just the normal hatchet job
visited upon women writers who are daring and gifted?" (1997, 33).

Our contemporary cultural landscape is cluttered with sexual stories, and Harrison's memoir does not shy away from one of our culture's
most compelling and problematic performances: the narrating of sexual
aberration. Given the national brouhaha caused by the intimate relationship between President Clinton and Monica Lewinsky, we can no longer
argue that our sexual lives are private matters and sexual stories the
venue of pulp fiction only. We should not underestimate the importance
of such stories. Harrison's memoir and its reviews provide fertile ground
for examining the relationship between the telling of sexual transgressions and the virulent enmity felt by some and the communal compassion experienced by others.

The Kiss itself gracefully shifts back and forth between Harrison's childhood, adolescence, and young adulthood. Harrison takes a great risk in breaking the silence and courageously telling the astounding family secret of her affair with her father. She had already addressed father-daughter incest in her first novel, *Thicker than Water* (which many critics did suspect was a memoir in disguise), and father-daughter obsession in her novel *Exposure*. But apparently fiction did not grant Harrison the confessional release her psyche required. Although she repeats significant events in both novels, she still needed to write the memoir for psychological catharsis.

In *Thicker than Water*, for example, the first-person narrator, Isabel, relates the time when she forced open the eyelids of her grandmother's nine-day-old purebred Persian kittens: "One thumb against the upper lid, the other on the lower, gently, slowly, I pulled one tiny, delicate membrane of flesh from its mate until the skin tore apart neatly. . . . Underneath was a bleary, pale, ice-blue eye. Methodically, and with almost surgical attention, I opened each of the five kittens' eyelids" (1991, 81–82). A day passes, and the kittens' eyes become infected. Again Isabel decides to open their eyes: "I pressed gingerly against one of the tightly shut lids with my index finger and, horribly, a thin worm of pus shot out" (82).

In *The Kiss*, Harrison again describes this highly symbolic rupturing of the innocent, helpless kittens' eyelids, but this time it is Harrison herself who confesses to us that it was she, not the fictional Isabel, who executed the symbolic molestation: "With one thumb on the upper lid, the other on the lower, I carefully pulled its eyes open, separating one delicate membrane of flesh from the other. . . . I held it up to see its eyes— bleary, watering" (1997b, 90). Here too the kittens' eyes become infected, and Harrison echoes the fictional Isabel: "I picked one up and tried to brush away the yellow crust. . . . A worm of pus shot out" (91). Such remarkable similarities continue throughout the novel and the memoir. That Harrison, à la Coleridge's Ancient Mariner, had to revisit the story suggests that the redemption and release she hoped to achieve when she published *Thicker than Water* in 1991 were not granted. This recursiveness suggests that we have yet another attempt at purging a haunting life story with the memoir.

The Kiss received negative reviews, then, not only because of its subject matter and its confessional ethos but also because the memoir mirrors the novel so closely. Michael Shnayerson describes the memoir as

Harrison's premeditated, "wholesale lift" of *Thicker than Water* for the sake of bettering her career or, in short, for greed. Yardley regards *The Kiss* as contrived "for personal gain and talk show notoriety." Editor Julie Grau corroborates this motivation, stating that in today's market, "issue memoirs by articulate, *attractive* memoirists" receive attention a novel cannot (qtd. in Shnayerson 1997, 60). Like my colleague who accused me of "spilling my guts" in order to publish, many critics seem comfortable accusing Harrison of telling the truth merely to sell books.

When my friend Leslie read my memoir, she urged me to publish it, believing we all need to know more about the sexual exploitation of adolescent girls. However, she urged me to publish it anonymously. Leslie anticipated the same hostile audience that intimidated Harrison and me into silence about our pasts. Struggling with her own painful history of childhood sexual abuse, Leslie felt I would be making myself too emotionally vulnerable if I were to put my name to my story. I understand Leslie's cautious advice. I know she is not yet ready to link her tormenting secret past with her gregarious, optimistic public self. But my purpose has never been simply to tell an engaging story with a worthwhile message. To publish "Bearing Sorrow" anonymously would be comparable to Harrison's attempt to mask her debilitating past in the fictional *Thicker than Water*. Like most serious memoirists, I have made the move to public disclosure because I believe that revealing my own vexed past will lead to a better life, even if it entails criticism or condemnation. Harrison wrote *The Kiss* with the same confidence. "It is my conviction," she told the *New York Observer*, "that secrets are more costly in the long run than honesty" (qtd. in Giles 1997a, 62).

In an article for *Vogue*, Colin Harrison, Kathryn's husband, reveals that he encouraged her to write and publish *The Kiss*, even though he knew it would expose her to "all manner of criticism, name-calling, [and] cheap psychologizing" (1997, 376). His words sting. As an interpreter of texts, my own included, I find myself doing a great deal of self-reflective psychologizing, which I believe is informed, not cheap. But Colin Harrison is correct: *The Kiss* resists simple interpretation and invites all kinds of psychological speculation. Frank McCourt suggests that Harrison is writing a "subconscious vendetta" (qtd. in Alther 1997, 33). Mary Gordon finds her a victim of "posttraumatic stress" (1997, 136). Elizabeth Fagan, a psychoanalyst who has worked with incest victims, suggests a more deep-seated psychological motivation for Harrison's memoir.

Fagan maintains that because Harrison accepted her father's abuse as adoration, which she still craves, now she "may be offering herself up to the world the way she offered herself to her father, . . .to get attention at any cost to her psyche and her self" (qtd. in Shnayerson 1997, 60). These words, like Colin Harrison's, must give all memoirists pause. Am I displaying my family secrets simply to get attention?

Perhaps all writers do, in part. But I believe more strongly that Harrison and I have been driven by another need—acceptance, both self-acceptance and the acceptance of others. Harrison had to move out of the shelter of fiction and into the unguarded memoir to fully admit to the horrifying events of her past. Like me, Harrison was eventually compelled to stop harboring festering secrets. She too needed to allow all the concrete actualities of her experiences to emerge in their intimate and complex specificity. I suspect that like me, Harrison could not feel entirely worthy of genuine love or legitimate admiration as long as she felt forbidden to tell the truth about her past, her parents, and herself. She could not fully love because she was not fully present, not fully herself.

In a conversation with Mary Gordon, who has also written a memoir that exposes her father, Harrison herself reveals the following about *The Kiss* and her motivations:

> I believe in the form of confession. For so long in my life—particularly with my mother, who never really wanted a child—I was an expert at shape-shifting, at being the person who the other person wanted. The pleasing one, the one who got good grades, who was thin, who was amusing. The challenge for me was to strip all that away. Good memoir writing is a kind of self-vivisection. . . . I believe disclosure is better than secrecy—one of the most terrible things about my experience was knowing that I had to hide. There would have been something unreal about writing a book I wasn't going to publish. The demand to get it right wouldn't have been there. (qtd. in Gordon 1997, 136)

Brenda Daly reiterates Harrison's insistence that incest is a secret that must not be kept in her academic memoir, *Authoring a Life*. Daly, whose father sexually abused her three sisters, notes, "One tragic consequence of society's taboo of speaking about incest is that it leaves children to bear the guilt for crimes committed by fathers (and in rare instances, mothers) against them" (1998, 135). Only when Daly realized that her silence had been unjustly exacted to protect her father and that her reality had been injuriously denied could she begin to claim her strength as a survivor. "Only when a daughter tells her story . . . is she able to reconstruct a meaningful life" (155).

And so Harrison retells the story of *Thicker than Water*—how she became her father's sexual partner. Harrison's parents divorce when she is six months old. She is raised in her maternal grandparents' home, where her mother is frustratingly unapproachable. One of her most unsettling early memories becomes a haunting refrain throughout the memoir. Waiting quietly for hours for her mother to awaken, Harrison watches her sleep behind a black satin sleep mask. The mask becomes emblematic of her mother's unwillingness to acknowledge her and respond lovingly to her, to recognize and approve wholeheartedly of her. She grows up feeling unreal, "a trick of light, a phantom that might evaporate" (1997b, 158), for when her mother refuses consciousness by escaping behind the mask, Harrison contends, "she refuses consciousness of me: I do not exist" (8).

As a child, Harrison perceives herself as a taxing, burdensome annoyance. When she dares to interrupt her mother by reaching for her lipstick or to awaken her by touching the smooth sheen of the black sleep mask, her mother lashes out wildly, hitting her wherever she can reach with a hairbrush. When Harrison is six, her mother moves out, making it clear that she does not want to be available for the daily exigencies of parenthood. Her leaving is her bid for independence from her own dominating mother, Harrison's grandmother, but for Kathryn, it is blunt, painful abandonment. She is furious with her mother and, at the same time, desperately in need of her love.

The psychological battle between the three generations of women—Harrison's grandmother, mother, and herself—is significant and alarmingly unhealthy. Her tyrannical grandmother and her harsh mother compete with one another to win Kathryn's loyalty, though neither want her affection. Harrison learns the wisdom of keeping her feelings to herself, "a lesson reinforced often during a childhood of female warfare and trickery, shifting alliances" (36). She grows into an expert at evasion, remarking, "[My mother] may sleep with a mask, but by the time I am a teenager I have made one within myself, I have hidden my heart" (36).

Many memoirists write about the existence and importance of the mask. I also learned to disguise my emotions as a child and, in so doing, became unusually passive and tractable. Harrison too becomes crafty at "shape-shifting, at being the person who the other person wanted." Alice Miller, in her classic *The Drama of the Gifted Child*, maintains that denial of one's own emotional reactions "begins in the service of an absolutely essential adaptation during childhood and indicates a very early injury" (1994, 63). Such children learn the art of dissembling, of how to make others happy by not crying, by not being angry, by not even being hungry. They create what Miller and other psychoanalysts refer to as a false self, an "as-if personality" that reveals only what is expected of them, and represses all that is vivacious, spontaneous, and, therefore, irritating to their caretakers (36–37). Such children vilify their more authentic, but aggravating, selves and learn early to forbear legitimate, but displeasing, emotions. Consequently, they develop a readiness to conform, and this willingness to comply with parental expectations transcends the family circle. As adolescents and adults, such acquiescent individuals, eager to please at all costs, willingly enter into exploitative relationships (63). Harrison creates her own compliant mask and learns adeptly how to "hide her heart," but as Miller warns, it leaves her susceptible to the manipulations of others, including her mother and father.

For example, when Harrison is about to leave for college, her mother insists that she be fitted with a diaphragm, even though she is still a virgin. With no mettle, no sense of her right to her own body, no ability to defy her mother's perverse wishes, Harrison submissively lies prone on a gynecologist's examining table. With her mother watching, the doctor inserts a series of graduated green plastic penises until he breaks her hymen and fits her with the diaphragm. Humiliated but powerless, Harrison does not have the self-possession or confidence to stop the procedure. Instead, the "as-if" willing daughter helplessly complies with her mother's demands.

Then, because of her mother's continuous nagging about her weight, Harrison stops eating and drops to ninety-five pounds in an attempt to match her mother's ideal. With no sense of her own capability and promise, Harrison is desperately vulnerable to her father, a minister, whom she meets for only the third time when she is a college junior. His highly emotional reaction to his newfound daughter is immediately suspicious to the reader but not to the defenseless Harrison. He cannot stop staring at her, and she admits, "this kind of besotted focus is intoxicating, especially for a girl schooled in self-effacement" (61). She continues: "[M]y father, holding himself so still and staring at me, has somehow begun to *see* me into being" (63).

How do we construct a healthy sense of self? How did Harrison's up-bringing deprive her of that stability so that now her father's gaze becomes so compelling and so necessary to her? Much of our self-concept comes from the way those people around us reflect us. We learn about our selves from the gazes of others. D. W. Winnicott notes that young infants define themselves by the gaze of the mother. If she smiles with warmth and adoration at the infant, the infant absorbs that gaze; it becomes the child's way of seeing herself in the world, worthy of affection and love (1971, 112). Given the black mask that greeted Harrison when she gazed longingly at her mother, it is no wonder that she finds her father's enraptured eyes spellbinding. The fact that her father yearns to see her, taking hundreds of pictures of her so he can summon her image even when they are not together, is so intoxicating to Harrison that she begins to feel that her life depends on being seen by him. Because, as Winnicott states, "the mother's role of giving back to the baby the baby's own self" is never completed (118), Harrison becomes deeply reliant on her father's gaze. "His look," Harrison asserts, "gives me to myself, his gaze reflects the life my mother's willfully shut eyes denied" (63).

With an unhealthy ferocity, Harrison attaches herself to her father because she believes he too suffers from an impoverished selfhood, given the similar rejection they have suffered: "For half of his life and all of mine, we have defined ourselves as those who love *her*, the one who won't love us back" (79). Hungry for attention, acceptance, and parental love, she simply cannot see that her father is, in fact, selfish, narcissistic, and dangerous. At the end of their first intensely emotional and sensual weeklong reunion, Harrison's father kisses her good-bye, not with the innocent peck appropriate for father and daughter, but instead with "the kiss": pushing his tongue deep into her mouth, "wet, insistent, exploring, then withdrawn" (68). Harrison knows the kiss is wrong, but its very wrongness tells her that it must be kept a secret. Ingenuously, she decides to overlook the sexual transgression so that she can continue seeing her father. She begins a process of denial: "*Don't think about it*, I tell myself, and I don't, but it seems to require an enormous effort of will" (75). In fact, her energy is completely usurped by her father, who is pleased when she drops out of school and withdraws from her family, boyfriend, and friends. He tells her, "Everyone will have to understand that for now I am your school. I am what you have to learn" (81).

The step to actual sexual intercourse with her father is not one she takes easily. She resists for months, but finally succumbs under the barrage of her father's theological arguments as to why the two of them are exceptions to the rules, why God gave her to him, why it is, in fact, divine will that they seal their bond by making love. Finally, he makes the one argument that she cannot resist: he threatens that without the reassurance he needs by way of their "expression of love," he will stop loving her. Exhausted, she gives in.

Later she will be angry, angry at her mother for raising her to be so defenseless against her father's relentless declarations of love because her mother was "so unwilling for so long to love [her] just a little"; angry at herself because she, the good girl, "the thin girl, the achiever, the grade-earner, the quiet girl, the unhungry girl, the girl who [would] . . . perform any self-alchemy to win her mother's love," failed and became so bad that "what she [did was] unspeakable" (139).

Of course, Harrison is incredibly ashamed about what she has agreed to, but what shames her even more is her capacity for secrecy. Her father reinforces the necessity for secrecy when he dashes her hopes for a future with a husband and children. He tells her: "You've done what you've done, and you've done it with me. And now you'll never be able to have anyone else, because you won't be able to keep our secret. You'll tell whoever it is, and once he knows, he'll leave you" (188). Walled in by a kind of psychological famine for parental love, she relinquishes her life entirely to her father's control. The affair can come to an end only when her mother dies of cancer, and Harrison's complex reasons for surrendering to her father die with her. Again, a kiss galvanizes Harrison. As she kisses her mother's corpse, a "slick, invisible, impenetrable wall" comes tumbling down, one that has kept her from taking paths that she could have chosen for her *own* life.

For Harrison, renouncing her father has to be absolute; there was never any realm of normalcy to which they might return, but exiling him does not resolve the past. Harrison notes that not only does she still pay, but so do her children "by having a mother who carries this darkness inside her" (174). In her marriage, she and her husband have made a place for her father and for what happened. "It's a locked place, the psychic equivalent of a high cupboard, nearly out of reach" (175). But carrying such forbidding darkness inside is psychologically unhealthy. The cupboard has to be opened; light must shine on the actual events. In so doing, Harrison has made incest real for us. She has taken us through her childhood, showing us why and how she became so needy, so vulnerable. Failing to grasp the differences between memoir and fiction, many critics and reviewers do not see the necessity (or have not learned how) to read intimately and do not extend or employ the empathy necessary for appreciating Harrison's memoir. But those of us who are willing to intimately identify with her hunger for love understand how she accepted her father's rationalizations and consented to his demands. We do not condemn her; we understand her. And in doing so, we achieve a new depth of empathy. How could a young girl transgress our culture's deepest taboo? Now I know.

Through an intimate reading of Harrison's memoir, I can also better understand how easily I was seduced by men I mistakenly believed could fill my own desperate vacancy. Like Harrison, I too was emotionally destitute and, therefore, terribly vulnerable. Culturally constructed to believe that marriage must be the answer to my emotional needs, I pursued it unmindfully, almost mechanically, more than willing to compromise my own fragile sense of self-worth and embark on doomed relationships with men I hardly knew and who certainly did not know me. I was driven by a need akin to the need that drove Harrison to her father. Hers was for parental love; mine was for motherhood. There I would find, I believed, the wholeness and comfort I longed for. A baby, my own baby, would bring an end to the ache of Sorrow that haunted me, drove me, consumed me. One loss, one raw, unmended wound, prompted me to squander my judgment for too long, propelled me to move from one incompatible man to another, searching desperately for balm, for surcease, for healing. Along with other memoirists who have written to fill their emptiness, I believe that Kathryn Harrison would understand completely.

Slow Motion: A True Story

> I've been lying to myself for so long now that I don't know what the truth might feel like. But now, ready or not, the truth is all around me.—Dani Shapiro

The Kiss helps us comprehend how it is that a bright, attractive, promising young woman can be so easily manipulated by a powerful man. Slow

Motion: A True Story, by Dani Shapiro, gives more narrative shape to this troubling occurrence.[2] Trying to describe her self-alienation because of her relationship with a man who has captured her will, Shapiro says: "My life has become unrecognizable to me. I have slid slowly into this state the way one might wade into an icy lake, . . .pushing past all resistance until the body is submerged, numb to the cold" (1998b, 3). Shapiro gives herself over to a powerful, loquacious, married man who is much older than she. He is a prominent New York attorney, so well known that she gives him the pseudonym Lenny Klein, because some readers would recognize his real name. Shapiro describes herself early on in the memoir as "a fuckup, a college dropout, a high-class drifter," and, in a more psychologically injurious way, as "a thing"—one of the many objects in Lenny's collection of fine things (4, 11).

As a "fuckup," Shapiro characterizes herself in a highly negative way, but she at least grants herself subjectivity. She is still the active framer of her life, no matter how disappointing that might be. However, as Lenny's "thing," she sees herself as pure object, and given that, she relinquishes all sense of self-authority, all efforts at self-control: "Something has gone wrong, terribly wrong, with my life. I don't, in fact, think of my life as 'my life' " (94).

An only child, she grows up in an Orthodox Jewish home in an expensive neighborhood in New Jersey. Her father, also a powerful man with a seat on the New York Stock Exchange, is in many ways emotion-

---

2. *Slow Motion: A True Story* receives much more uniformly positive reviews than *The Kiss,* most likely because although it is revealing a sexual story, it is not an incest story that confesses the ultimate taboo—complicity. The following are laudatory descriptions of Shapiro's memoir gleaned from a variety of reviews: "spare," "unflinching," "taut," "richly introspective," "seamless," and "a literary and personal triumph." Diane Cole, herself an author of a memoir about pain, finds Shapiro's vision "unblinking," although she notes that there will be those readers who will find her focus too "narrowly self-centered." Still, Cole identifies the social good that "the gritty honesty" of Shapiro's "cautionary confession" can do: "alert[ing] others to listen for and respond to wake-up calls of their own" (1998, 8). However, not all reviewers are kind. Sheena Joughin critiques not only Shapiro's memoir, but, in fact, all "contemporary writing-school memoirs" by comparing them to Marguerite Duras's thoughts on loving men: "You have to be fond of them. . . . Very very fond. Otherwise, they're simply unbearable" (1999, 32). Reviewer Malcolm Jones Jr. notes that the Library of Congress is classifying certain memoirs such as Shapiro's as "bibliotherapy," and although he maintains that Shapiro "skates around the ugly bumps in her narrative," he finds the library classification "dead on" (1998, 59).

ally distant, though she recognizes a defeating sadness in him. He has been addicted to painkillers of all kinds for as long as she can remember, and it is from him that she learns there are easy chemical solutions for tension and pain (84).

Shapiro's childhood, like Harrison's and like mine, is often solitary and lonely. "I grew up alone in a room . . . inventing a self out of thin air. I had no one to reflect this self back to me" (30). She constructs intricate stories about a girl with brothers and sisters, a healthy father, a happy mother (30). Childhood loneliness is a key to understanding the unappeasable need young women like Harrison, Shapiro, and I had for intimate companionship at any cost.

Alice Miller wonders if we will ever be able to grasp the extent of the loneliness of some children. She is speaking not of those children who are conspicuously uncared for or wholly neglected, but of children she labels as "the poor rich children," whose parents are emotionally unavailable to them (1994, 30). My own sisters were ten and six years older than I, so by the time I was thirteen, they had both moved out of the house. My parents had satisfying careers that they rightfully enjoyed, but even when the three of us were home together, I kept both physical and emotional distances among us. I knew they did not approve of the emotional turmoil of my early adolescence, so I kept myself well concealed either in my room or in our huge basement "rumpus room" that was equipped with a TV, record player, Ping-Pong table, and dartboard. Though we conscientiously and ritualistically came together every evening for dinner, I was already a skilled dissembler. I knew I could not appear without my mask of composure; there was no tolerance for overt emotional fanfare.

Alone in our big house, I invented peculiar ways to fill the space with pretend companionship. I too wrote meticulously illustrated miniature books about make-believe brothers and sisters. By dialing a special number, I could get our telephone to ring back: I would dial the number, eagerly pick up, and spend the late afternoon having long conversations with the dial tone about the complicated confusion of being part of a large family. One summer, I went to sleepover camp and for the entire twelve-day session entertained my fellow campers with the exciting adventures of me and my willful twin sister, Judy. In my hunger for engagement and companionship, imaginary siblings served as ephemeral substitutes.

Harrison, watching her mother sleep behind the black sleep mask;

Shapiro, alone in her house, "as still and quiet as a war museum" (30); myself, chattering earnestly into the empty telephone receiver—all of us waited for someone to come along and show us who we might be beyond the docile girls our parents expected. Certainly, we were well cared for, each raised in a comfortable home, well dressed, and well fed, but we were languishing in our worlds of good manners. Instead of permitting the kind of family discourse necessary to help us understand our insecurity, sorrow, jealousy, anger, and fear, our families required that we hold our jangling, discordant emotions in check. Left to ourselves, we were unable to create the conditions that would ensure a healthy self-confidence, incapable of doing the difficult emotional work necessary to develop as serious, purposeful young women, capable of discerning decision making and responsible action.

Rather than prepared for a life of self-reliance and entitlement, Shapiro is trained instead in submissive behavior. Only twenty when Lenny Klein takes her out on their first date, his wealth, power, and urbanity mesmerize her. As she thinks back on her first ride in his white Rolls-Royce she remarks, "Everything I knew about right and wrong seemed to vanish" (23). Later, outwardly embarrassed by his barrage of phone calls (several dozen a day) and the bouquets of roses piling up in her dorm room at Sarah Lawrence, she admits that "secretly, Lenny's attentions made me feel like the most special girl in the world" (24). Lenny knows that the surest way to seduce her is to feed her hunger for approval. She says, "He never stopped telling me how beautiful I was, how special I was, how he thought from the moment he first saw me that I was the most perfect creature he had ever laid eyes on" (146). His words have a narcotic effect on her, and she spirals quickly downhill into the material world of Lenny Klein.

Although she lives primarily on what Lenny gives her, she also works halfheartedly as an actress and model. Despite her indisputable beauty, Shapiro admits, "As far as my looks go, I am seething with insecurity, a bottomless pit into which compliments fall for a brief, shining moment, then disappear" (21). She has become, she confesses, a "physical instrument, slicing my way through the world with nothing but youth, long legs, and long blond hair" (21). Once she objectifies herself, assessing her worth solely by the criteria of youth and beauty, her appearance becomes even more crucial. Lenny always addresses her as "Fox," never "Dani," and she becomes "the Fox," his wild sex pet: "I am reduced to body parts: breasts, hips, stomach, cunt. Lenny tells me women are over the hill at thirty. It seems an age I will never reach" (63).

Ashamed of the role Lenny has cast her in, and having relinquished all means of self-control, she turns to alcohol, cocaine, and starvation to suppress a lurking sense of degradation. If she is drunk enough or high enough, she can deceive herself that, first and foremost, she is desirable. By keeping herself wraithlike and halfheartedly going to auditions for parts she does not get, she can temporarily pretend that being Lenny's "babe du jour" is not her full-time job. Shapiro's sense of self is that of a pawn, numbly moving in the limited directions allowed by Lenny, the powerful manipulator. None of her actions feel sincere; her more genuine emotions are lost behind the requirements of her performance. Keeping her most fundamental impulses dulled by alcohol, honesty is no longer even presumed.

Although she begins the affair with Lenny believing him when he implausibly tells her his wife is mentally ill, that he has cancer, that his youngest daughter has leukemia—all reasons he cannot get a divorce— she does eventually develop a sixth sense for his deceitfulness, partly because she has so little regard for truth in her own life. As she puts it, "It takes one to know one," and his layers and layers of lies are not that different from her way of constructing a life (59).

The central event that causes her to admit the extent of her self-deception is a deadly car crash in which her mother and father are critically injured. She is forced to become "Dani" again—daughter rather than sex kitten. At first, she is helpless; all she can do is stay drunk and depend on Lenny to provide her with limos and plane tickets to get her to her parents' bedsides. She cannot silence the voice that screams in her head, "I can't make it on my own" (75).

Shapiro's father dies two weeks after the accident. Powerless to face the funeral without him, she asks Lenny to accompany her even as she admits, "I hate him, and I hate myself" (114). Afterward, as she and Lenny dine at a fancy French restaurant, a seemingly trivial incident allows Shapiro that flash of "revolutionary grace" that Lessard has described. The incident itself is veiled in such tawdry trappings that it hardly seems possible that such a moment could call forth her epiphany—yet it does.

Lenny has become furious with Shapiro for momentarily abandoning him in order to call and check on her mother. He hisses, "How dare you leave me sitting here like this?" Astounded by his petty selfishness, her vision suddenly clears. "As if someone has peeled back [her] eyelids" (135), she can see Lenny not as the powerful, suave, fabulously rich attorney, but as "a middle-aged man with a trace of chocolate around his upper lip and a linen napkin up over his belly, his face flushed like an angry toddler's" (135). Empowered by her new and inexplicable discernment, she walks away and hails her own cab, insisting that he leave her alone. Isolated that night, she seeks solace alone, without Lenny, alcohol, or cocaine. At dawn, as she ends her nightlong vigil, she is not even sure she still exists. "The whole world," she says, "seemed empty, for a moment washed clean" (147). Though she will occasionally fall back on cocaine, alcohol, and even Lenny, this is her turning point; she will now begin to take the steps to reclaim her life, to define her existence.

The steps involve a return to college, AA meetings, generous care of her mother whose injuries take years to heal, and enrollment in graduate school. With confidence, she takes these steps and chooses the direction she wants her life to take. Her vision restored, she observes: "One of the few gifts of spending so many years doing the wrong thing is the clarity with which I can see when something is right" (225). Although she says she "will never be out of the woods" (243), she concludes the memoir with a "fairy tale" ending, even suggesting in her acknowledgments that she has found her handsome prince. She thanks her husband who "helped [her] feel safe, read every word, and made [her] believe in happily ever after."

After following Shapiro's formidable journey toward self-reliance, I shudder when she thanks her husband for helping her "feel safe" and cringe when she declares her belief in "happily ever after." Perhaps my reaction is ironic given that it was also because of my husband that I was roused from my reverie into a life-altering moment of clarity; nevertheless, I am certain that "happily ever after" is a dangerous myth for women. We must finally strive to locate feelings of safety from within. Shapiro's conclusion feels sappy and naïve. Happy endings are suspect even in fiction; in the memoir, which purports to be true-to-life, Shapiro's ingenuous closing is not just dubious but downright disappointing.

Still, like The Kiss, telling the truth appears to have been cathartic. Explaining how and why a young girl can get so lost serves as a cautionary tale. I read Slow Motion confident that Shapiro was revealing her secrets as completely as she could, making herself as transparent as possible. It is the nature of the confessional memoir to appear trustworthy; after all, if the memoirist's purpose is to reveal the truth, then why doubt the version we receive? The reader expects a reliable narrator; a pact is established, one in which the memoirist claims, "I am doing my best here to tell you the truth." All except the most jaded readers temporarily relinquish their postmodern skepticism. That this stance is perhaps naïve was brought home to me when I began reading a nonfiction piece by Shapiro, "The Secret Wife," that appeared in the *New Yorker* several months after the publication of *Slow Motion*.

In the essay, Shapiro reveals details about her father's previous wife, Dorothy, Dorothy's tragic death, and the secrets that surrounded that marriage. It makes sense; Shapiro has every right to flesh out the story and the lasting impact Dorothy's death had on her father and on her parents' subsequent marriage. In *Slow Motion*, it would have been an unnecessary detour away from the immediate story of Shapiro's own psychological struggle to reclaim her life.

Nevertheless, a key and fascinating component of *Slow Motion* is the long digressions Shapiro does take back into her childhood as she works to understand how she became so vulnerable to alcoholism and Lenny Klein. Part of the answer seems to be the ongoing tension in her parents' home that left her lonely and withdrawn. In "The Secret Wife," Shapiro returns to this theme: "My parents kept secrets. Dorothy was only one of them. My mother's first marriage, an aunt's nervous breakdown, an uncle's attempted suicide—all were kept secret. On the surface, everything seemed perfect, by why was my father so unhappy all the time? Why did my mother seem so constantly on edge?" (1998a, 86). Behind her parents' brittle politeness, which would sometimes escalate into booming arguments, were secrets that alienated her parents from one another and from Shapiro herself. Certainly, given my own experience with family secrets, I can affirm that secrecy can be a chronic disease, infecting the trusting affinity of healthy family life. How surprised I was, then, to find disclosed in the *New Yorker* essay another secret—one Shapiro inexplicably omitted from *Slow Motion*. In "The Secret Wife," she reveals: "I have been married three times—once at nineteen, then at twenty-eight, and now, for the third time, at thirty-five. My first husband was a shop owner, a boyish free spirit. He took off on buying trips for months at a time. I was a teenager, unprepared for marriage or solitude. I threw dinner parties . . . and pretended to be a grownup. Less than a year after the wedding, I left. I don't think either of us was surprised" (81). After identifying so closely with Shapiro's childhood in *Slow Motion*, and inspired by her courageous confessions of sexual humiliation and the extremity of her addictions, I was amazed to find we also had in common a first marriage of which we were both ashamed.

Why did she not include in the memoir the details of this marriage that ended the same year she met Lenny? Why did she mislead me as a reader by suggesting that she was sexually inexperienced when she met him? In *Slow Motion*, she contends: "The first time Lenny kissed me I thought I was going to throw up. I had been kissed only by boys at that point—young, handsome boys with firm jaws and soft stubbled cheeks, whose hands roamed my body in fits and starts. . . . [W]hen he . . . kissed me, his tongue pushing deeply, immediately, into my mouth, at first I felt sick" (144–46). Perhaps her editors advised her not to go into the first marriage: it would make the book too long; it was immaterial. After all, she does not tell us about her second husband and mentions her third husband only in the acknowledgments, so why bring up this first marriage?

Still, it feels like such a lapse because she does give us seemingly extraneous details in the memoir such as descriptions of her adolescent aversion to her bas mitzvah tutor, Miles, and of her affection for her black miniature poodle, Poofy. In *Slow Motion*, we learn details about a dish that she prepares for her parents' visit, but not until "The Secret Wife" do we learn it was the only dish she knew how to cook for her secret husband. How disconcerting that the memoir gives us the precise details of the recipe's ingredients but tells us nothing about the first man she cooked it for. Did she deliberately elide details that would not fit neatly into the narrative she needed to construct the Dani Shapiro of *Slow Motion*?

Perhaps the stories about the marriages are for another memoir, but I am struck by Shapiro's wording when she does choose to tell about that secret husband in the ironically titled essay "The Secret Wife." She states, "I was a divorcee at twenty, and ashamed of it" (81). Shame—that crippling emotion that makes us falsely rebuild our world according to our needs and fears—is behind this omission.

Is Dani Shapiro lying in *Slow Motion*? No, not outright, but her authenticity has been compromised by this significant ellipsis. As readers of confessional memoirs, should we be more wary of their first-person narrators? Perhaps. The memoirist has a profound emotional involvement with her text. Intense shame can be offset by newfound self-respect. However, self-disclosure will probably not occur unless self-respect outweighs shame.

Memoirs such as Harrison's and Shapiro's are about devitalizing disgrace and the strength that disclosure can generate. They signify the memoirists' optimism that a better life will be reconstituted by way of narration and understanding. But telling the truth is never simple and, perhaps, not a reasonable expectation, even of the memoirist. Though objectivity is a useful goal, it is of little relevance when one is trying to decide what sort of person to be. According to Richard Rorty, "Nobody knows what it would be like to try to be objective when . . . answering the question of who one really is oneself, what one's individual past really adds up to. We raise questions about our individual . . . identity as part of the process of deciding what we will do next, what we will try to become" (1998, 11). For Shapiro and perhaps for all memoirists, decisions about which parts of a life to reveal and which to conceal are predicated by what we will allow ourselves to admit and what we must still forgo as we try to become more authentic, capable individuals.

The memoir is a genre of hope, but finally our identities remain unfinished. Readers of memoirs are best served if they take the pragmatic stance that truth is a selective process, constructed by human hands. Rather than use valuative terms such as *truth* and *honesty* as relating to some a priori life script, readers are better served to see the memoir as an expression of progress, part of an ongoing solution to a problem. "Progress is . . . measured by the extent to which we have made ourselves better than we were in the past" (Rorty 1998, 28). Dani Shapiro writes so that her past will cause her less shame, so that she can give up her habitual, impairing retrospective stance, so that her future will be larger, fuller, more resourceful, and bold.

The memoirist sees her identity as still to be achieved rather than as needing to be preserved. The memoirist and her memoir are social constructions, but her discursive practice conflates mind and heart in an attempt to reconstruct a subjectivity that will be more capable of richer human possibility.

Drinking: A Love Story

The drinking was a different kind of secret and a more dangerous one. It wasn't hidden, it was completely visible. Because it was completely visible, the drinking was a secret that we kept from ourselves.—Susan Cheever, *Note Found in a Bottle: My Life as a Drinker*

In her memoir, *Drinking: A Love Story,* Caroline Knapp provides a poignant example of the memoirist who willingly journeys to the very core of her mind and heart, not only to reconstruct her subjectivity without the augmentation of alcohol, but also to reveal to us her slow seduction into its irresistible web.[3]

Like Harrison, Shapiro, and myself, Knapp grows up in materially comfortable surroundings—a spare but elegant home in Cambridge, Massachusetts. Her mother, an artist, her father, a psychiatrist, Knapp and her brother and sister are raised with subtle but incontrovertible rules. With a certain reserve, the family ritually sits down to dinner every night at seven-thirty, "the white twelve-inch candles flickering in the center of the table, the silence punctuated by the periodic clatter of a knife or fork against a plate, the actual sound of people swallowing" (1996, 42). Nothing is identifiably wrong, but as Knapp grows and visits other people's noisy homes, she realizes: "The lack of storminess in our household spoke to its own set of problems, to a quality of subterfuge, as though difficult and dangerous things lay beneath the surface, too difficult and dangerous to speak of or even acknowledge" (43). Her childhood is imbued with unarticulated tension. Her parents never hit the children, but at the same time, they are unaffectionate and eccentrically frugal. Carolyn and her siblings receive music lessons and books, but they are never indulged with a frivolous outfit or unnourishing "junk" food. Knapp grows up with an unappeasable "yearning for *something*, something outside the self that will provide relief and solace and well-being" (60). As a child, it is *things* she craves: patent-leather party shoes, horseback-riding lessons, knee-high riding boots, the tallest Christmas

3. *Drinking: A Love Story* received conflicting reviews. Meryl Gordon remarks: "[W]hile [Knapp] can be a talented stylist, she hasn't recognized one basic fact: other people's hangovers are boring" (1996, 34). On the other hand, Lehmann-Haupt finds it "eloquent," and as a critic clearly aware of the social significance of her portrait of the alcoholic, he names the book an "important" and "remarkable exercise in self-discovery" (1996b, C18). In his review "I Drink, Therefore. . . ," Mark Cunningham reveals more about his uneasiness concerning his own drinking habits than provides a critique of Knapp's memoir, but he does finally ascertain that she treats her recovery with a "clear-eyed" and "proper caution" (1999, 52).

tree in the lot. She admits, "I still don't know, today, if that hunger origi-
nated within the family or if it was something I was simply born with,"
but no matter (61). As a child and as an adult, she faced an incessant
paean of absence. Giving this psychological craving a voice, she pro-
claims: "Fill it up, fill it up, fill it up. Fill up the emptiness; fill up what feels
like a pit of loneliness and terror and rage; please, just take it away, now"
(61–62).

Like a generous lover, alcohol complies. Not only does it take away
the longing, but it also brings out a new identity, one she likes better
than the inhibited, cerebral, and confused girl she grew up as. She likes
the way drinking helps her turn into someone "more hardened and re-
bellious and cynical . . . someone who could scoff and tell stories and
make other people laugh" (73). In her family she was taught to always
hold back, but alcohol slackens the reins, allowing her ease, connection,
relief. Now she is equipped with the missing element of the equation
that had always stymied her, leaving her bereft and hungry: "Repression
+ *Drink* = Openness" (74).

I am not an alcoholic, but I too have depended on the inflatable
buoy of a drink; in a twinkling, alcohol can erase my shyness and self-
doubt. Perhaps my physical intolerance for too much has saved me; I
have never been able to get utterly drunk without also getting ill. Without that, would I have resisted tapping into the exhilarating power of
glasses of wine, gin, vodka? Those magic liquids could ease my sorrow,
numb my shame, free me from isolation, and release me for a while. Psychologically, I may have been ripe for alcoholism; my mutinous body,
however, has been a sober and fortunate ally.

That I am not an alcoholic does not mean that I have not learned
from *Drinking: A Love Story* about myself and the obsessions that led me
down my own self-destructive escape routes. In fact, I share many of the
psychological characteristics of the alcoholics Knapp has known and
describes, as do Kathryn Harrison and Dani Shapiro. Knapp, for example, could have been describing both Shapiro and me when she relates,
"alcoholics . . . end up leading double lives—and sometimes triple and
quadruple lives—because they never learned how to lead a single one, a
single honest one that's based on a clear sense of who they are and what
they really need" (90). I am still surprised when I realize I no longer have
to juggle my secret lives with my day-to-day life, that I have given up my
secrets, that I can live one life—its past, present and future—unpro-

tected by lies, out in the open. Yet, I still feel insecure, afraid of rejection, awkward, ashamed, and embarrassed about who I have been and what I have done; I still have to fight the urge to hide, dissemble, elide, and edit. I still have to do the difficult work of constructing a clear sense of who I am in plain sight. It is hard to give up the lies, but each time I do, I discover myself again.

As memoirists, Harrison, Shapiro, Knapp, and I hold in common a disempowering compliance—a willingness to turn our lives over to inflexible, authoritarian men. A woman at an AA meeting astutely describes this habit of submissive attachment as "a fundamental inability to be honest . . . with the *self* . . . as a way of avoiding the messy, fearful business of growing up, as a way of cashing in the chips of [our] core being by simply handing them over to someone else, letting others define [us]" (90). Unable to cope with my loneliness, needing to be validated and defined by others, I told men—first Alec, then Allen, then Ricardo, then on, and on again—"*You* tell me who to be. And *you*, and now *you*" (Knapp 1996, 91). Harrison asked her father; Shapiro asked Lenny; Knapp asked several men—David, Julian, and Michael.

Given that within patriarchal culture most men expect young women to be emotionally dependent, naïve, muddled, and in need of direction and guardianship, they are more than willing to take charge, especially because our culture tells them they are supposed to. Grown-up, self-reliant, discerning, purposeful women are often viewed as unattractive and certainly not alluring, even today. For Shapiro to attract Lenny, for Harrison to attract her father, for me to attract the decisive men I gave myself over to for what I believed to be necessary refashioning, we had to look powerless, assailable, exploitable.

Accustomed to transforming ourselves into new and improved versions of male desire and cultural acceptability, we become vulnerable to much more than an addiction to alcohol. Knapp uncovers the complexity of female compulsions. Like Harrison and Shapiro, she also suffers through an obsessive eating disorder, a dangerous period of anorexia when she pares her weight down from 120 to 83 pounds. Because almost all of the women she meets through AA also struggle with "food issues" as well as alcoholism, Knapp draws a convincing connection: women who are hyperconscious about their weight (that is just about all the women Knapp knows and just about all the women I know) are suffering from a form of culturally induced self-hatred that can lead to a cycle of self-sabotage. She provides the following illustration to show how easily food compulsions segue to other addictions: "A bout of compulsive overeating fills you with shame and sexual inferiority, which fills you with self-loathing and doubt, which leads you to a drink, which temporarily counters the self-hatred and fills you with chemical confidence, which leads you to sleep with a man you don't love, which leads you circling back to shame, and voila: the dance can begin again" (137). When describing this "dance," Knapp makes clear that she is talking not just about female alcoholics, but women in general, for, she says, "I don't think I know a single woman . . . who doesn't engage in that dance to some extent, sporadically or regularly, fueled by varying substances and propelled by varying degrees of self-destruction" (137).

My own "food issues" keep me in the dance, on my own relentless seesaw of overeating versus dieting, pursuing thinness but perennially ashamed of my pudgy thighs. Harrison danced the dance to foil her mother and to free herself from her own sexuality. Shapiro danced the dance in order to stay in Lenny Klein's destructively sexualized whirl-wind. Whether it is binging on alcohol or food or carving away pounds through starvation, all serve to keep women at a distance from their more authentic bodies and selves, which in themselves are so intertwined for women that one hesitates to differentiate between them. Through a ritu-alized, perverse self-control or an induced oblivion where all our self-hatred can temporarily fall away, too many women attempt to escape from a mind and body they believe to be fundamentally inadequate. The "real" body (the shameful) and the "real" mind (the fearful) must be se-creted away behind screens of diet tricks and inebriated antics.

Secrets. Knapp, like so many memoirists, grows up in a house with particularly injurious family secrets. Her parents, as parents will do, have gone to astonishing lengths to keep the secrets, and it is not until Knapp graduates from Brown that her mother finally tells her the one that has been the most damaging to their family circle: Knapp's father has been having an affair for more than seven years. However, for Knapp, finally knowing the truth is not harmful. Instead, it helps her see her silent, dis-tant father in a more intelligible light: "Of course he was preoccupied; he was leading a double life. And of course he relied on that martini every evening: coming home was a painful thing, an exercise in guilt and be-trayal that needed easing daily. The information might have been shock-ing but it also made him human" (98). The truth is illuminating; she can understand where all the "veils of sadness and tension came from; all the energy went into hiding things, keeping the lid on feelings" (100). Furthermore, Knapp can establish a connection between secrecy and alcohol. How did her father handle his sexual conflict and deceitfulness? Drinking was his solution; he drank vodka, he drank gin, he drank and drank. Drinking allowed him to live with his dishonesty, keep the secret, quiet the ambivalence and guilt.

Looking back at the memoirs that I have discussed, alcohol plays a role in all. Suzannah Lessard's father drank so much that he could not remember entering his daughters' bedrooms at night and molesting each of them. Mary Karr's mother bought herself a bar so she could make a living doing what she liked best—drinking. Kathryn Harrison admits, "There are drugs and alcohol, and there is food, too much or too little, with which to bludgeon the senses. Over time I make use of each of these, and perhaps others of which I am still not aware" (1997b, 137). Dani Shapiro admits, "If I hadn't been drunk whenever I was with [Lenny], would there have been any possibility I would have stayed with him for nearly four years? I try out this equation in my head: Lenny without alcohol. It doesn't compute" (1998b, 204). And in my family, too, alcohol has been the magic elixir that allows us all to be as sunny and ebullient as is expected around our family table. Gin, scotch, and lots of wine keep all secrets at bay, all shadows in exile. As I look back through my scrapbooks, I find so many of the family pictures have us gathered around that table, lifting high our sparkling goblets of chilled wine, gleefully welcoming the lighthearted harmony those brimming goblets promise. Are we wrong to do so? I do not think so. Are we wrong to do so in order to circumvent the onerous truths of a complicated yet enduring family life? Yes.

Knapp cogently explores one of the great paradoxes of alcoholism: "alcoholics drink in order to ease the very pain that drinking helps create" (208). One of the great paradoxes of lying is that liars prevaricate in order to ease the very shame that lying helps create. For a long time, Knapp simply cannot see that it is her drinking, not her boyfriend, Michael, or her ex-boyfriend, Julian, that is making a huge disaster of everything. For a long time, I simply could not see that it was my dissembling, not my partner, not my ex-husbands, not even losing Sorrow, that was making me so unhappy and alone. Knapp eventually comes to see that in order for her to have made a solid relationship with Michael or with Julian and to end her loneliness, she will have to live through "those moments of profound disappointment when you look into the eyes of someone you love and see that they are unable to meet every single one of your needs" (209–10). But, she continues, "alcoholics . . . can't do that kind of work when we're actively drinking. All our impulses tell us to reach for a bottle at the first stirring of emotional distress" (210).

I have come to see that in order for me to foster dependable relationships and to find solace from the deep loneliness that periodically descends on me since I lost Sorrow, I too will have to live through those seasons of despondency when those people I love will not or cannot satisfy my needs or address my distress. Always in the past I simply bailed out—unable to live through those seasons without looking for frenzied diversion in new connections, a fresh challenge, secret escapes. Some of those escapes proved productive; I ran away to the challenges of parenting, academia, and life in the countryside, life in the South. But I was also like the woman Knapp meets at an AA meeting who admits one night that when her husband was acting like an idiot, her solution was, "Get a new husband" (61).

In all my running, I could never get to the richer sort of relationship that occurs only when we begin to tell the truth. Plagued by the same problems I had been carrying with me from one man to the next, I finally hit bottom by betraying the man I had come to love quite desperately. I squandered the self-respect I had managed to stockpile because I was too afraid to live in plain sight. Nevertheless, this time something was different. Reacting in the same old way—hightailing it once again for new territories—was untenable. This time escape would also mean leaving a tenured job in academia just when I was finally making a passable income that I needed badly to support my children through college. I had to stay put, so it was either live in a quagmire of self-loathing and deceit or attempt to live in a radically different way.

When Caroline Knapp stops drinking, she gives up her own slough of self-loathing and claims agency, though at times she feels she is still "stagnating . . . [or] just muddling along, trying to make up . . . for lessons lost to all that liquor" (278). Like me, she cannot put to rest once and for all her confusion and ambivalence. She still does not have a clear sense of her own needs and expectations; she lacks tolerance for other people's limits. But she has something new, and by way of her memoir, she has given it to me. It is faith. She says: "Faith is a new concept to me, too, but I seem to have acquired a bit of it; as long as I don't drink, as long as I expose my doubts and fears to the clear light and refuse to drown them in liquor, I believe I'll find my way, as a person, as part of a couple" (278). The promising relationship she refers to here is with Michael; nevertheless, in *Pack of Two*, Knapp's book that follows *Drinking*, she reveals that she ended her relationship with Michael. Her primary and sustaining relationship is now with her dog, Lucille. Knapp admits that she is still filling in the outlines of the new identity she began to sketch in *Drinking*: "there is still a lot to be filled in, a great deal of fuzziness around the outskirts . . . but at the center I can see the clearest image, the most important one: a woman holding a leash instead of a drink" (237). That Lucille has never seen her drunk is highly significant to Knapp, for it is sobriety that has allowed her to give to Lucille and to herself "consistency, continuity, connection. In a word, love" (238). In loving Lucille, Knapp has had her "sense of being filled anew and essentially redirected, an old identity shattered and new one emerging in its stead" (237).

Often pessimistic if not outright cynical about the possibilities of sustaining love (with a man or a dog) and nourishing faith, I once would have skeptically shaken my head at the naïveté of such declarations of conviction as Knapp's conclusions to *Drinking* and *Pack of Two*. But my task as a memoirist has shaken that skepticism, and I find myself believing in the tender promise of lifelong love with my husband (and our dog). Like Knapp, who has written and learned to live without liquor, I am learning to live without deception and with equilibrium, dependability, and permanence. Like Knapp, I too have that sense of being integrally redirected, my old way of coping abandoned and a new one materializing in its place.

Much of what Knapp tells us is what she has heard and what she has revealed before in the accepting, supportive, and reassuring community of Alcoholics Anonymous. However, with *Drinking* she has braved a potentially less intimate audience that will not necessarily identify with her addiction, a more general public that may be quicker to judge and possibly condemn. To tell her story outside the more sensitive confidentiality of AA, she has risked disapprobation, and she has also put herself more on the line. She has acquired a substantial audience to whom she has, in a sense, pledged her ongoing sobriety, her continuing pursuit of physical and emotional health. She has invited us to witness her journey, and we feel invested. But she, like Harrison and Shapiro, has increased her responsibility. We want Harrison to have succeeded in exorcising her diabolical father; we want Shapiro to continue to write, abstemious and centered; we want Knapp to live soberly and contentedly with Lucille; readers want me, I hope, to live on forthrightly and balanced.

As audiences for memoirs, we are asked to read with greater intimacy, cherishing the sense of familiarity we discover in the texts and expanding our limited realm of experience by the differences we detect. Intensely personal bonds can be fostered within this distinctive reading transaction. As readers of memoirs, we can vicariously encounter actual life events that may have little to do with our own set of circumstances, and most important, we can intimately identify with women who face unfamiliar challenges, understand their vulnerability, sympathize with their struggle, respect their courage.

As memoirists, we give our audience a kind of promise, testimony of our hopefulness, of our trust in richer forms of human happiness and understanding. It is with faith that we uncover our pasts, our shame, and our fears in the clear light of narrative. With faith, we refuse the destructive lure of deception and betrayal. With hope, we write in order to find our way to a renewed existence. With anticipation, we conclude.

5

"I WOULD RATHER GO NAKED"
Narratives of Sexuality

We need the stories, the feelings, the situations, the characters, the humor, the ro-
mance, the memories, and the affirmation of the recent sexual and communal and
emotional past that novels and poets can give us. . . . We need our formidable
imaginations and the resources of our style, our aesthetic sense, our sexual memo-
ries.—Robert Davidoff, at an AIDS Memorial Day Rally

Confessional narratives work to foster within readers the sympathy and understanding that emotional connection requires. If the intimate bond between the memoirist and her audience is to be made, disclosure must elicit empathy and compassion. In each of the memoirs I discuss, readers are provided with multiple overlapping stories about intricate secrets, secrets that heretofore have been kept within complex and diverse communities. That the secrets are freighted with shame is obvious, because shame is most often the catalyst for our dissembling. As members of various interpretive communities, we judge each revelation on a continuum from deviant to normal; each unlocked secret enters the wider cultural discourse that inscribes certain sexual practices as permissible or not, levels of drinking or drug use as extreme or not.

Narrative theorist Susan Sniader Lanser observes that getting a story told involves far more than the specialized formalities of narration: "narrative entails social relationships. . . . [T]he narrative voice and the narrated world are mutually constitutive" (1996, 183). In other words, the memoirist is not "outside" the world that equips her to constitute that story. Each sexual or drinking story is assessed not by an essential morality or immorality, but by complex and changing conventions that are produced interactively in and by the receiving community. A provisional, historically contingent, ideologically charged consensus implicates the memoirist, her story, and the reader. Ever shifting discourse communities encourage or silence storytellers, willingly interpret or defensively confound their stories.

What kept Dani Shapiro from being able to tell of her first marriage in *Slow Motion*? She gives us an answer in "The Secret Wife" when she admits that she is still ashamed of being a "divorcee" at twenty. Because the shame is still so palpable, we must assume that she remains fearful of rejection or censure or both by an audience unsympathetic to the truth. What allows her to finally be able to move toward an authentic rendition of her past in "The Secret Wife"? She surmounts her shame and fear because of a more pressing necessity—to live with a more exigent conception of herself. Urged on by a moral earnestness, the memoirist's telling remains an emotional struggle between the need for public approbation and sympathy and the fear of familial disapproval and rejection, between the personal desire for authenticity and veracity and artistic demands of narrative.

However, it is not only the telling that causes both apprehension and hope but also the more far-reaching social consequences that may be unleashed by the narrating. Painful stories of incest such as Kathryn Harrison's, child molestation such as Suzannah Lessard's, or rape such as Mary Karr's could hardly be told twenty years ago because there were almost no receptive communities to hear them. But by the early twenty-first century, we confront such stories regularly not only in memoirs, but also on talk shows, in tabloids, at "Take Back the Night" marches, in therapeutic support groups, and in our daily news (for example, the unappealing details of President Clinton and Monica Lewinsky's affair in the "Starr Report"). Personal sexual stories are everywhere, and they make a difference in our lives, our communities, our cultures, our politics. By hearing and analyzing them fairly, we may be encouraged to advocate victims' rights, contest homophobia, deter sexual harassment, combat sexual violence, even impeach a president. Contemporary audiences are multiple and diverse. Some listen with predetermined, inflexible standards, their minds set, their hearts closed; others listen with tolerance, compassion, and flexibility, able to reconsider their principles. The memoir is an especially apt genre to foster strong, sensitive communities that can receive stories such as Harrison's, Shapiro's, and Knapp's with empathy.

However, stories can be constructive and affirming only when they can elicit receptive audiences. The narratives that sexual perpetrators such as Harrison's father or Lessard's father could tell, if they dared, serve as good examples for discerning whether certain stories may be told. Fathers who have sexually molested their children are unable to tell their stories because of their own shame, their need for secrecy, and, of course, the potential for imprisonment. Once targeted, the molester's story in his own voice would not be received with forbearance or sympathy. Todd Solondz's film *Happiness* (1998) is a good example because his sympathetic treatment of a pedophile outraged many enlightened critics. In part, this reaction is certainly because of our socialized narrative restraints: we simply do not want to hear Harrison's father's version, his justification, reasonable or not, for seducing his daughter. Even though current literature on marginality, outsiders, and silenced voices grows, it allows little space for perpetrators of incest, rapists, or pedophiles to tell their stories in detail and in their own voices. If openly heard, a community would be forced to make sense of the story. But for the most part, on these specific issues, communities are not ready for empathy with the perpetrator. We have already condemned Harrison's father and Lessard's father and want not broad-minded, unbiased interpretation, but our uncomplicated, unexamined outrage confirmed.

What Falls Away: A Memoir

> The only way through pain . . . is to absorb, probe, understand exactly what it is and what it means. To close the door on pain is to miss the chance for growth. . . . Nothing that happens to us, even the most terrible shock, is unusable, and everything has somehow to be built into the fabric of the personality.—May Sarton, *Recovering: A Journal, 1978–1979*

Stories of sexual abuse continue to be told from the point of view of their victims. Unable to receive the child molester's story as a fully realized and problematized narrative, we comfortably receive it through the eyes of those people who have suffered molestation or seduction. Mia Farrow's memoir, *What Falls Away: A Memoir*, is a good example of this idea.[1] It is Farrow, not Woody Allen, who has written a best-selling mem-

---

1. Reviews for *What Falls Away: A Memoir* have been generally good, but include much sarcasm from critics who do not want to recognize Farrow as a serious writer and do not want to recognize any memoir as serious literature. Mim Udovitch, who found *The Kiss* "somnambulant," finds *What Falls Away* "a lot of fun, especially the icily sweet in-

oir about the debacle of Allen's seduction of Farrow's daughter, Soon-Yi Previn, and his possible molestation of their daughter, Dylan.

Talk shows and tabloids that prey on the sensational serve as amplifiers of permissible and impermissible sexual practices.[2] True to form, they relentlessly covered the Farrow-Allen breakup, the relationship between Allen and Soon-Yi, and the child molestation charges brought against Allen by the State of Connecticut. However, such venues, which go to great lengths to narrate the lurid and scandalous, are unhelpful contributors to our expanding cultural narrative of threatened children.

---

sincerity with which Farrow dices, cubes, and disposes of Allen" (1997, 58). Ironically, when Kathryn Harrison herself reviews Farrow's memoir, she becomes preoccupied with psychoanalyzing Farrow's motivations for adopting ten children: "the reader begins to suspect that what Ms. Farrow is really collecting is order, solace, meaning, redemption. That she arms herself against her demons with children." Interestingly, although Harrison finds the memoir "affecting," even "unnerving," she concludes by using the same kind of language that has been leveled at *The Kiss*: "a lot of it is melodramatic . . . manipulative" (1997a, 9). Farrow's memoir is also described as "eloquent but unnervingly opaque" (Jackson 1997, 88), with "deft touches of comic understatement and . . . quiet, spare and evocative sketches" that show "Farrow has the writerly chops to compete with other memoirists on the glutted scene these days" (Beram 1997, 25).

2. In her discussion of the Allen-Farrow trial, Janna Malamud Smith observes that "the subtext of contemporary celebrity 'news' often explores the question of how much power women should have, and examines their status as victim or perpetrator: Anita Hill versus Clarence Thomas, Woody Allen versus Mia Farrow." Journalists attempt to figure out which partner was "bad," but in so doing, they irresistibly sensationalize the sexual content, and their descriptions become titillating and pleasurable (1997, 205, 90). Nevertheless, "the media attention to these struggles signals a larger issue. Traditional power divisions between the sexes are shifting. . . , and people feel anxious. This anxiety leads the public to examine some stories very closely as it seeks knowledge about what these changes might mean to private life and relationships" (205). Reactions to Farrow's memoir and Allen's culpability or lack thereof provide a rich array of reactions to our culture's sexual anxieties and its concomitant unwillingness to relinquish certain heroes. When Nell Beram was asked to review Farrow's book in the *Women's Review of Books*, she was cautioned: "Farrow has an ax to grind." Nevertheless, she counters such typecasting of the scorned, thus vindictive, woman with the following tough but deserved observations: "Could it be that Allen, whose films' popularity hasn't suffered critically or commercially since the scandals, has inoculated himself against lasting public enmity through his moralizing, endlessly romantic, quasi-autobiographical sensitive-guy film incarnations? White liberals seem as hell-bent on believing his innocence of child abuse as many blacks are on believing O. J. Simpson's innocence of murder, despite the profiles of our heroes that have emerged" (1997, 25).

They continue to exacerbate the cultural anxiety that began in the 1970s over child abuse and came to encompass "kidnappers, child molesters, child pornographers, drug pushers, pimps, Satanists, Halloween sadists . . . abortionists, drunk drivers, people with AIDS," and so on (Plummer 1995, 118–19). Sensational formats such as the tabloids that deal with these sexual stories in an unproblematized mode can only disrupt rather than consolidate potential communities by generating pervasive distrust, sanctioning stereotypical thinking, and fostering sexual panic. Their reporting does not, I would argue, encourage the social intervention or communal guardianship that would better protect children. After all, despite decades of sensational reportage, children are still at risk, and the number of abuse cases is not abating.

Harrison, Lessard, and Farrow give us insights into how sexual stories should be told. Rather than tabloid headlines, we need to hear the specificity of the private stories, the particular feelings, the unique attachments, the singular memories. We need the clear delineation of a life. Mia Farrow takes us beyond the oversimplifying tabloid synopses and into the specificity of her private story. She begins with her childhood, so that we can slowly come to understand the sexual stories of her adulthood—how it could happen that she would love a man who could seduce her adolescent daughter and sexually pursue their daughter.

Despite being a middle child in a family of seven children, Farrow, like most of the other memoirists I have discussed, spent a great deal of time alone. At nine, she suffered from polio and was isolated not only by her illness but also by the fear that surrounded the disease and made her a kind of pariah among her classmates. Although one would assume that growing up the daughter of wealthy movie stars in the lavish, protected environs of Beverly Hills would be not only idyllic but also supremely safe, Farrow was extraordinarily insecure. Sounding remarkably like Lessard describing the underlying ominousness of the Place, Farrow says that "over the years, a creeping awareness of the precariousness of [our parents'] place fed the dark, hidden things that grew, malignant, demanding light, punching through the cracks in the smooth, polished surface" (1997, 17).

The family's perilousness is realized with the death of the oldest child in a plane collision: "everything was overturned, broken into senselessness" (52). Money is no longer plentiful, and her father, "morose, difficult, and demanding," drinks heavily (60). Mia is placed in the terrifying position of having to protect her mother, Maureen O'Sullivan, from her father's rage, and her early loneliness is intensified by the family's disintegration. As she puts it, "A feeling of failure slowly settled around me. My brothers and sisters were now in trouble too. We had been through too much, too separately; and now in the isolation our grief had imposed on us, we could not reach one another" (61). Because the family needs money, her mother returns to acting in New York, and Farrow accompanies her. One night, while O'Sullivan is out very late with her director, the telephone rings for hours. Farrow refuses to answer it, assuming it is her father calling from California, trying desperately to reach her mother. The next day, she learns that her father died the night before with the phone in his hand as she listened to her mother's phone ringing and ringing in New York City.

These early traumas may seem unrelated to Woody Allen's future sexual seduction of Soon-Yi and sexualized pursuit of Dylan, but they are crucial to the purposes of the memoir—to arriving at an understanding of how Farrow becomes the irresolute woman who ingenuously loves the wrong man. The psychological harm done to Mia seems insurmountable, and we can appreciate why she begins her adult life with no firm underpinnings for a well-defined, resilient selfhood and why she is so vulnerable to the manipulations of others. Rather than being protected and nurtured through the pivotal years of her adolescence, she had to brave violence, danger, and dumbfounding anguish. Nevertheless, she looks back not with a sense of unfairness at having to cope with her family's collapse at such a young age, but instead with guilt and remorse for not doing enough. She asks, "Why didn't I hold them there, my family, why didn't I hold them in their places, help them take up arms, to stand firm against demons, not to falter, and above all, to make no exits?" (76).

Farrow's guilt is generated by her own interpretation of her milieu and her experience within it. Her self-chastisement is a perspective, and different perspectives have different implications for how a person expects to be treated. Rather than seeing herself as a young casualty of disturbed, erratic parents, she sees herself as lacking the strength and wherewithal to hold a disintegrating family together. Postmodern theorist Kenneth Gergen maintains, "In this era, the self is redefined as no longer an essence in itself, but relational" (1991, 146). If there is no originating and genuine essence to direct our path through life, we construct our selves by way of the relationships established for us and by us. For Farrow, the construction of this relational self was early on encumbered with feelings of guilt and inadequacy. Similarly, when I look back, I cannot counter guilt with forgiveness. To me, I shattered the tranquility of my parents' lives and failed Sorrow too by giving her up. In constructing our interpersonal selves, both Farrow and I saw through lenses of guilt and deficiency and then instinctively brought that perspective into our future relationships.

When I have shared my memoir with readers, their first response has consistently been perplexity at my overwhelming sense of shame. My friend Andrea asked me, "The one thing I don't understand is why have you felt so guilty for so long? Why did you agree to keep the secret when you were the one wronged?" Like others, Andrea simply read me as a victim of excessive and unreflective social coercion. Although I appreciate the reasonableness of her comment, in my felt experience, I still see myself as a blameworthy teenager who let the currents of desire carry her into a whirlpool of harrowing but *deserved* consequences. I read Farrow as an undeserving victim; my readers read "me" the same way; but I cannot grant myself much forgiveness, at least not yet. All of us read texts through highly personalized lenses, refracted through experience and cultural baggage, even if we wrote those texts.

Inhibited by her construction of her relational self as inadequate, and also exceptionally naïve and unprepared, Farrow is faced with making a living. Almost instantaneously she enters the starstruck atmosphere of Hollywood, followed promptly by the frenetic world of Frank Sinatra. In Sinatra's preserve, she is again overwhelmed by a sense of helplessness and ineptitude and simply gives herself over to him, careening into the life he chooses for her. As an immature teenager with a tormented past, she comes into the relationship with Sinatra (who just happens to smell exactly like her father) with enormous and complex needs. As women will do when feeling desperately helpless and wretchedly lonely, she blindly seeks security by turning to a domineering man, though in this case, Sinatra proves as emotionally and psychologically muddled as she. Like Farrow, I too turned to my first husband, Allen, looking for loving assurance and finding only a venomous possessiveness.

Her marriage to Sinatra, like mine to Allen, is a catastrophe, and with its failure, Farrow feels "returned to the void" (129). When she meets Andre Previn, she admits that what she finds most attractive about him is that "he was more interested in me than anyone had been in my life" (156). I am a completely sympathetic reader of this uncertain, emotionally needy young woman who so craves approval that she is incapable of resisting the attention and affirmation of anyone. Again she rushes in, and before she even has the opportunity to get to know Previn well, she finds herself pregnant with his twins. I too rushed in, and before I had the chance to know Ricardo at all, I was blissfully pregnant with my son, Todd. Farrow's second marriage lasts longer than her first, but also ultimately fails, though not before she and Previn have six children: three biological boys and three adopted girls. My second marriage lasts five years, and also fails, though not before I have two more children, my daughters, Helen and Kezia.

Farrow adopts another son, Moses, after she and Previn are divorced. Hence, it is with these seven children that she meets Woody Allen, who admits readily, "I have zero interest in kids" (195). Despite his distinct uninterest in her children, she finds herself again attracted to a wealthy and powerful man. I cannot help but recall Dani Shapiro's observations about our compulsion to repeat: "It is safe to say that at the root of all basic neurotic wounds—at the center of most of the functioning citizens who lie on [the psychoanalyst's] couch—is the repetition compulsion. We do the same things over and over, and expect different results. We are prisoners of our own repressed infantile wishes" (1997, 143). Still helpless, still searching futilely for the nonexistent strong father who will finally bring her home to safety and certainty, Farrow again falls in love with a man who sometimes praises her and sometimes makes her happy, but also rouses in her a sort of "generic fear." She describes her apprehension as a "fear that comes from feeling unsafe, fear that his feelings were nothing like mine—it was hard to know what he really felt— fear of something in him, or something not there in him, fear of surrendering my last shred of power" (200).

I find it telling that Farrow describes succumbing to her love and need for Allen as surrendering all her power. Why is this capitulation so often a requisite part of heterosexual relationships? Why do so many women look for both fathers and lovers in one man? Why can't Farrow enter the relationship as Allen's equal, as his peer? Perhaps one answer is that just as dependent women are attracted to dominant men, dominant men are attracted to dependent women. If we look at Farrow's material circumstances when she meets Allen, she is far from dependent or helpless. She is financially self-reliant, a resourceful, talented actress, and a capable and giving mother. However, if we look at Farrow's psychological situation, we find a childlike emotional fragility and lack of confidence that make the ostensibly all-powerful Woody Allen perversely attractive to her.

Although Farrow does gain Allen's approbation at least some of the time and they become committed partners, her dream of creating a secure family with him is continually thwarted. Although over the years he sees the children almost daily, and although the children themselves try to earn his affections, he either scarcely acknowledges them or overtly objects to them. Again, as she did for the dissolution of the Farrow-O'Sullivan family, Farrow takes full responsibility for someone else's faults—this time Allen's. She blames herself for exposing her children to his cold, disapproving propensities, maintaining, "One of my greatest regrets is that I permitted this to continue though twelve irreplaceable years of their childhood" (211). Nevertheless, she remains controlled by her own psychic wounds, unable to extricate herself from this powerful and eventually predatory man who will not adapt to her lifestyle or share her priorities. She continues: "But then he was king in our midst: the one who knew everything, whose concerns were greater than most, a *superior* person. His opinions were the final word. And he could cut you quicker than you could open your mouth. We admired him and we were afraid of him, each in our own way" (211). Her abrogation of self-determination and self-confidence is striking and alarming.

Driven by the need to secure her family, she seizes upon the idea that by conceiving their own child, Allen will automatically love it, and from that connection will grow enduring relationships with all the children: "[T]hen he would know all they mean to me, and finally he would understand who I am; and knowing my heart, he would feel safe and love me back with certainty . . . and we would all be there together, a family" (228). Unable to conceive, Farrow adopts an infant girl, Dylan.

Again, I identify with Farrow's desire to secure her marriage by having a child. When I was forty-one, a confluence of events made me desperate to have another baby. Neither my husband nor I were seriously committed to making our gloomy marriage fulfilling—only functional. I had just completed my Ph.D. and had fortuitously landed a solid, tenure-track job in North Carolina, which meant moving the family again, across the country this time. But it also meant leaving my son to begin college in Seattle, a separation I dreaded. Despite the precariousness of my marriage, the inevitable demands of my new career, and the difficulty of moving two temperamental teenage daughters to the South, all I could think about was conceiving, and I drove my husband to insane lengths to do so. Nothing worked.

I was downhearted over the separation from my son, exhilarated by the newfound responsibilities of my highly motivating job, absorbed with my daughters' difficult transition, and thoroughly disconnected from my husband. I had no way of envisioning our marriage continuing without the conception of a child; that seemed the only possible way to reunite us. He returned to the Northwest shortly after our arrival in North Carolina. Tellingly, my foremost regret was not that another marriage had ended, but that I had missed my last chance to conceive. I could not reach any vantage point for self-reflection. I knew that when my marriage to Ricardo had failed, my new baby, Kezia, had been a comfort to me, bringing intense gratification to my life. All I wanted now was the solace of a baby. Only recently have I come to understand that I will always have an irredeemable yearning to restore the original void caused by the loss of Sorrow. And knowing that this kind of deep desire can never be sated, I can intimately understand Farrow's lasting need for children. When others shake their heads at her fourteen children, I can defend her. Had I had the means, I probably would have done the same—yes, partly out of an irrational need caused by an irresolvable psychological wound, but also out of generosity and love.

To understand the emotional complexities that make Farrow's choices merit our empathy, we must return to the specificity of her memoir. Because Allen and Farrow are not married, Farrow alone legally adopts Dylan, but Allen takes on the role of being Dylan's father—sort of. Allen's endeavors at fatherhood have to be questioned because from the beginning, his passionate attentions to Dylan are eccentric. Farrow, now pregnant with their biological child, is alarmed but emotionally powerless to effectively intervene when she notices Allen looking at Dylan in sexual ways, fondling her, having her suck his thumb, putting his face in her lap, putting his hands under her covers, pinning her shoulders to the bed as she thrashes her head to avoid his kisses, entwining himself around her in bed "like a python in Jockey underpants" (257). When Farrow questions Allen, he reacts with angry defensiveness, leaving her feeling stupid, worthless, even afraid of him.

In retrospect, Farrow realizes, "I seemed to have lost whatever definition I had once had of myself as an independent working woman, and in the process I had also lost confidence in my ability to survive without him" (241). Taken out of context, one might expect these words to have come from a poor, battered, defenseless woman, but they come from Mia Farrow—a beautiful, privileged, and respected actress. Her helplessness demonstrates just how vulnerable women from all social strata can be to the paralyzing self-doubt that keeps them from acting in their children's and their own best interests. When Allen argues that she is misinterpreting normal paternal affection, she admits that because she was "accustomed to thinking he was right about everything, he had to be right about this" (257). Because he has persuaded her that she will be unable to locate work as an actress outside of his movies and, therefore, to support her family, and because she fears he will end their relationship if she does not allow him to legally adopt Dylan, she concedes to him over and over again.

Allen next turns his attention to the innocent and unsophisticated Soon-Yi Previn, whom he has known since she was eight. What follows is the well-known tale of Farrow finding the nude pictures of Soon-Yi taken by Allen and the astounding discovery that Allen has been having an affair with Soon-Yi for the past year. One would assume that these bombshells would bring an instantaneous end to Farrow and Allen's relationship, but the emotional neediness that Farrow has for Allen is so compelling that she does not separate from him. They continue to see and speak with one another, and she admits that although there are times she is furious with him for what he has done, other times she finds herself saying, "Please don't leave me now, I'm so afraid." She admits, "In my worst anguish, he was the one I needed the most" (284).

They carry on the pretence of normalcy with Allen visiting at Farrow's Connecticut home to see Dylan and their new baby, Satchel. It is during one of these visits that Allen disappears with Dylan for a short time, and when Dylan is later located, she is not wearing underpants. Readers learn firsthand from the child what occurred after her father took her up to the attic. Dylan recounts: "He was kissing me. . . . I got soaked all over the whole body. . . . I had to do what he said. I'm a kid, I have to do whatever the grown-ups say. . . . It hurt, it hurt when he pushed his finger in. . . . [H]e said the only way for me to be in the movie is to do this. I don't want to be in his movie. Do I have to be in his movie? He just kept poking it in" (299). When Farrow takes Dylan to the doctor, Connecticut child-welfare authorities take over, but while he is under investigation by the state, Allen files for sole custody of Dylan, Satchel, and Moses, claiming that "the children are in great fear" of Farrow "by reason of her emotional instability and abusive conduct" (303).

Here, at this crucial juncture of conflict, readers seem to have the option of believing Allen's allegations about Farrow or trusting Farrow, our narrator. But by this time, it is unthinkable that we would switch allegiances to Allen and accept his version of Farrow's unsuitability as a mother. She is without a doubt the more credible witness. How so? First, she has preceded this crisis with three hundred pages of specificity about herself and Allen that has led us to harbor significant distrust for him and a host of convincing grounds for believing her. Second, she has earned our sympathy by her earnest forthrightness, by her deliberate endeavors to tell all—even the disturbing admissions of her ongoing, self-destructive emotional dependency. Third, she demonstrates her willingness to shoulder much of the blame for what has occurred. At one point she asks:

> Why did I expose my children to [Allen's] disregard for so long, and place them at risk? . . . Wasn't it my own appalling denial of the facts that permitted him to inflict his damage on those I love most?
>
> I could protest that I didn't know . . . what he was capable of. . . . I could argue that the world I had occupied with him for a quarter of my life was so utterly removed from any other that it was impossible for me to envision a life for myself beyond it. . . . I could tell my children all this, but no explanation seems adequate. In the end all I can do is accept my share of responsibility, and hope they can find it in their hearts to forgive me. (259–60)

Farrow wins our respect and trust by accepting responsibility for her actions and inactions and by admitting her own faults as well as Allen's without resorting to rationalizations.

Generously, she allows Allen to speak in his own defense within her memoir by quoting interviews he gave at the time to *Time* and *Newsweek*. To *Time's* Walter Isaacson, he defends his relationship with Soon-Yi by claiming, "I didn't feel that just because she was Mia's daughter, there was any great moral dilemma." When asked if his relationship with Soon-Yi could be a healthy one, he replies, "Who knows? . . . The heart wants what it wants" (306).

Certainly, there is a kind of truth to what he says; we are all driven by our desires and needs, sometimes in perverse ways. I have always been a fan of the awkward and unlucky schlemiel of *Manhattan, Annie Hall,* and *Hannah and Her Sisters.* I have enjoyed his movies and relished his fiction. So when I first heard him repeat this line about the heart in a television interview, I was more than willing to suspend my initial dismay at the troubling turn of events and acknowledge that there was validity to his statement. After all, I had followed my own "heart" into unhealthy, ill-fated relationships. But after reading Farrow's memoir, I had to differentiate between the good-hearted schlemiel Allen plays on screen and the controlling man Farrow portrays. Given Farrow's perspective, Allen's rationalization sounds selfish and arrogant—a self-deluding excuse for a lack of self-control, his aberrant sexual seduction of Soon-Yi, and, possibly, the sexual molestation of his six-year-old daughter, Dylan. (This accusation is eventually dropped by the Connecticut police with Farrow's consent.) Because of the specificity of her memoir, we understand why Farrow was driven by the traumatic events of her own childhood and young adulthood to go to such lengths in her attempt to forge a strong, devoted, loving family with this disinclined, inappropriate, and finally corrupt man, why she was willing to grant him intellectual and moral superiority for so long.

In the legal judgment that denied Allen custody of Dylan, Satchel, and Moses, Justice Elliot Wilk notes: "Ironically, Ms. Farrow's principal shortcoming with respect to responsible parenting appears to have been her continued relationship with Mr. Allen" (qtd. in ibid., 323). Unflinchingly, Farrow accepts the culpability. She ends her memoir with an appendix that provides the entire state supreme court decision, her purpose being "to reassure the reader that extracts from it [in the memoir] have not distorted what was decided by the Court" (343). Again, she makes an extraordinary rhetorical gesture to assure the reader that she has given a truthful rendition of the events that brought about the end of her relationship with Allen.

Farrow's purpose in writing her memoir was not first to convince the public of Allen's guilt and her own innocence, though that is the outcome on which I have focused. She clearly wrote for self-understanding:

to resee herself in a variety of fractured relationships in order to enter her future with more self-consciousness, more insight, more self-esteem. Like most memoirists, Farrow wanted to locate memories that were deeply expressive. Indeed, at the memoir's conclusion, she does achieve a new awareness of and liberation from long-standing destructive patterns: "Through this awareness, and the falling of the walls, and the evolution of self comes meaningful direction, strength, and security" (332). Farrow has arrived at that pivotal place in a woman's life where she can rewrite herself as emotionally independent, capable, focused, strong, and finally safe at home, which, she says, "feels absolutely right" (340).

Farrow's memoir demonstrates how a sexual story can be revealed so that it will garner sympathy and patronage for the teller rather than dismissal or condemnation. From her we learn how sexual abuse can happen even in the most privileged of families, and rather than condemn the irresolute parent who allowed the abuse to occur, we respond with compassion, even sharing her outrage. Readers come away with an understanding of the menacing power certain men can have over emotionally dependent women and the psychological damage that can occur in families where women are made to feel stupid, worthless, and insecure.

The telling of sexual stories such as Farrow's has constructive social purposes. Insight into the ways children become exposed to harmful sexual aggression helps us guard against such endangerment. But there is another kind of sexual story, one that, rather than delineates permissible and impermissible sex, expands the boundaries to include behavior that demands to be accepted as normal. Memoirs by men and women who grow up knowing they do not fit conventional sex roles contribute to a better understanding of homosexual and bisexual orientations that are still often marginalized.

Like stories of sexual abuse, public coming-out stories were inaudible before the 1970s. These narratives were dormant. There was no point in telling them because there were so few receptive listeners who could be supportive audiences and tolerant interpretive communities. Coming-out stories were first told more easily at the very moment when the decriminalization of homosexuality became common, and they have progressively acquired sympathetic audiences that enable them to be told with detailed specificity in a variety of personal voices—all of which has helped the wider community to understand what was a mysterious and often tormented way of life. Even so, we clearly cannot dismiss homophobia as an aberration of the past. Given the rise of hate crimes, we can understand why lesbians and gay men may need to keep their sexual orientation a secret: they still have good reason to fear the enmity of intolerant communities. Communal hostility, whether it is fostered by homophobia, racism, sexism, or just fear of difference, can inhibit certain narratives even as it sanctions the repetition of stories that confirm similarity, affinity, and unquestioned convictions. Memoirists run the risk of rejection by such communities, but the risk is worthwhile and the benefits great for those readers able to read with open minds and hearts.

Dorothy Allison's *Two or Three Things I Know for Sure* and Claudia Bepko's *Heart's Progress* foster empathetic and compassionate reading communities whether those communities are straight or gay, feminist or not. Both memoirs are coming-out narratives, and both work to reveal the pain, risk, turmoil, and joy that can and will be found by honoring one's sexual orientation and choosing to live out of the closet.

Two or Three Things I Know for Sure

> *Women lose their lives not knowing they can do something different. Men eat themselves up believing they have to be the thing they have been made. . . . [E]ven children go crazy, believing the shape of the life they must live is as small and broken as they are told.*—Dorothy Allison

Allison's purposes in writing her brief memoir are twofold: to bear witness to childhood sexual abuse and to declare her lesbian orientation. In her novel *Bastard Out of Carolina*, published in 1992 and dedicated to her "Mama, Ruth Gibson Allison," Allison creates a fictional character, Bone, who seems highly autobiographical. Allison maintains that as a fiction writer, her task is private revelation, the truthful re-creation of a life: "I'm a storyteller. I'll work to make you believe me. Throw in some real stuff, change a few details, add the certainty of outrage. I know the use of fiction in a world of hard truth, the way fiction can be a harder piece of truth. . . . The story becomes the thing needed" (1996, 3). But, finally, fiction is not sufficient for Allison; consequently, after writing her novel, she is compelled to compose her memoir, *Two or Three Things I Know for Sure*.[3]

As a child, given the assignment to make a family tree, she finds it impossible to unearth all the names she needs because, like many families, hers also guards secrets. Past family members have just vanished. Later, while rummaging through a box of old family photographs, she comes across a picture of two anonymous women with toddlers on their laps, framing a sullen, adolescent girl who might, her mother and aunt surmise, have married "Bo." But when Allison presses her mother for more information, asking, "Were they the ones who died in the bridge accident? . . . The one Granny told me about?" the only response is "Oh, you know your granny." Allison persists: " 'Then what did happen?' Mama's grip on the photograph tightened, the tips of her fingers going white while her mouth set in a thin hard line. 'Nothing happened to them,' she said. 'Nothing at all' " (18–19).

Allison is left with an enigma obscured by shame, for why else would her mother not tell her the story if it ends with a tragic but surely admissible bridge accident? Given what I have learned from my own family secrets and the tenacity with which they have been kept, I am certain something much more disgraceful must have occurred. What else explains her mother's mouth, set in that "thin hard line"? Unable to ac-

---

3. Because of the literary success of *Bastard Out of Carolina*, Dorothy Allison's memoir (first a performance piece) was greeted, for the most part, with less skepticism than most. Andee Hochmann observes that although "this monologue seems indulgently self-therapeutic, . . . Ms. Allison is at her most powerful here when she ponders the uses and limits of fiction in a world where truth can be the most brutal story of all" (1995, 16). The reviewer in the *Times Literary Supplement*, P. P. R., describes this memoir as "a portrait painted with fierce eloquence . . . [that] rises high over the pile of grief that is the modern public confession or the chat-show revelation" (1996, 32). In his review for the *Advocate*, the national gay and lesbian magazine, David Drake concludes that there is "no mushy *Fried Green Tomatoes* here." Instead, Allison's storytelling is an "act of profound healing, a survival tool for mending the heart, sending you back into the world strong, ready, and deeply, deeply loved." Most important, Drake makes a comment that demonstrates the power of the memoir to cross gender lines. He observes that although Allison wrote the memoir "for [her] sisters . . . I'll tell you one thing I know for sure—I felt included" (1995, 63–64). Mary Ann Daly gives Allison a remarkable review: "Her best stories, with a deep bow toward pain, transcend it to reach some ecstatic moment that is part belly laugh, part orgasm" (1995, 25).

knowledge moral wandering, families simply cut off branches of the family tree, leaving cryptic lacunae.

Unlike our parents, Allison and I want to know all the stories; we long to be able to tell what really happened, not to shame but to accept our relatives in all their hotheaded and cautious, lustful and chaste, tragic and fortunate complexities. As an adult, Allison understands that we must "name our own"—all of them—for if we do not, "we are cut off at the root, our hold on our lives as fragile as seed in a wind" (12).

Allison identifies with her mother and her aunts and the mistreatment they endured at the hands of their men because she too suffered terribly within that family. "My family," she observes, "has a history of death and murder, grief and denial, rage and ugliness—the women of my family most of all" (32). She states her history outright: "The man raped me. It's the truth. It's a fact. I was five, and he was eight months married to my mother" (39). For Allison, it is important to say these words over and over again, to become "a woman who can talk about rape plainly, without being hesitant or self-conscious, or vulnerable to what people might be saying this year" (42). Like Suzannah Lessard, Allison understands the danger in keeping the secrets of family violence. Because silence pardons, we must adamantly name our experience, resist undeserved shame, and risk the consequences of revelation. Even when people we love plead, "Why? . . . Why do you bring that up? Must you talk about that?" we must inscribe what we know (43).

Talking about sexual violence makes change possible. But the resistance Allison faces comes not only from her family. She provides the example of the therapist who worries that if Allison tells about being raped and beaten by her stepfather, "People might imagine that sexual abuse makes lesbians" (45). Allison, irritated by this exasperating concern, is ready with an astute and persuasive response: "Oh, I doubt it," she replies. "If it did, there would be so many more" (45).

Allison's other purpose for her memoir is to discuss candidly her sexual orientation, her growing up to be "a lesbian, a dyke, stubborn, competitive, and perversely lustful" (45). She is concerned about the ways women talk about sex, "carefully, obliquely, cautiously, almost shamefully," and she wants to change it (54). She wants to tell her story, and while doing so, she refuses to take on the shame, humiliation, or self-pity that an incest survivor is supposed to feel in order to gain our sympathy, nor will she play the role of the unsure, self-effacing lesbian to gain our acceptance: "Two or three things I know for sure, and one is that I would rather go naked than wear the coat the world has made for me" (71).

Allison will not tell a story of herself as a broken and debased victim. That may be the one that our culture expects, but that is not hers. Her ardent narrative names the crimes that were committed against her, but she goes on to tell her readers that she did learn to enjoy sex, that she did learn to love and to trust love. She feels compelled to tell that story, because "stories are the one sure way I know to touch the heart and change the world" (72).

Luminously, as an act of love for all women, Allison recounts her horrifying beginnings so that she may conclude with her gratifying present, her honest and loving relationships with her sisters, the joyous birth of her son, a healed life, and a vision of a better world for girls, women, families. Both Farrow and Allison write their memoirs not only to recuperate themselves, but also, adeptly, with self-awareness and self-respect, to contest the victimization of women that is so interwoven into the fabric of our culture. They have learned a great deal at the hands of hard, cruel men, but they do not retreat; instead, through writing, they courageously act to provide social critique and social change.

The Heart's Progress: A Memoir

> *Why not just love a woman? . . . There is a reason why not. Loving a man, you gain a place in culture—you get a husband, a baby, and a house with a white picket fence. (Or something along those lines.) Heterosexual love, as Freud was not the first to notice, grants a woman admittance to the "real world."*—Suzanne Juhasz, *Reading from the Heart: Women, Literature, and the Search for True Love*

Like Allison's, Claudia Bepko's memoir, *The Heart's Progress: A Memoir*, is about her journey to live openly as a lesbian.[4] Her message is relevant to all women who for reasons of their own lead lives of deception. Bepko

4. *The Heart's Progress* has not been widely reviewed; however, in the *Lambda Book Report*, it is lauded as "cause for celebration" and "the lesbian memoir" that reviewer Susan Rogers "hadn't yet dreamed possible." Rogers identifies Bepko as a woman whose life is not exceptional, "not the life of a leader or a hero," but in the telling of her life, "something extraordinary happens," and she writes "the model from which . . . other [lesbian memoirs] will certainly grow . . . and a model for what lesbian love is, how our 'hearts progress'" (1997, 12).

describes her own spiritual path: "It has not been an easy one, but no authentic path ever is. That's what a path is—something that teaches, hones, and shapes you, that fires you in the kiln of exposure. I didn't choose this path; it chose me. All these years I have just followed it, being led where I seemed meant to go" (1996, xi). Reading intimately, I can immediately relate to Bepko's words, for I too found how difficult the authentic path was. In fact, for me, that path was so fraught with peril that it seemed impassable. Nevertheless, even the unauthentic paths I took taught me and shaped me, and, often, particularly duplicitous paths felt like Bepko's fiery kiln, even if the shameful intensity was fueled by my secrets rather than my exposure. Like Bepko, I wandered; paths rose up for me, and skirting detection, I took them as far as I could. Without self-consciousness about the psychological forces that propelled me, I took paths that led me to hide from others and myself, paths I thought were safe. Now I self-consciously seek a more authentic road—one of straightforward and intimidating exposure. Even so, the reach of the past is long. One's past is never past.

One day as I sat working on this manuscript, the phone rang, and my husband inadvertently overheard my conversation with my friend Jess about getting together with her for dinner. But what he heard was me making evening plans with a male colleague, Josh. He was not spying, and I was not hiding; in fact, I was using the phone in the study we share. Nevertheless, when he heard "Josh" rather than "Jess," he placed me back on that other path, the one of duplicity and betrayal, the one he knows I followed for most of my life, and his distrust bubbled up despite his best efforts to silence it. Can I fault him? He was profusely apologetic once we got the misunderstanding straightened out and more than willing to say his suspicion was his own psychological shortcoming, his own insecurity taking precedence over the trust and confidence we have fought hard for.

Afterward, we saw the incident as a minor lapse in a trusting and gratifying attachment. Nevertheless, I also see "the lapse" in its larger context, for it is a discouraging confirmation that the other path of crafty deception and betrayal will always be there in his memory and in mine. I followed it for so long that no matter what, it will invariably offer the comfort of the customary. Like the alcoholic who must each day intentionally seek direction from something other than a half bottle of gin, I must be always vigilant. To choose the high-wire act of honesty will always require conscious, deliberate steps rather than the old, automatic swerves and dodges away from exposure and self-knowledge. Every once in a while, I will have to stop and shout, metaphorically at least, to whomever will hear me—"Look! Watch me! I'm keeping my promises; I'm living my truth!" Perhaps that declaration is what this book is, in fact, all about.

Bepko forecasts that someday, we who keep secrets will not need to wear our mantles of disgrace any longer (xi). I can hardly believe her, because I still find myself suddenly burdened with the bleak and heavy mantle of guilt and shame, even when I know it is undeserved. If only confessing our sexual stories could once and for all cleanse the soul of shame and permanently banish guilt; if only there really were "clean slates" or "fresh starts." Though the memoirist may hope for an everlasting emancipation granted by her confession, I fear that more often than not, the shadow of shame and fear will inevitably darken and complicate such unclouded liberation. As Barbara DiBernard observes in "Being an I-Witness: My Life as a Lesbian Teacher," coming out is "not one act but many" (1995, 103); each disclosure is hazardous because intolerance and suspicion endure. Unfortunately, confession is not an elixir but simply an endless but necessary process. Nevertheless, though we may not ever be able to at last and forever throw off our history, the best course is to follow Bepko's advice when she suggests, "the different among us [must] tell our stories, because we are all only human and so much need a witness to the truth" (xi), and I would add that those stories need to be told again and again.

In *The Heart's Progress*, Bepko, like most of the memoirists discussed, reveals that she spends much of her adolescence alone and lonely. In order to find a structured community for herself bound by love in what seems an otherwise friendless world, she decides in high school to become a nun, but after experiencing a consuming infatuation for her university campus priest, followed by a passionate sexual affair with her first college friend, Molly, she realizes she is not cut out for celibacy.

After Molly leaves college and marries, Bepko tries to fit herself into a heterosexual lifestyle and after graduating marries a longtime friend, David. She wants the conformity that the title "Mrs." confers; it makes her a "good," acceptable woman. For a short while, she convinces herself that her sexual conflicts are over, and that with David, she can better focus on the work she wants to do in the world. Nevertheless, she discovers: "[T]here was a deep and dangerous fracture in the bond that David and I had vowed to keep. The fracture was my dishonesty with myself, my belief that I was doing the right thing by ignoring my feelings. . . . My marriage was only a detour from my true path" (52). How often do women, lesbian and straight, overlook their more genuine feelings and choose dishonesty over forthrightness? Straightforward women who fearlessly speak their minds are still not the norm in the dominant culture. Women are either taught outright or learn intuitively that to honor their convictions and expound on them either privately or publicly will be threatening. Rather than be respected for their sincerity and backbone, vocal, articulate women are more often considered discourteous, impudent, even ill-bred. All too often, outspoken women are spurned or, even worse, ridiculed.

To avoid dismissal, astute women learn how to be decorous, inhibited, and, at times, false. Unfortunately, the counterfeit often infects the more authentic self to the point where women forfeit their genuine desires. Time and again, I find my women students surprised when I ask them the very simple question, "What do *you* want?" Although they are all enrolled in the university and following the structured, acceptable path that should be leading them to autonomy, the question is a bombshell; it is the kind of self-interrogation that too many young women have never felt authorized to ask themselves.

At the time of her marriage, Bepko cannot ask herself that question and answer it honestly, and she also cannot quell her deepest sexual desires. Because she is ashamed of her sexual longings for women and, at the same time, striving to repress a growing awareness that she does not love her husband, it takes her several years before she can discern that she is compromising her most authentic self for the increasingly insufficient consolation of conformity. In the journal she keeps at the time, she notes: "I think that I must say, I am gay. . . . There would be a tremendously freeing power to that declaration. A direction, an identity. . . . Isn't the basic issue one of coming out to people in general, being who I am, even beyond defining a sexual preference?" (61). Insightfully, Bepko recognizes that coming out is more than declaring sexual preference. It means being authentic in all our subject positions: at our work, within our families and our circle of friends, as well as in our larger communities. It means having the resilience to be able to say this is who I am, this is who I have been, and this is what I want in my life despite the fact that such declarations will be greeted by some with disapproval or outright denunciation.

Bepko does leave her husband and comes out by beginning what will be a long, passionate, and evolving relationship with Alice. They buy a home in suburbia with a white picket fence and build a prosperous business together as therapists. Bepko has longed to be a writer for years, but has been stymied by self-doubt. When she can finally subdue her anxiety long enough to get started, she and Alice become successful writing collaborators. Bepko finds that writing allows her finally "to work with ideas, with my own mind. . . . I needed to write to articulate it all, to say it. I felt centered and alive, and so did Alice" (104). One might think that the memoir should end here with two women who, after significant struggle, can now live together in plain sight, happy, productive, loving. But happy endings of blissful fulfillment are for fiction—not the memoir.

Instead, Bepko is plagued by ongoing depression and a pervasive loneliness. Despite her partnership with Alice and many supportive friends, she continues to feel unacceptable, uncared for, isolated. She wonders if she is good enough to be loved unconditionally. "There are no mothers—not when you're gay," she observes. "[E]ven the most loving are uncomfortable at some unvoiced level with this sexual differentness, with any difference" (134). Her sense of alienation is chillingly real, and her inclusiveness of "any difference" as a factor of unavoidable rejection reaches out to encircle intimate readers.

She embarks on a useless, defeating quest of unrequited love for a married, heterosexual woman who tells her early on that she is committed to her marriage and interested in only friendship, not a love affair. But most wrenchingly, Bepko is involved in a car crash near the home that she shares with Alice in their small Maine town. Proceeding into an intersection, she fails to see an oncoming Wagoneer and grazes its back bumper; however, this jolt sends it flipping end to end, landing on one side of the road and bouncing to the other side before it stops. The woman driving the Wagoneer is killed.

Bepko is incapacitated by her grief and guilt over the horrifying accident. Although her memoir is ostensibly to celebrate "the freedom and normalcy of loving whomever one is destined to love," according to the book jacket, the car crash becomes the most riveting event of the book. How would we fare given similar stunning circumstances? Bepko describes her own responses in a series of wrenching rhetorical questions:

Shall I tell you how I wanted to kill myself? . . . [T]hat I knew I did not deserve to go on living? Shall I tell you . . . that the woman I killed was . . . an upstanding heterosexual wife and mother, and that she was probably much more valuable in the world than I, the middle-aged lesbian? . . . That all of my life was now open to question, that there were questions of meaning and reason and random terror and my own value on the planet? (200)

Bepko seeks help from responsible people. One doctor is especially helpful when he tells her about the time a patient of his died because of his mistake. She later learns that there is a label for people like them: "accidental killers" (202). Nevertheless, her resolve to continue does resurface as she realigns her values, putting her family and her relationships first, relinquishing her long-standing need for the security of money, and willingly going heavily into debt in order to settle without acrimony the lawsuit the dead woman's family pursues.

Bepko does the ethical thing by giving the woman's family a great deal of money. Then she resumes her life, always with "a chronic sorrow," but also with the determination "to savor the good as much as I could, to create as much good as I was able, and to accept the bad as a necessary part, but not the whole of the story" (206). Echoing the prologue of the memoir when she maintained that she did not choose her path, that it chose her, she ends this provocative chapter with the following deterministic declaration: "After all, I did not design the plan, if that's what it is, so what made me think I should have any say about it? What made me think I had the right to do anything other than accept the good with the bad and stay alive until I was dead?" (206). Bepko's affirmation is reassuring because it provides a way for dealing with a tragedy that we cannot imagine living through. Yet, we find we must, for we are, after all, still alive. When our choices are suicide, or living a life of what Rorty calls "bottomless self-disgust" (1998, 33), it is helpful to hear Bepko's decision of acceptance and her determination to stay alive.

Nevertheless, rather than entertaining grand designs, I prefer to trust our individual potential for agency—the self-conscious "attempt to live so as never to do such a thing again" (ibid.). Here I am speaking not just of avoiding deadly car crashes, but also of Caroline Knapp's struggle never to drink again, of Farrow's endeavor never to give away her power again, of my striving never to deceive myself and others again. Although

Bepko understandably flirts with the idea of a prior design, she, in fact, does not back out of responsibility. In writing her memoir, she is explicit about her sexual orientation and adds to the growth of insightful lesbian discourse. Furthermore, she shoulders the catastrophe and shame of the car crash by revealing it, even though it does not necessarily fit the theme of the memoir. She does not withhold; she does not edit; she discloses all, telling of her own journey out of the shameful dark into the potentially liberating light of authenticity.

Allison's and Bepko's memoirs make important contributions to our current discourse on sexuality and sexual orientation. Foucault gives us some historical perspective here in charting the ways our sexual ideology has been influenced by this continuing discourse: "Western man has been drawn for three centuries to the task of telling everything concerning his sex. . . . [T]his . . . discourse . . . [has] yield[ed] multiple effects of displacement, intensification, reorientations and modification of desire itself" (1980, 23). Foucault obliges us to consider a constructionist account of sexuality. He throws into doubt the notion that sexuality is the natural, unalterable result of the body, biology, or an innate sexual drive. It is important to think along the social constructionist lines Foucault suggests even though we will have to hear reductive oversimplifications, as did Allison, from those people who will want to argue that the reason a woman becomes a lesbian is because she has been sexually molested by a man. My purpose here is not to get sidetracked by a discussion of the origins of sexual orientation. Homosexuals do not need to be cured, and it is insulting and dangerous when our politicians so suggest; instead, gay men and lesbians must be welcomed in our families, our workplaces, our churches, our culture.

Nevertheless, if we view atypical sexual drives as innate and biologically determined so that we can avoid the argument that homosexuality is an aberrant and immoral turn away from "normal" heterosexuality, we might risk having to also exculpate sexual predators such as Dorothy Allison's stepfather, and Kathryn Harrison's and Suzannah Lessard's fathers. If we see such predators as irreversibly propelled by their own biological impulses, we risk convincing ourselves that social knowledge about incest, rape, pedophilia, and sexual molestation is superfluous and that clinical intervention will always be ineffectual or worthless. I want to argue that intervention is not only possible but also crucial if we are to create a culture where women and children are safe from sexual violence.

In his book *Telling Sexual Stories*, Ken Plummer demonstrates convincingly that the sexual stories we tell are deeply affected by the winds of our moral and political climate. Stories depend upon communities that can hear those stories. Without the publication of lesbian and gay narratives, their struggle may not have flourished. Plummer observes: "Moving out of a silence, the stories helped shape a new public language, generating communities to receive and disseminate them on a global scale, ultimately creating more and more spaces for them to be heard" (1995, 149). Plummer maintains that without the stories told by abuse survivors, the antirape movement would probably also have foundered. Public sexual stories can change lives, communities, cultures, even a nation. Sexual storytelling is the critical component to our ongoing interrogation of sexual ethics, and serious critique of these narratives is central to an understanding of sexual politics and communal ethics. Rights and responsibilities for gays and lesbians, for abuse survivors, and for victims of sexual harassment depend upon communities that make those rights plausible and possible. The protean influences of our communities—the discourses they allow, the stories that get told, the identities they construct, the ethical codes they champion—are at the center stage of contemporary ethics.

A good example of this centrality can be found in Allison's stories of her childhood, adolescence, and adulthood. All are embedded in the narratives of the communities she moved through: as a child in Greenville, South Carolina; as a member of an extended family of sisters, mother, stepfather, aunts, uncles; in the cities she moved to; at the sites where she worked and learned; as part of the causes she was committed to; within the circle of friends she made; and in the family she now builds with her son and partner. As she has evolved, the narrative parameters of these communities have made significant psychological and ethical differences. Each community has situated Allison in the broader culture and given her life its ethical particularity by forbidding, allowing, or encouraging her to tell her truest stories.

Allison's and Bepko's memoirs demonstrate that communities can grant the permission for lesbian desire: being sexual, pursuing pleasure, possessing bodies, claiming visibility, acknowledging and respecting relationships. Farrow's memoir demonstrates that communities will refuse permission for sexual desires that seem incestuous. Allen's libidinous pursuit of Dylan was not sanctioned by either the legal community or the familial one, and he was, therefore, ostracized from Farrow's family, and his visits with his children were severely regulated. That he is now married to Soon-Yi, that they have been permitted to adopt their own daughter, and that his reputation as a great film auteur continues to hold him in good stead speak to the willingness of our culture to grant artists a wider moral berth than politicians, teachers, or any other profession.

Readers can function within communities as alert and sensitive listeners to an ever growing array of stories. Memoirs help us to resist relegating unique personal experience to the oversimplified polarities of right and wrong. We need to hear these unique stories and theorize how we and our communities might think otherwise, how we might move beyond putative ethical norms. Rorty argues that human sufferings can be reduced only through an imported sensitivity to the voices of the suffering, which is "a matter of detailed description" (1989, xvi). The detailed description to be found in memoirs can make us highly sensitive to unique voices of those people who have suffered and, in so doing, can assist us in committing ourselves to the abatement of affliction, abuse, and intolerance.

The memoir acts as the bridge between isolated individuals and receptive communities, between the rigid "ought" of ethical principles and the "is" of narrative specificity. Memoirs such as the ones I have discussed help the flow of communal interaction, help to bind us together, help us to renegotiate the shifting boundaries between the degenerate and the moral. Suzannah Lessard, Mary Karr, Kathryn Harrison, and Dorothy Allison have all been victims of sexual abuse. To tell their sexual stories means merging the spheres of what is public and private, liberating secrets into the agora, and, hence, opening them to interpretation and negotiation. As we can see, not all stories reinforce communal norms. Some tellers refuse to simply replicate ritualized, conventionalized forms and content. Instead, they challenge and subvert dominant narratives; they threaten boundaries. Such stories portend change.

With few exceptions, serious women memoirists will not give their readers the ritualized but unrealistic "happy" ending for women—love, marriage, and the haven of the home. Yet, the endings of the memoirs discussed are realistically optimistic. Our memoirists end their transaction with their readers having established a connection to a community of intimate readers that now knows and accepts them. In so doing, readers offer solace and understanding for the victim of incest or rape, the addict or the alcoholic, the anorectic or the "accidental killer," the lesbian or the liar, the mother who has made her children prey to the molester or lost them to the more powerful.

As readers, we become the wider, diverse interpretive community for their stories. Deliberate or not, the memoirists' ideological mission is to produce new mental habits. Despite our diversity, when we read empathetically, the memoirist accomplishes this mission, for memoirs can destabilize us; they can shake us up. Serving as catalysts, memoirs ask us to interrogate our own ethical givens, to rethink sexual codes, and to reevaluate our culture's powerful influence on desire.

The memoir that elicits autobiographical criticism can further break down distinctions between cultural and literary analysis and art, not just for the sake of the new, but for social change and transformation. Blending my own memoir with my intimate reading of the contemporary memoir enables me to elide the limiting and unwarranted distinction between creative writing and theory. As memoirist, I can tell my story of what was allowed and what was forbidden. As cultural critic, I can then examine the allowable and the forbidden in dialectical tension rather than with theoretical absolutes.

This is not to say "anything goes," that to know all is to forgive all. Recognizing the nebulous boundaries between sexual wrongs and sexual rights does not mean I will stop insisting, for example, that sexual molestation is harmful to children, to families, to communities. But as cultural critic, I can mediate the stories that memoirs provide, reading them in ways that keep at bay the imposition of unexamined, monolithic "rules" and keep open the ever shifting social process by which sexual boundaries are reconstituted.

Memoirists make a promise. Because the future that the memoirist anticipates (without alcohol, or secrets, or a powerful man) will be so hard, the memoir helps her to solidify the statement, "I won't do that again." The memoir makes one's past and *future* accessible, even communal; it ups the ante. But finally, the memoir exists not just for the individual memoirist's well-being; its ultimate purpose is the cultural community's betterment, the citizenry's ongoing struggle. Bepko's and Allison's voices can be likened to what bell hooks calls the "liberatory voice" because they seek meaning in language in order to contest bound-aries and disrupt the certainties of more dominant narratives: "The liber-atory voice . . . is characterized by opposition, by resistance. It demands that paradigms shift—that we learn to talk—to listen—to hear in a new way" (1989, 15). Serious memoirs do serious work.

6

"OUR RITE WAS SILENCE"
Narratives of Trauma

Where did you come up with the idea that if you simply pretended something didn't happen, then it lost its power over you?—Pat Conroy, *The Prince of Tides*

Our culture faces profound ethical dilemmas not only in the more rarified professional fields of medicine, law, ecology, and biology, but also in our local police forces, courts, city councils, and state legislatures. Our popular magazines, newspapers, television dramas, docudramas, newscasts, contemporary music, and films all provide contested sites where we confront topics such as family values, pornography, reproductive rights, privacy, and sexual mores. Ethical issues are everywhere even if they seem difficult to locate in the pedestrian concerns of our particular lives. Ethical questions are both pervasive and elusive, appearing not in isolation, but as part of discussions about honesty, integrity, morality, virtue, responsibility, and power. Because they are intimately reflective of our deepest values, memoirs provide dynamic locations for readers to enter the ethical conversations of the day.

The memoir invites the writer and the reader to compose and clarify ethical positions, encouraging and deepening our sense of ourselves as ethical agents. Because the memoir is so grounded in the texture of our lives, it can serve as a corrective, an antidote to abstract, theoretical pronouncements. Deploying the terms of traditional ethical philosophizing, I want to think of the memoir as the *is* and of ethical principles as the *ought* of human behavior. Memoirs are grounded in lived specificity; ethics serve as their thematic soul. In the blending of the two, readers acquire an enriched sense of themselves as immersed in the ethical discourse of our culture.

130

Encouraged by the possibilities of postmodern antifoundationalism, I see ethics not as concretized strictures, but as a process of interpretation agreed upon through ongoing, fluid discursive power struggles within our cultures. Mia Farrow, for example, has convincingly interpreted appropriate sexual family conventions and persuaded me that Woody Allen crossed sacrosanct boundaries in pursuit of sexual gratification. And within my own memoir, I maintain that even though adoption might be an ethical and healthy societal practice, I am painfully aware of the lifelong anguish such unnatural separation causes. I want my story to alert readers to the negative consequences of the institutionalized secrecy that still circumscribes adoption procedures and to the ethical benefits of open adoptions and open records. It is my hope that memoirs such as Farrow's and mine can add to our ongoing ethical conversation.

I also want to address the postmodern fragmented self of the contemporary memoirist, one that is never fully present to itself and deeply but not inextricably written by our culture's invasive discourses. Consequently, in writing my memoir, I hoped to shed our culture's definitions of me as betrayer and to see myself in a more transparent, more understanding light. Even so, I cannot now pretend to fully know myself. I know I will not always be able to anticipate and curb my shame, needs, desires, fears, or my propensity to deceive. The mysterious emotions that plague me emanate from unknowable sites that remain within me and beyond me, resisting absolute understanding. The memoir is not a passport to lucidity.

One of the memoirist's tasks is to raise awareness of the complex and intimate connection among her experience, ideology, and power, and to make her readers conscious of this link. By re-creating the context within which I had to give Sorrow away and begin decades of secrecy and deception, I can better see how my experiences have been shaped by powerful ideologies that for a long time I could not contest. I can see why I acted as I did, and I can (most of the time) forgive myself for those actions. Now, with greater self-awareness, I want to resituate my first daughter within my life experience, speak with honesty, and desist from harmful duplicity. I agree with Zygmunt Bauman in his *Postmodern Ethics* when he observes: "Contrary to one of the most uncritically accepted philosophical axioms, there is no contradiction between the rejection of (or skepticism towards) the ethics of socially conventionalized and rationally 'found' norms, and the insistence that it does matter, and *matter morally,* what we do and from what we desist" (1993, 250). While admitting that there are no ethical absolutes, that my ethical beliefs are contextual and susceptible to modification and even transformation, I want to simultaneously assert that my hard-won convictions are worth defending—a seemingly postmodern paradox but one, I maintain, the memoir encourages.

Memoirs provide a way to keep our focus on ethics because they demonstrate that ethical principles always animate the stories we tell about our lives. By interrogating the norms behind personal narratives, readers can begin to see the unexamined influence of ethical principles on our lives. In their particularity, diversity, and contextuality, memoirs can sustain, contest, or subvert universal ethical norms and thereby encourage readers to ground their ethical commitments in the concrete, such as in fully realized narratives.

The memoir enacts ethical choices, is imbued with values, and asserts implicit positions on the big questions of ethical theorizing: What does it mean to live morally? How should I treat others? How should others treat me? How honest can I be? Likewise, in reading memoirs, our own values come to the fore when our own social conventions are challenged. Memoirs such as Allison's and Bepko's, for example, make explicit our conflicting discourses on lesbianism, and readers can see how we have been constructed to see homosexuality as immoral, or desirable, or forbidden, or intriguing, or perhaps a little of each. The memoir positions us to understand the degree to which received values permeate our consciousness. Such awareness can offer the possibility of ethical ownership. The memoir asks us to locate ourselves within its discourse, to think about the problematic of right or wrong, to search for the source of our ideas, and to wonder who benefits from these values and who loses.

My own ethical beliefs were created by the daily exhilarations and losses of my childhood, by the dramas and traumas of my adolescence, by the antiwar movement, by women's liberation, by feminism, by my evolving professional development, by my allegiance to and struggles against the institutions that have taught me and employed me, and constantly by the lived specificity of my everyday existence. I have been written by complex, intersecting, and conflicting discourses, and I have worked hard to locate and critique these inscriptions with the hope that awareness can facilitate agency. Writing my memoir and reading the memoirs of others has helped me if not to unearth the essence of my "self," then at least to locate the multiple cultural and social influences that connect me to some and alienate me from others. Furthermore, it has allowed me to probe my psychological history and delve into events that not only left me inhibited with self-doubt and prevented me from acting, but also animated me to persist in my quest for acceptance and fulfillment.

After Silence: Rape and My Journey Back

> The part played by the body in memory is comprehensible only if memory is . . . an effort to reopen time on the basis of the implications contained in the present, and if the body . . . is the medium of our communication with time as well as space.— Maurice Merleau-Ponty, The Phenomenology of Perception

A memoir that has shown me a way to better understand how the terrifying early morning hours of March 20, 1965, changed me forever has been Nancy Venable Raine's After Silence: Rape and My Journey Back.[1] I am lucky. Unlike millions of women worldwide, I have never been sexually assaulted. Nor do I want to suggest that those frightening hours of labor that I endured alone before giving birth to Sorrow are akin to the horrendous violation that is rape. Yet, the effects of that night on me and the repercussions of trauma on Raine and other survivors about whom she

1. Thankfully, I have been unable to find a bad or even mediocre review of Nancy Venable Raine's After Silence: Rape and My Journey Back. Each reviewer finds it an incredibly necessary book, not only for Raine herself, but also for our world. Reviewer Richard A. Shweder, a cultural anthropologist, maintains that Raine's purpose is to construct "a blameless and shameless modern narrative about the meaning of rape" and to contest the idea that "surviving rape implies consent, in the mind of the victim at least." Shweder concludes: "After Silence is a book that dignifies the human spirit. It should be read by everyone" (1998, 13). Linda Williams praises Raine's account of the "isolation of the aftermath of rape and its life-altering transformations . . . associated with . . . PTSD." Williams also advocates that Raine's book be read by everyone, especially because it "eloquently reaffirm[s] that a necessary part of any national strategy to prevent rape is ending the silence" (1999, 22). Carol Birch notes that Raine is a poet by profession and that she "brings to her account a gentle eloquence that unfolds layers of meaning, cultural, psychological and even mythical" (1999, 31). In Writing as a Way of Healing, Louise De Salvo uses Raine's book to demonstrate how one can write a healing narrative. Raine "does this brilliantly . . . by contextualizing her rape: she writes about its prevalence, discusses attitudes about it, and shows how the subject is treated in works of literature" (1999, 60).

writes reveal striking similarities that have enabled me to comprehend more clearly how the ripples from that traumatic night wash over me still.

In the months and years that followed her rape, Raine learned that it was emotionally troublesome not just for her but also for those people with whom she was trying to talk about her ordeal. She relates: "It pained my family and friends to remember. To acknowledge my experience might bring up what they hoped I had forgotten—that terrible day, those hours of horror. They hoped to spare me that. For me to remind them that I had not forgotten seemed unkind, even cruel, because I knew they needed to believe I had. Our rite was, therefore, silence" (1998, 3). However, seven years after the rape—seven years of near silence concerning it—Raine realizes that she needs to write about what has become the most profound experience of her life. She composes an essay for the *New York Times Magazine* titled "Returns of the Day" in which she writes publicly for the first time about the rape, about her silence "that tastes a lot like shame," and about the pain of millions of women who must celebrate like her in silence and isolation the anniversaries of their rapes (1994, 34).

Although she receives praise and gratitude, especially from other rape survivors, many women find the essay disconcerting. One tells her bluntly, "Let's face it, people don't want to read about such terrible things" (1998, 5). In the memoir, Raine reiterates what I have learned so acutely and what is worth repeating: "silence has the rusty taste of shame" (6). Because the crime of rape is so unspeakable and degrading, rape survivors suppress the truth. Shame usually follows the binding contract to maintain one's silence.

Raine makes it possible for me to pinpoint the catastrophe in my own life. My parents and my Aunt Jo thought the chronology they created for me throughout 1965 would be linear: I would carry a fetus to full term, give birth, and then erase the hazy recollection from my life. Though they probably fretted about the physical pain, that was apparently all they anticipated. I do not believe they actually thought of that pain as different from, say, the pain of a broken limb. The trauma of my solitary labor, the exquisite reality of Sorrow herself, and my immediate and profound attachment to her were never imagined as part of their carefully plotted narrative sequence.

But I have known for thirty-five years that the sequence they devised, with its significant gap on March 20, was an unequivocal fiasco. Rather than the minor dislocation they hoped for, Sorrow's birth was an irreparable rent in the fabric of my adolescence, an opening that became the most meaningful and consequential event of my life. Raine helps me see why: "The losses in catastrophes are like the birth of a universe, matter exploding violently outward into an infinity of consciousness, moving outward in all directions at once from the moment of creation. Memory, unreliable and inventive, returns again and again to this center, because it is the beginning of changes. . . . A catastrophe, an overturning of normal living, moves forward in this way along with everything else" (36). Linearity is futile when it comes to trauma. The night of Sorrow's birth ignited an explosion of the selfhood I had tenuously pieced together by sixteen. It was hardly stable, but the center that provided the centrifugal force that kept me together—a bold, bright, sturdy girl—was obliterated that night as I turned into a helpless, unfamiliar, straining body. In my sharp and unforeseeable pain, I had no idea what was going to happen to me, who would finally find me as I waited in the hall at Florence Crittendon. That I was found and delivered to the hospital did not make it easier to cope with the next blow of the night—surrendering my baby, whom I loved instantly and completely, while tied to a table. She was, I believe, the only thing in the world that might have repaired me, recentered me after the pain and terror of that lonely labor, but she was taken away. And so my selfhood exploded into fragments of hysteria. The tranquilizer the doctor administered was simply the first of thousands more I would take in order to quell that hysteria, to silence the screams, to restrain my grief, to hide Sorrow.

When I woke up the next day, a metamorphosis had occurred: the girl I had been was gone—thoroughly dissipated. I can remember that first girl. She was so unformed, so insubstantial, that looking back it is easy to see how easily she was erased. In a way, I was like my daughter; two births could have been registered that day. Sorrow had to begin her life; I had to begin my life again. But this time, I had to start over hobbled by a complex psychological wound, shell-shocked from a night that had shattered an irreclaimable girl. Raine describes the transformed person who surfaces after the trauma: "It is the traumatized self that emerges from the dust, not like the Phoenix, the mythological bird that rose from its own ashes every five hundred years to live on as before, but more like an alien creature bearing little resemblance to the earlier one. It is a metamorphosis. . . . Life goes on. But it is not the same life" (139). Expected to be the phoenix, my fledgling identity was painfully complicated by the fakery that had to be a critical part of the new me. Not only did I need to construct a new self, but it also had to be necessarily split: one half was the more genuine but deeply troubled child who emerged from a secret trauma, the other a counterfeit teenager, pretending to be that first girl. But I could never again retrieve her optimism. Together we became collaborators, grooming a woman who pretended she was fine, just fine.

In *Soul Murder*, Leonard Shengold observes that we all have "an intense need for psychic synthesis, continuity, and causality. . . . What goes on within and without our minds may be ultimately unknowable; yet sanity and survival depend on comparatively accurate registration of the outer and inner worlds" (1989, 32). Thus I spun a personal narrative, weaving my memories, constructing an identity, but I could not faithfully register either the outer world that included Sorrow's birth or my inner world that persisted in grieving her loss. In fact, I created a tangled system of selfhood, an intricate orchestration that consistently failed me. An inexorable past kept insinuating itself into my present, and I kept breaking apart, falling into sloughs of depression that felt like sheer crevasses so deep I would fear I might never climb out.

Now I can appreciate why these periods of deep-seated unhappiness kept returning. When Sorrow was taken away, I gave into churning waves of hysteria, a multitude of overwhelming emotions were born, becoming parts of who I am. Most of the time I can pretend those repressed emotions are not there, but inevitably I return to them as surely as the tides ebb and flow. The triggers are not always the same, so I have never been able to identify exactly what provokes a recurrence, but inevitably I find myself drawn back to the same terror, helplessness, grief, sometimes even the transforming hysteria. The anesthesia I have pumped into my system through hard work—my busy family and demanding career—always wears off, and I lose control, falling off a teetering edge into inconsolable melancholy.

Shengold speaks directly to what I experienced then and have lived with since: "Soul, or psychic murder involves trauma imposed from the world outside the mind that is so overwhelming that the mental apparatus is flooded with feeling." Shengold calls this feeling "the terrifying too-muchness," and though it is born out of the original trauma, it can continue to overwhelm the survivor in the present (24). Despite my parents' unspoken dicta not to feel and not to recall, the night I lost Sorrow will never remain in the past. I encounter the memory over and over again: the coldness of the delivery room, the precise sounds of Sorrow's cry and my own wailing, the numb feeling of my legs in the stirrups, the sight of my tiny baby, so vulnerably naked except for the whitish, chalky substance that covered her, and my own outstretched arms. Despite my earnest, most concentrated efforts, I am inundated by the flood of feeling this memory releases, leaving me in disarray—discomposed, stranded, utterly alone.

Forced to deal with her own debilitating condition years after the rape occurred, Raine comes to understand that she is suffering from posttraumatic stress disorder (PTSD). I was fascinated to learn that the key to PTSD might lie not in a psychological scar born of a traumatic event, but in an actual chemical change in the brain. "Overwhelming terror, even a single instance of it, can physically alter the brain forever" (Raine 1998, 60). In his book *Emotional Intelligence*, Daniel Goleman explains that any traumatic event can leave a memory "emblazoned in the emotional circuitry," a "kind of emotional wounding that leaves its imprint on the brain" (1997, 201, 202). Because trauma causes a temporary infusion of adrenaline and noradrenaline, the memories of the event remain stronger, more vivid, and the brain system that mobilizes the body for an emergency "becomes hyperreactive, secreting extra-large doses of these brain chemicals in response to situations that hold little or no threat but somehow are reminders of the original trauma" (205). Now it makes sense why I can remember with such crystalline clarity that entire night, hour by hour, even minute by minute. I can also see why I have not yet ever been able to get through a retelling of the night's events without sobbing, terribly shaken. But it is not only explicit memory links that leave me crushed. Events will occur that initially seem entirely unrelated, yet they can defeat me with the same mysterious acuity.

For example, a couple of years ago, I was being considered for an administrative position. In discussing my qualifications, none of my colleagues doubted my commitment to the program, my organizational skills, or my ability to mentor. I am known and respected as an energetic hard worker who has good rapport with students. But objections were raised that had to do with my emotions. I am not supposed to know it, but even professional confidentiality, I have learned, is rarely kept. One colleague said I was too passionate, another too volatile for an administrative role that requires levelheaded composure. Of course, I was insulted and angered by these observations—both made by men—and chalked them up to sexism.

I did get the job, but I have to admit my two colleagues were prescient. In certain situations, when I see blatant unfairness and glaring inequity, others see moderate disagreement. Other times, when I read people as treacherously manipulative, pushing their egotistical strategies, others see a typical dispute over agendas. I can be eruptive. In a recent tenure decision meeting, a colleague was criticized in ways that seemed unjustified. Unfortunately, I could not rise to the occasion to defend my colleague with sound argument and sensible rhetoric. Instead, I felt helpless, dumbstruck by my powerlessness, crushed by the unfairness, embarrassingly reduced to tears in front of my colleagues. Why couldn't I take a forceful, rational stance when called for? Why did I still, after all these years and all these degrees, dissolve into useless tears?

Understanding PTSD helps me understand why. Although I do not believe I suffer in a significant, incapacitating way from PTSD, I do struggle with some of its manifestations. Raine lists the symptoms of the disorder: *"flashbacks, nightmares, depression, denial, a sense of estrangement and isolation, guilt,* rage, emotional numbness and constriction, *insomnia, being fearful and easily startled,* loss of capacity to symbolize, fantasize, or sublimate, difficulty concentrating" (1998, 56). As I italicize the eight symptoms out of twelve that I myself have had to confront, I have to wonder. I have been able to do so much: I know I have been a reliable, loving mother and friend, a conscientious, giving teacher, a prolific reader and competent writer; I have made a comfortable home; I add joyful companionship to my husband's life. Yet, I am haunted by recurring nightmares of lost children; I fall into days of depression and despondency; I denied so much in my life that it became difficult for me to differentiate between the factual and fallacious; there are times that no matter how close I try to draw in my family and friends, I can feel only helpless and alone, irrevocably separated from them all; guilt has been a primary motivating force in my life; I am an insomniac; I am terrified of being alone in my own home between two A.M. and dawn. But what I can do is sublimate. All my guilt, fear, self-doubt, sleeplessness, loneliness, and sorrow have been channeled into what looks like a productive, healthy life of goals accomplished. I have achieved, achieved, achieved. I thought that I fooled almost everyone, but I was wrong. Perhaps the only people I have truly fooled consistently are my parents, whom I have wanted most to please and protect, but maybe I have not fooled even them.

Is there a plausible explanation for my inexplicable tears and irrational retreat from composure? Faced with situations that somehow resemble the original trauma, I am apparently once again unhinged by a feeling of uncontrollable helplessness, and, remarks Goleman, "the operative word is *uncontrollable*": "If people feel there is something they can do in a catastrophic situation, some control they can exert, no matter how minor, they fare far better emotionally than do those who feel utterly helpless. The element of helplessness is what makes a given event *subjectively* overwhelming" (204). The helplessness I experienced on the night of Sorrow's birth was immense. Now, when I feel helpless, for example, when I see unexpected, unjust, and seemingly irreversible decisions being made by people in power without regard to those they control, adrenaline surges through my brain and my body with such ferocity that all I can do is grip my chair, shiver with agitation, weep as quietly as possible, and try to ride it out until I am alone. It takes me days, sometimes weeks, to recover my composure.

The other symptom that I can trace directly back to March 20 is my struggle with insomnia. When I returned from the hospital to the Florence Crittendon Home for the necessary two weeks before I could return to the outside world, I literally stopped sleeping. I was zombielike: an unwashed body with dirty, tangled hair, awake hour after hour. Stupefied during the day, by three, four, five A.M., I would be hysterical as the house once again slept so peacefully around me—again I was the only one awake, the only one in pain, though this time it was mental anguish rather than labor pains. Since that time, I have to read myself to sleep. A reading light is as crucial as my sleeping pills. A stream of words about someone else's life is necessary if I am to distract an overactive mind that will not stop flitting from one nagging memory to the next. Nor have I ever slept through a night again. For the past twenty years, I have had a hypnotic sedative to help me with my struggle to find sleep. But if the pill does not put me out, I am still awake at three, four, five A.M., completely distraught. By this time I am long past being able to focus my tired eyes or exhausted brain on a book. My husband, a sound sleeper, used to awaken when I was in this state and try to comfort me by rubbing my back, holding me, but we both agree that this kind of sweet attention is ineffective. All I can do is get up, walk around the house, weep quietly, try the couch, the futon, the floor at the foot of the bed. Sometimes I panic and cry like I did for those interminable two weeks at Florence Crittendon; sometimes I can soothe myself, taking on five minutes and then another five, breathing as regularly as possible—like getting through labor pains—trusting that I will get to morning. If I am away from home, it is a given that I will not sleep, and so my pills are the first things I pack, and if I am flying, I make sure several times that I have put them in both my carry-on and my checked bag.

Without medication, the sleeplessness compounds, multiplying into not just one bad night, but an entire week, and then another until my days are like fuzzy theater sets that I walk through as a visitor who is watching the real world from the outside. I am completely cut off, desperate for release from my loneliness and anxiety, so quick to cry that nothing more than an abrupt grocery clerk can send me into a tailspin of sobbing, so hungry for sleep that I have wished for death as a way to find it.

I have had doctors tell me I am seriously depressed; therefore, I cannot sleep. I have insisted in return, I cannot sleep; therefore, I am depressed. I am grateful to the doctors who have trusted me, understood my plight, and prescribed the medication that makes it possible for me to live with this affliction. I love sleep; sometimes I can feel it overtaking me, and I savor the feeling of giving myself over to the gentle, cushiony waves that will bear me away for a while and return me refreshed, eager, full of energy and anticipation for my life that I love—if only I can sleep.

I have always known that since I lost Sorrow, life has never been the same. Reading Raine's memoir has given me another perspective, helping me to see that being high-strung and sleepless may be because of an altered brain. Overreacting may be the result of adrenaline automatically flooding my brain and my body, leaving me helplessly adrift in troubled waters. It helps to know that I will make it back to the shores of emotional stability and self-esteem.

Raine, surprised by her rapist from behind while tranquilly doing her dishes, emerges from the rape a new person. She goes to stay with her mother and father, terrified and needy, and they care for her patiently and gently. But, like me, she realizes she must continue as if her former, capable, self was still existing. Raine remarks: "I thought of her—of myself before that terrible instant at the sink—as a character from a film. Her story—my life up until that moment, and I decided to imagine how it might go on. Acting *as if* I were she—although I didn't feel like her in the slightest—was the only available alternative to never leaving Mommy and Daddy again" (1998, 69). Raine's memoir teaches us that we cannot ask trauma victims to emerge from the event and return to the former self. True, we are always in process; the self is never fixed, is continuously constructing and reconstructing. But the radical shifts brought about by trauma leave victims fundamentally transformed. Because of our own discomfort, because the trauma is so devastating, we ask survivors to be convincingly strong, to heal quickly, to hide their scars, to restore that prior self so that we can have our own sense of well-being reestablished. Although the people who denied the reality of Raine's experience did so because they loved her, Raine begins to see that denial is an aftermath of trauma for the survivor and those who witness that survival. In her influential text *Trauma and Recovery*, Judith Herman states, "The will to deny horrible events and the will to proclaim them aloud is the central dialectic of psychological trauma" (1992, 1). To deny or to proclaim—two roads diverge for survivors. To their disadvantage, too many take the road of denial not to shield themselves, but to accommodate others.

Although shortly after the rape Raine works with some success with a therapist to regain feelings of control and self-confidence, she continues to suffer. Nevertheless, in the years that follow and for the sake of her family, friends, and her husband, she successfully plays the part of the woman before the rape, consequently never getting to know herself as a raped woman. *After Silence* is the result of her struggle to stop performing, stop constructing a self in whom repression is necessary for survival and sanity. Although she tries to forget what happened, she has also tried to forget how what happened continues to shape her. Once a woman is raped, once we live through trauma, not only are we irrevocably changed, but we also process the experience of our everyday lives through the distorting filter of the trauma. No matter how vigorously we beat back our memories, we are, as F. Scott Fitzgerald observed, like "boats against the current, borne back ceaselessly into the past" (1995, 189).

Eventually, Raine's strenuous efforts at repression are defeated. The burden of holding the memory of her rape outside of her personal narrative becomes too onerous, resulting in a loss of cohesive identity. Unable to construct an authentic view of reality that includes the rapist and the woman he left behind, she begins to falter. Events, memories, and feelings connected to the rape begin to insinuate themselves in Raine's life, but in transformed ways she cannot understand. She identifies this transmutation as "dissociation": the psychological malady in which memories and feelings connected to a traumatic event, although seemingly forgotten, "return not in their original form but as intrusive flashes of distorted recollections, as overwhelming anxiety and panic unwarranted by current experience, as emotional stupors covered over by acting 'normal' " (173). Years after the rape, Raine suddenly begins to suffer from panic attacks and severe depression. She finds a therapist who deals specifically with rape survivors and begins the long process of integrating the rape and the woman who was raped into her life narrative.

In her quest to understand her trauma, Raine reads Judith Stewart, a trauma-recovery clinical psychologist whose observations ring true for Raine and for me when she describes overinvolvement and overachievement. These strategies that hold rage and guilt at bay are common to women suffering from PTSD. "By working three jobs, getting multiple degrees, and being extremely active" (qtd. in ibid., 185), many women are able to hold off the symptoms of PTSD.

I have kept myself absurdly busy for decades, raising three children as a single parent, completing my M.A. and my Ph.D., moving from L.A., to Idaho, to Seattle, to North Carolina, building a career in each location, publishing, teaching, and taking on the responsibilities of being an administrator, all the while never feeling complete enough unless I have read at least one novel or, now, memoir a week, and have kept up with the *New Yorker* and the *New York Times*, entertained friends and students, and maintained my ongoing correspondence with old friends and distant family. Even when I go on vacation, I find myself tearing through places of great beauty, would-be serenity, and history, determined to see every location mentioned in the guidebook that I have used to organize our excursion. My brother- and sister-in-law still tease me with some measure of seriousness about the day I almost killed them by dragging them as quickly as possible to thirty-six points of interest around Nantucket in humid ninety-degree weather. When I was awarded several months off from teaching to write, I awaited the sabbatical with trepidation. What would happen to me when I had to stay home alone? How soon would that black cloud of depression descend on me, leaving me incapable of composing anything?

The cloud did not descend, partly because I rigorously structured my days and made sure that I built in time with friends and family. Also, although my task began as a literary analysis of contemporary memoirs by women that would include my own memoir, the project soon evolved into a personal exploration not only of the girl I once was, but also of the woman who has so assiduously avoided confronting the effects of my early loss. The courageous women memoirists I have encountered on this journey have served as my mentors, helping me to interpret my own identity forthrightly.

I knew there was no forgetting Sorrow, but by keeping the secret, I believed she could live within me as a memory. Nevertheless, her birth and her loss would not stay neatly compartmentalized in my past. Instead, roiling emotions and injurious habits continually surfaced. Although I intuitively sensed their origin, I would not or could not understand how directly they were linked to this early ordeal. Raine explains: "Defenses, no matter how well built, cannot hold the raw, submerged forces of traumatic memory at bay forever. Denial is a trickster, capable of astonishing disguises. . . . Invisible, it sets about its destructive business. Denial is a presence disguised as an absence. You cannot see it even when it is staring you in the face" (186). For me, denial had its pragmatic side; it allowed me to manage the practicalities of living as long as I kept up a frantic pace that did not allow for reflective interstices. But I too could not maintain these ultimately insupportable defenses that my denial required.

Although I knew that my inability to sleep through the night started at the Florence Crittendon Home, I convinced doctors and myself (perhaps) that I had a physiological disorder. Only recently, by reading Raine and Herman, have I recognized that my insomnia is intrinsically bound to that night; the hysteria I fall into before dawn is a reenactment of the fear and hysteria I experienced then. When I am rested, the memory stays in place, but when circumstances simulate the early morning hours of March 20, 1965, I seem compelled to relive the terror and loneliness all over again.

Intellectually, I know that a compulsion to repeat is often an attempt to master a sense of fear and helplessness. In fact, in my dissertation I took 317 pages to distinguish between compulsive and creative repetition. But emotionally I have not yet integrated that night into a narrative that will diminish its persistent power to return. Raine too encounters these repetitions and comments:

> My own experience suggests that all of these reenactments can be, and often are, a part of the attempt to make trauma survivable. There are aspects of my own behavior since the rape that I can explain in no other way. The trauma, for one reason or another, resurfaces. Feelings such as dread, failure, helplessness trigger it. Sometimes the resurfacing is straightforward and I can identify my dread as a remembrance of the rapist. Other times, the trauma resurfaces disguised, and all I know is that I feel helpless and out of control. (194)

Unfortunately, because I have made a connection between my insomnia and Sorrow's birth does not mean that I have been cured of my sleeplessness. Nor have I suddenly eradicated all self-doubt, emotional susceptibility, or a consuming need to keep busy. Raine herself says: "I have only a little more understanding now, but a deeper appreciation for the predicament that consciousness presents—it is a work in process, its limits unknown. There will always be a shadow, despite the occasional flicker of light I can cast upon it. What has changed, I suppose, is I now accept it is there" (252). Unlike Raine, whose shadow was cast by a vicious rapist, my shadow was not cast by any one demonic perpetrator. Certainly, the shadow is not Sorrow, whom I have always accepted, always wanted, always treasured. Nor is the shadow my parents or my aunt whom I love. I know that they wanted more than anything to protect me.

The fateful events of that night were caused by a tangled confluence of circumstances and a bit of bad luck. There was no demon, not even the tired and abusive nurse. Nevertheless, the shadow is there. What I did for too long was to deny that it should have any significance in my life. I knew I was emotionally unstable—obsessive, insecure, dishonest, lonely—but I could not imagine how to change. Perhaps several years of dedicated therapy would have helped me, as it did Raine. But with the frenetic pace I have maintained since losing Sorrow, I have never given myself the time for such an undertaking. The few times I have seen a therapist for counseling as my marriages were crumbling, I never took the opportunity to open the door that I have pried ajar in this memoir.

Reading women's memoirs did finally allow space for self-reflection and a new kind of perception to emerge that would not surface twelve years ago when I wrote "Repetition and Redemption." I have had serious, emotional, resonant responses to the memoirists I read. Raine's story, for example, allowed me to continue my story, demonstrating firsthand how secrecy and silence block the paths to social change that could prevent sexual violence. Rape will not stop until the culture knows the stories of rape survivors, until we can grasp the horrendous costs women pay year after year because of sexual violence. If we are to create a culture where women and children are safe, we need to heed Adrienne Rich's advice when she urges us to talk to each other, to tell our life stories, to read aloud to one another the books that move and heal us, to read our own words to each other, to remember what has in the past been forbidden to mention (1979, 13). Raine accomplishes this goal in *After Silence* by uncovering what she was encouraged to conceal.

One image she provides especially drives home the harm rape does to women in the United States. In order to give a dramatic visual image that transcends mere numbers, she uses the Vietnam War Memorial as a point of comparison. The wall lists every name of the 58,135 Americans killed in the Vietnam War. Having been to the memorial, I know the emotional impact of walking along the wall, reading the name of each man and woman sacrificed. Raine explains that if we take the most conservative figure for the number of rapes committed in 1991 in our country—106,593—and compare it to the number of Americans killed in Vietnam, we will find that in 1991 alone, 48,458 more women were raped than military personnel died in the entire Vietnam War. This statistic means that if we were to list the name of each reported rape victim for that year alone, the wall would have to be twice as long. However, Raine goes further by noting that according to a 1992 study by the National Victim Center and Crime Victims Research and Treatment Center, only one out of six rapes is reported to the police. Hence, if we were to combine the number of reported rapes and the probable number of unreported rapes, "the wall would need to be eleven times longer just to accommodate the names of women raped in 1991" (1998, 69). Raine's visual image has me reeling; I had never fully comprehended the appalling magnitude of rape in our country.

Rich claims our culture nourishes violence at its core by actively opposing women who want to narrate their own lives (14). One form of this opposition is the perverse and damaging way the shame of rape has been unjustly transferred from the rapist to the victim. "The feeling of shame seems to make being the victim of rape an act of wrongdoing. When others ask her to 'hide' or 'disappear,' she has no hope of 'corrective action' " (Raine 1998, 132). Victims of rape and sexual violence have been continuously checked by shame from laying claim to their experience. They are also silenced because their stories make women feel too threatened, too uncomfortable, too much like sexual targets when we are trying hard to be recognized as competent, empowered individuals. Our culture asks survivors to live in an especially dangerous form of denial. By denying rape, we cut off the hope, the opportunity, and the agency for corrective action not just for the victim herself but also for our mothers, our sisters, our children—for all of us who do, in fact, live at risk. Raine's memoir is a vital antidote for a cultural denial whose cost is no longer bearable.

Memory Slips

> Incest is not so crazy. . . . In order to call incest crazy, I would have to believe that the world is only a wonderful, just, loving place where people know how to respect each other. I know that isn't true. . . . The crazy feeling is the denial, the figures pretending that nothing happened.—Louise Wisechild, The Obsidian Mirror: An Adult Healing from Incest

Another memoirist who explores the long-term effects of trauma in her memoir, Memory Slips, is Linda Katherine Cutting, a concert pianist and writer.[2] Like Raine, she turns to Herman's Trauma and Recovery to make sense of her own disabling memories of incest at the hands of her father, a minister, and the silence that inhibited her recovery. Cutting observes:

2. Memory Slips is reviewed by Margaret Moorman, who herself has written a memoir about giving her infant son up for adoption, titled Waiting to Forget. Moorman observes an important approach for Cutting and for any memoirist: "Ms. Cutting describes her memories of incest and violence through carefully chosen details. . . . The slant of Ms. Cutting's descriptions protects readers from a sense of voyeurism and allows them to join with her as she struggles . . . to recover," and in so doing, Cutting writes a "dignified, eloquent book" (1997, 18). This method is in direct contrast to another recent memoir by an incest victim, Because I Remember Terror, Father, I Remember You, by Sue William Silverman (1996). Silverman's language is so graphically detailed that as a reader, I found myself horrified, even at times assaulted by her explicitness. Rather than allowing for an intimate reading, Silverman's lack of aesthetic subtlety makes the memoir one I wish I had never encountered, while Cutting's remains a poignant and persuasive indictment of a father, a mother, and a culture that willingly overlooks parental cruelty and abuse.

So much has been done to discredit the memories, and silence the voices of those who have struggled against great odds to be heard. Survivors of atrocities, whether they were at the hands of strangers, trusted clerics, or in the private sanctum of family, do not speak easily of their experiences. They "long to forget," as Dr. Judith Herman . . . put it. "But healing requires the reconstruction of memory; the unspeakable must be spoken and heard." (2)

Cutting grows up the daughter of a Congregational minister who savagely beats her and her two older brothers and also sexually molests her. Her brothers, Paul and David, tormented beyond endurance by the debilitating psychological consequences of their traumatic childhoods, both commit suicide in their twenties. Severely traumatized herself, Cutting copes with her past, but also eventually finds herself in such emotional crisis that she must be hospitalized. There she meets a psychiatrist and Holocaust survivor. He advises her, "Stay alive so you can tell," and his words provide her with a newfound tenacity to resist suicide and to bear witness to the truth.

She begins by refusing to obey her parents' ploy to tell people that her second brother died in a car crash. She knows that to do so would be to dishonor her brother's suffering, and, more important, acceding to the lie would make her complicit in her parents' denial. Like other memoirists, she turns to writing for resolution and redemption—"to recover ownership, to restore honor, to save" (Cutting 1997, 3). Herman explains this move from private confinement to public engagement: "These survivors recognize a political or religious dimension in their misfortune and discover that they can transform the meaning of their personal tragedy by making it the basis for social action" (1992, 207). A crucial component of Raine's and Cutting's recoveries is their dedication to raising awareness. Their memoirs become missions of social action.

Cutting exhibits several trauma symptoms, including insomnia. For a long time, she does not connect the muscle tension that keeps her awake with the sexual abuse in her past. Suffering from posttraumatic amnesia that keeps painful memories split off from ordinary awareness, Cutting has forgotten why "the night was not for sleeping," why she sometimes goes to bed with a baseball bat, her brother Paul's afghan, her brother David's T-shirt, her ex-husband's nine iron (11). Although the memories that created this need for nocturnal talismans elude her consciousness, her "muscles were holding their own memories" (12). They keep her tense, alert, and awake in the dark, prepared to fight off an attacker.

Cutting also stays excessively busy in order to keep the past at bay. By tirelessly studying the piano and moving through her twenties at breakneck speed, Cutting distracts herself from her past. As a child, she was able to avoid her father's abuse by playing the piano. As long as she was practicing, he would not approach her, and so she became increasingly skilled. The piano becomes her shield: a means to safety, a method of denial, a necessary ingredient for composure. As an adult, traveling and upset by insomnia, she can fall asleep only when she can hear her husband play her piano for her over the phone. By ceaselessly memorizing and incessantly practicing the music that she performs in concerts all over the country, she suppresses her past. However, even this masterful example of sublimation is only partially successful. She confesses: "Nothing sticks inside me, not my house, my husband, performing, nothing. I'm twenty-seven. I ought to feel like I exist in the world. I only exist in the music. When I stop playing, everything vanishes" (46). Cutting's mental health relies on her music, her piano, and, ironically, her memory, for it is her acute memory that grants her the acumen to retain long, complex Shostakovich concertos, Beethoven concertos, Schumann sonatas. Without her monopolizing talent, she would have to contemplate herself alone—a perilous undertaking. Like many of the memoirists we have encountered, she avoids self-confrontation by being extraordinarily productive and rigorously self-disciplined, but, in fact, she is desperately driven.

At the center of many contemporary memoirs, we find not a centered "self," but the postmodern subject that, Chris Weedon observes, is "precarious, contradictory and in process, constantly being reconstituted in discourse each time we think or speak" (1987, 32–33). It is helpful to think of Cutting, the speaking subject of *Memory Slips*, in these terms—not as an essential individual, but as "a dynamic subject that changes over time, is situated historically in the world and positioned in multiple discourses" (Bergland 1994, 134). Depending on context, we constitute our subjectivity differently. Cutting, however, gives us an example of how this process can lead to the unhealthy "false" self that Winnicott posits. Winnicott's "true" self can originate only when "the potential space between baby and mother, between child and family" is based on trust (1971, 102–3), a quality that is painfully missing from Cutting's abusive upbringing.

In order to maintain a relationship with her mother, Cutting does what so many women do to preserve relationships: she learns to dissemble, to be the girl her mother wants her to be, to construct a self that her mother will find likable and acceptable. She even has a name for this other "self"; she becomes "Betty," her mother's actual best friend, in the hope that her mother will treat her with comparable care and affection. This masking of her more authentic subjectivity is not psychotic, but rather a harmful swerve from authenticity. Women everywhere have Betty-like masks that we don for our mothers, our partners, or our bosses. Cutting describes her "Betty": "Betty is my outer shell, a second skin. . . . She's not really part of me inside. I don't lose control or consciousness when I'm putting on Betty. She's more like a piece of clothing I wear in public, a mask. For a long time people were fooled. My mother has always been fooled. Or maybe it's just that she can't really look at me until I've put on Betty" (53). In fact, her mother refuses to speak with her after her brother David's suicide until Cutting puts "Betty" back on, or, as her mother puts it, "until you restore the warmth in your voice" (52).

Masks are sometimes effective. We resort to them because of our cultural expectations about how children should talk to adults, how employees should talk to superiors, how the marginalized should speak to the privileged. Self-consciously donned, the mask is expedient and protective, permitting a surreptitious agency. But masks can be harmful, as Raine's and Bepko's dissemblings demonstrate. I have seen masks of honeyed docility work well for those who are willing to employ this form of manipulation. The mask is often easier than the truer mien, but it is finally detrimental to all who seek honest relationships.

I know how difficult it is to remove the mask, for I too have worn one for too long in order to be acceptable. Will I be able to relinquish my own rendition of "Betty" the next time I visit with my extended family or speak out at work? Perhaps. Certainly, I have resisted expectations in the past and spoken in a more authentic, outright manner, but I have learned that that kind of discourse can sound unreasonable, overly emotional, and "out of line" in hierarchical groups. Such reception has been so alarming to me that I have found myself deliberately putting my own cautious and compliant "Betty" mask back on.

Part of Cutting's recovery involves saying good-bye to "Betty." She asserts: "When I put on Betty, I am nobody, I am invisible. I need to get to know the parts of myself that I hide when I put on Betty, the parts that control me even when I'm wearing Betty like a coat" (54). As an intimate reader, I can follow Cutting's example, trusting those hidden parts of myself, those parts that control me even behind the mask. Long ago, I put on my mask in order to leave the Florence Crittendon Home, return to my family, resume high school, and jump-start the life that was envisioned for me. Like Cutting, I too struggled to make the disturbed young girl behind the mask invisible by ignoring her sorrow, hiding her despondency, making up for the disappointments she caused with accomplishments. The speaking subject of my memoir is not the prudent, tractable "false" self I created long ago. Yet, even as I write about the need to resist masks, I am also apprehensive about "unmasking" myself. I both want and fear my exposure. What price will I pay when this more honest voice claims its public place, asserting its right to speak?

For Cutting, the memory slips that allowed her to repress childhood trauma begin to fail; memories become so intrusive that they keep her from performing solo concerts. She can no longer manipulate her memory by remembering music. While hospitalized and highly suicidal at the Denver Trauma Center, Cutting learns from her therapist the difference between admitting trauma and pretending it never happened. Either way, the trauma is going to cause pain; that is a given. For me that means that no matter what, losing Sorrow will always cause pain. For Cutting that means that whether she acknowledges the molestation and her mother's complicity, the fact that the trauma occurred is always going to cause her great suffering. Pretence will only inhibit her recovery.

Cutting's therapist gives her permission to feel "good pain" for the *real* thing that did happen. I underscore *"real"* because in postmodern theory asserting the "real" is highly suspect. But no matter how concerned literary analysis is with postmodernism, mental health requires that at some point we assert for ourselves and others, "This is what really happened." Nancy Raine is urging a culture that is in denial to allow rape survivors to acknowledge their "good pain," their legitimate anguish about the *real* thing that did happen. More damaging for me than Sorrow's birth was the ensuing instruction: "Nothing happened." I have paid a high price for my obedience. To tell of Sorrow's birth, to say "it happened," restores the right denied me: to mourn for the real thing that happened.

When Cutting confronts her father about the abuse she and her brothers endured as children, her mother and father deny the severity of the childhood beatings and maintain she was molested by a baby-sitter, not her father. In a letter, her father tells her, "It is necessary to reconstruct memory tapes" (166); her mother tells her that she has demons. When she conclusively recognizes the extent of her father's sexual molestation, and remembers the power he holds as a minister, she realizes, "No longer does the secrecy affect only my life, whether I could stay in it or not with unbearable truths inside, but whether another life could be destroyed by my silence" (133).

Cutting decides she must tell what she knows to the National Association of Congregational Churches. The director of pastoral relations judges her accusations as unsubstantiated and, therefore, comparable to hearsay. He will not consider advising her father's congregation about her charges; in fact, even with verifiable evidence, the church would be unwilling to act until she filed a civil suit against her father. Cutting must come to terms with an audience as unreceptive as her mother, one that does not want to believe her accusations of incest. This willful denial is one of the most intractable problems for the truth teller. Abused women are not believed because "We have been required to tell different lies at different times, depending on what the men of the time needed to hear" (Rich 1979, 188). Cutting's father's church prefers the easier route, believing in the rectitude of its ostensibly moral pastor. Her mother needs to believe in a wrongfully accused, misunderstood father and the fiction of a happy though inexplicably tragic family. If she were to believe her daughter, she would have to leave him, and she says she cannot live without him. Unfortunately, neither is an atypical response to accusations of sexual molestation or abuse. Our culture continues to overlook, misdiagnose, or negate the allegations of abused women and children, leaving vulnerable family members in dangerous circumstances.

As Cutting's intimate reader, it is my desire and my charge to believe Cutting, and I do so unequivocally. Like Rich, I know that women are made to feel insane "when cleaving to the truth of [their] experience" (190). Given the history of depression and suicide in her family, some may contend that Cutting is genetically flawed—an undependable, mentally ill witness. When Cutting confronts her father with her memories of the incest, he immediately responds by taking this tact, questioning her sanity, past and future. He knows how to wound her in the tenderest places, saying, "I hope you never have any children of your own. . . . [Y]ou will never be free to be a mother" (162). In a letter, her father warns that if she insists on believing her own memories, she will lose what he describes as "the beautiful relationship of love and affirmation that you have always known from your father and mother" (163). These words are written by the father who French-kissed her the last time he saw her (146).

Cutting willingly relinquishes a relationship with her father, but to give up her mother is much more difficult. She always wanted her mother to touch and comfort her, and although she was always stonily refused, her need has not diminished. She continues: "But worse than death, I fear the death of someone I need. . . . I fear my own death less than I fear my mother's" (235). Nevertheless, her parents have made their ultimatum clear: if Cutting wants a relationship with either of them, she will have to renounce the truth and continue to honor their lies and secrets. Cutting must forfeit her mother. Her therapist tells her that she will learn how to mother herself, and that is the work she continues in therapy, with her friends, in her house, and with her piano. "Music," she contends, "is the language I understand best, where there are no words for longing, where comfort comes at the fingertips, where a simple vibration disturbs the stillness in the air, lets you know you are not alone" (237).

Although music remains the language she understands best, Cutting has learned that in order to maintain her mental stability and stay alive, she must honor the truth of her and her brothers' experience in words. She states: "I need music. But I know I also need words. Giving a voice to what was once unutterable has saved my life" (237). For a long time, she was able to render the anguish of her experience and to quiet the intrusive dissonance of her memories with her music, but finally, no matter how furiously she practiced, memorized, and played, her attempts at dissociation were insufficient. The truth needs the solidity and endurance of words. Through the written word, we reclaim our lives. For Cutting, the memoir has released her so that, finally, she can declare, "I am free to make music for its own sake" (240).

In her book *Shattered Subjects*, Suzette Henke suggests that it is the goal of the memoirist to "re-member the fragmented subject and regain an enabling sense of psychic coherence." She continues: "The act of life-writing serves as its own testimony and, in so doing, carries through the work of reinventing the shattered self as a coherent subject capable of meaningful resistance to received ideologies and effective agency in the world" (1998, xix). In writing the memoir, Raine and Cutting repair the shattered self by telling what happened. "This work of reconstruction," says Herman, "actually transforms the traumatic memory, so that it can be integrated into the survivor's life story" (175). However problematic for postmodernists, the truth telling of the memoir is indispensable for mental health.

Rich maintains, "When a woman tells the truth she is creating the possibility for more truth around her" (191). Raine and Cutting are examples of women doing just that. By reading their memoirs, we learn the vital importance of telling the truth about sexual violence. We see that "the unconscious wants the truth, as the body does" (ibid., 188). Both Raine and Cutting learn that the unconscious insisted on the truth, and their bodies refused to forget. Neither could escape the consequences of brutality, no matter how hard they worked to minimize the trauma by way of commendable, noble achievements. Denial simply does not work. By disavowing our experience, "we lose faith even with our own lives" (ibid.); by shielding loved ones from our harrowing truths, we remain in isolation.

Memoirs such as Raine's and Cutting's allow us to do justice to women's minds and bodies, to go the hard way together, to connect and face together the truth of the turbulent, often brutal world we live in, and to recommit ourselves to its reform. "Silence," says Rich, "makes us all, to some degree, into liars" (190). Raine and Cutting demonstrate how intimately dangerous the lie of silence can be, for they have lived through its perilous consequences. By ending their silence, their memoirs extend the possibilities for living a more informed and effectual moral existence.

7

"THE OTHER PERSON'S WORLD"
Narratives of Mental Illness

In reality, every reader is, while he is reading, the reader of his own self. The writer's work is merely a kind of optical instrument which he offers to the reader to enable him to discern what, without this book, he would perhaps never have experienced in himself. And the recognition by the reader in his own self of what the book says is the proof of its veracity.—Marcel Proust, quoted in *How Proust Can Change Your Life*, by Alain de Botton

Reading memoirs such as *After Silence* and *Memory Slips* helps us interpret our culture's conflicted responses to those people who suffer from psychological impediments while giving us strategies for unraveling the multiple influences that determine those reactions. Women, including feminists, are divided over the "correct" approach to take when considering the narratives of those people who suffer from such illnesses.

While working on this chapter, I spoke with a friend, Carol, a feminist and a practicing therapist in Seattle. I asked her what she thought of Kay Redfield Jamison's memoir, *An Unquiet Mind*, a candid account of manic-depressive illness. I was disheartened by Carol's reply: she had not read it because she had been told by another female colleague that Jamison's narrative reinforced "patient as victim" ideology rather than "patient as empowered."

Unfortunately, Carol's preference for "empowering" stories and impatience with "victim" stories is not atypical. Seizing on a critique begun by Katie Roiphe in *The Morning After* and continued by Naomi Wolf in *Fire with Fire*, many women—especially successful women who have the potential to be strong advocates for oppressed women—are reluctant to see merit in narratives about exploitation, injury, or adversity. Rather than taking the opportunity to read memoirs such as Nancy Raine's and

Linda Cutting's intimately, readers like Carol straightaway dismiss them as unproductive narratives by languishing victims.

Critics who take a hard line against narratives by those people who have been harmed maintain that we should spotlight the positive steps women have taken rather than focus on their maltreatment or persecution. Wolf maintains, "The focus of some feminists, like Andrea Dworkin, Catharine MacKinnon, and Adrienne Rich, on female victimization foreshadowed over female agency, derives from conditions that were once truer than they are now" (1993, 141–42). According to Wolf, the silencing and negation that women endured in the seventies has become obsolete. In opposition to "victim feminism," Wolf posits "power feminism" that encourages women to identify with one another "through the shared pleasures and strengths of femaleness" (53).

That articulate, professional women such as Carol unreflectively accede to the tenets of "power feminism" is especially discouraging, for by so doing they become insensitive to the significant needs of the thousands of vulnerable, disenfranchised women who continue to face injustice and violation. In her critique of Wolf, bell hooks cogently critiques Wolf's premise: "In keeping with its denial of any political accountability for exploitation and oppression, particularly in relation to class elitism, 'power feminism' is in no way inclusive. It resolutely chooses to ignore the lived experiences of masses of women and men who in no way have access to the 'mainstream' of this society's political and economic life" (1994, 97). There is value in listening carefully to all women's stories, but especially to women who have had to be silent. The memoir is a significant and insurgent genre for countering the current resistance to painful truths about women's lives. Intimate memoirs about mental illness such as Jamison's Unquiet Mind, Susanna Kaysen's Girl, Interrupted, and Lauren Slater's Prozac Diary offer literate antidotes to the intolerance of women's suffering. Reading their memoirs, we sympathize and identify with women suffering from debilitating mental illnesses. By reading intimately, we better understand the many adversities and the severe consequences they endure, as well as the arduous difficulties they encounter while recuperating. If we have suffered from any psychological affliction, these narratives can be reassuring, educative, even transforming.

In his lyrical novel Waterland, Graham Swift pursues the tumultuous history of a woman that has left her psychologically ravaged, incapacitated by grief. The narrator urges: "No, don't forget. Don't erase it. You can't erase it. But make it into a story. Just a story" (1983, 225). Telling stories can be a way for those people who suffer from psychological disorders to comprehend their illness and to reweave mental turmoil into a recognizable pattern. Memoirists struggling with mental illness cannot erase their disability, but they can create poignant narratives about their journey into and out of their personal maelstroms. Although I try to avoid metaphors of warfare in my writing, I find the struggles of these memoirists so intense and so life threatening that I involuntarily resort to words such as *battle*, *vanquish*, and *victory* to describe their dauntless efforts. It seems inconceivable that after reading these memoirs anyone could possibly label Kaysen, Jamison, or Slater as victims and not heroines.

Girl, Interrupted

Susanna Kaysen's *Girl, Interrupted* begins with a photocopy of her admission form from McLean Psychiatric Hospital, where she was voluntarily admitted on April 27, 1967.[1] She was eighteen. It states that she was profoundly depressed, suicidal, promiscuous, and desperate. Kaysen went willingly to McLean much like I went willingly to the Florence Crittendon Home. Both of us were acquiescent, passively submitting to the decisions made by others. We agreed to do what they thought was best for us; we believed them because we could not believe in ourselves. We handed ourselves over to those people in charge, trusting they had our best interests at heart.

Shortly after being admitted to McLean, Kaysen is offered a means

---

1. When Susan Cheever reviews *Girl, Interrupted*, she quickly identifies the crux of memoir: "At times in this country, troublesome women—whether their trouble is promiscuity, alcohol, depression, or just plain orneriness—have been confined to private mental institutions where, their families hope, they will 'get better.'" Although Cheever refers to it as a "triumphantly funny story," she makes clear the serious import of Kaysen's blurred line between sanity and craziness (1993, 1). Reviewer Andrea Sachs finds Kaysen's book "wary," "witty," "poignant," and "confessional," and finally claims it has a "feeling of universality [that] makes Kaysen seem like Everypatient" (1994, 60). Dawn Marlan raises the provocative issue that Kaysen runs the risk of "aestheticizing and exploiting those who severely suffer from mental illness for her own profit," but refrains from doing so by way of a "fragility [that] does not occasion reductive polarization; rather her juxtapositions draw relations, layer modes of perception. She has equilibrium enough to navigate tensions, but not at the price of subtlety or challenge" (1996, 93).

of escape by a friend who shows up in his red sports car ready to take her away. She can reply only that "I'm here now, . . .I think I've got to stay here" (1993, 27). What would I have done had such a friend shown up at Florence Crittendon? I fear my response would have been the same. By then I had jettisoned any lingering gesture of defiance. My confinement felt secure. I was entirely dependent on my family's beneficence and so overcome by guilt that I welcomed the opportunity to do penance for my egregious transgression. I too would have said, "I'm here now; I've got to stay." No escape was ever proffered, so at least I do not have that daring scenario to add to my many regrets.

Before Kaysen's institutionalization, she was having difficulties with perception: "Reality was too dense. . . . Anything might be something else" (41–42). Although she had made a suicide attempt, she knew she did not want to try it again, and she did behave normally around others. It was neither her suicide attempt, her impeded perception, nor any bizarre behavior that led to her admission to McLean. She agreed to be hospitalized because at that time her only satisfaction came from refusal. She resisted sleep, declined food, and rejected friendship. She remarks, "All my integrity seemed to lie in saying NO. So the opportunity to be incarcerated was just too good to resist. It was a very big NO—the biggest NO this side of suicide" (42). Although her obdurate negation of any gratification was alarming, she knew she was not mad. She admitted herself to McLean with the mistaken confidence that they would not keep her, as she puts it, "locked up in a loony bin" for long (42).

Kaysen is diagnosed as having a "borderline personality." One of her symptoms, "overload," makes her thoughts run wild. A single thought like "I'm tired" triggers the whole circuit board of her brain, turning it into an avalanche of speculations that can take her days to follow. And there is "underload," when her inner life stalls into mute paralysis. She speculates on whether her mental illness is hereditary or socially constructed: "[Overload] or [underload] would assert itself, rush or dribble through me, and pass on. Pass on to where? Back into my cells to lurk like a virus waiting for the next opportunity? Out into the ether of the world to wait for the circumstances that would provoke its reappearance? Endogenous or exogenous, nature or nurture—it's the great mystery of mental illness" (78). The "great mystery" is one I too ponder, as do medical doctors, psychologists, teachers, social workers, and criminologists. The riddle has recently become more confounding with the publication of Judith Rich Harris's *Nurture Assumption* in which the author complicates the dialectic with her central claim: "Children are born with certain characteristics. Their genes predispose them to develop a certain kind of personality. But the environment can change them. Not 'nurture'—not the environment their parents provide—but the outside-the-home environment, the environment they share with their peers" (1998, 147). Rather than clarify the ancient argument, Harris adds another element. Not only do we have nature and nurture, but we also have multifaceted environments to influence us. Knowing how much I was loved and cared for as a child, I wonder what made me so lonely as an adolescent. However unwarranted, it had serious consequences, generating within me an unreasonable need for approval and attention from my peers, especially my boyfriend. My loneliness seemed to go beyond ordinary adolescent misery. Could it have been depression? Harris notes that "from early adolescence on, females are twice as likely as males to become clinically depressed," especially "starting in early puberty, [with] unipolar depression (lows without highs)" (238). In one of the many studies to support female adolescent depression, *Reviving Ophelia*, Mary Pipher describes Charlotte, but she could have been describing me. "Charlotte . . . tried very hard to win peer approval. . . . She made choices based not on her own true needs but on her sense of what other people, especially her boyfriend, Mel, wanted from her. Because she was so dependent on peer approval, she got into a great deal of trouble and was utterly lost to herself" (1994, 71). Charlotte and I represent something dramatic that happens to girls in adolescence. Pipher calls it the "social and developmental Bermuda Triangle," where "the selves of girls go down in droves . . . deferential, self-critical and depressed" (19).

I believe I was born with a personality that has hungered inordinately for the acceptance of others and, at the same time, has led me to periods of immoderate depression when I experience rejection or alienation. Self-awareness is priceless. It allows me to anticipate the heretofore inextricable dejection I feel when I have been slighted, ignored, or disparaged. Knowing my emotional inclinations helps me to control my circumstances and to ameliorate those factors that provoke my depression's reappearance. When my eagerness is seen as injudicious, perhaps I will be reflective rather than pulverized by the critique. Perhaps the next rejection will not leave me sleepless and pessimistic. Perhaps I will someday subdue my penchant for self-doubt and need for approval. Perhaps.

If I have inherited the gene of "unworthiness," have I passed it on to my children, including Sorrow? There does seem to be an inescapable, gloomy chord that has reverberated through my ancestors and now resonates through me and my children. I see it in the depths of my children's grief. They have each already had to weather bitter losses—the anguish of the premature deaths of best friends from cancer, accidents, even murder; the heartache of unrequited first love; the anguish caused by their father's withdrawal from their lives. Like me, they are exquisitely sensitive to the nuanced slights of others. Interestingly though, they were never defiant as children or as adolescents. I think defiance was too risky for them, too threatening to the necessary equilibrium of our relationship, which was critical for all of us. We all seem extreme, unusual, perhaps too tenderhearted for the rough-edged hurly-burly, too emotionally defenseless for the jostling of our competitive, contentious world; we have to guard our hearts and watch out for one another, to know our vulnerability and respect our predisposition for depression.

I support them by telling them about their inheritance. With this knowledge, they will be better prepared for descents into grief or hopelessness that may be unavoidable. All I can do is give them the reassurance that their lonely despair is transient, that their sorrow can be borne. Because of a legacy of family secrecy, I had to learn this fact on my own. Now my children know what they are up against. Such knowledge is precious and pragmatic.

For years after her release, Susanna Kaysen did not tell people she had been institutionalized. There were no advantages to telling; instead, by creating an ellipsis, she could distance herself from that "crazy self." She remarks, "The longer I didn't say anything about it, the farther away it got, until the me who had been in the hospital was a tiny blur and the me who didn't talk about it was big and strong and busy" (125). Nevertheless, twenty-five years after her diagnosis, the past must finally be acknowledged, and Kaysen is compelled to find out what happened. In order to do so, she first gets her records; consequently, we see copies of her case that include day-to-day progress notes, her formal diagnosis, and her prognosis.

Part of writing a memoir is detective work. Not every memoirist needs to unlock actual records, as does Kaysen, but the memoirist must fill in the blanks, explain the ellipses—those unaccountable years. It is only now that Kaysen learns that she was diagnosed as having a borderline personality. By consulting the official description of her disorder in the *Diagnostic and Statistical Manual of Mental Disorders* (1987), she finds a fairly accurate picture of herself at eighteen, but from her clearer vantage point, she interrogates the manual's definitions and assumptions.

For example, one of the symptoms of a borderline personality is "uncertainty about several life issues, such as self-image, sexual orientation, long-term goals or career choice, types of friends or lovers to have" (qtd. in Kaysen 1993, 150). Given these criteria, she grants that her diagnosis was valid: she was (and continues to be) uncertain about life issues, about her self-image, her goals, and her choices of friends and lovers. But how peculiar is this uncertainty? She justifiably asks, "Isn't this a good description of adolescence?" (152). The grounds for her hospitalization begin to look more and more arbitrary, even capricious. Kaysen argues convincingly that another symptom, "social contrariness," is almost synonymous with normal adolescent rebellion (153). Were her refusals to go to university or become a dental technician so socially contrary as to justify her institutionalization?

Kaysen adds cogently that within the description of "borderline personality," the following are noted: "The disorder is more commonly diagnosed in women," and another significant symptom is "compulsive promiscuity" (157). Kaysen's admission report does, in fact, note that "symptom." Interrogating this term for its unconscious bias, she makes it clear that the medical discourse of the *Manual of Mental Disorders* is patriarchal. Kaysen comments: "How many girls do you think a seventeen-year-old boy would have to screw to earn the label 'compulsively promiscuous'? Three? No, not enough. Six? Doubtful. Ten? That sounds more likely. Probably in the fifteen-to-twenty range, would be my guess—if they ever put that label on boys, which I don't recall their doing. And for seventeen-year-old girls, how many boys?" (158). Kaysen nicely exposes the ways conventional morality infects the diagnosis of mental illness. The sexist double standard is still firmly in place and is still damaging. Kaysen interrogates language for its conscious and unconscious layerings, for the Foucaultian struggle over who gets to define insanity and sanity, whose discourse has the power to influence our definitions of "social contrariness" or "promiscuous," whose cultural norm and ethical position will be privileged, whose discredited.

Kaysen shows her readers how easy it is to slip over the ambiguous borderline from sanity into diagnosed neurosis, paranoia, psychosis, or a "borderline personality." She still thinks about "being crazy"; she always will. But she got well, well enough to leave; others she shared her time with did not. She admits: "I often ask myself if I'm crazy. I ask other people too. 'Is this a crazy thing to say?' I'll ask before saying something that probably isn't crazy. . . . It's a common phrase, I know. But it means something particular to me: the tunnels, the security screens, the plastic forks, the shimmering, ever-shifting borderline that like all boundaries beckons and asks to be crossed" (159). When we read the particulars of Kaysen's memoir intimately, we see the vagueness of that borderline and are prompted to ask ourselves how close we could come to it. How vulnerable would we be to a hasty diagnosis? Could it cost us two years? For the most part I am on the clearheaded, balanced side of the borderline, though there have been times of great distress when I have sensed the other side's proximity. When I read Kaysen's candid admission of uncertainty, I can be more patient with my own inner turmoil; I take comfort in reading her frank journey into illness, learning again the precious freedom of stability.

Throughout her memoir, Kaysen refers to a Vermeer painting that she saw at the Frick sometime before she went to McLean. The painting is titled *Girl Interrupted at Her Music* and depicts a young girl, perhaps sixteen, who has turned away from her teacher and her sheet music, seemingly peering out of the painting at something that has distracted her momentarily. Kaysen so identifies with this girl that she titles the memoir after her. I too felt attracted to this girl, for I too had been interrupted in the turbulent task of growing up, obliged to detour from a sheltered life to a very different, unexpectedly severe place.

I was so fascinated by Kaysen's description of the painting that I had to visit the Frick myself; the painting was all I had hoped it to be. I bought a small reproduction and have hung it above my desk. Looking up at it, I am amazed and comforted to find a face so emblematic of my own. In the seventeenth century, Vermeer captured a young girl's cheerless gaze as she is forced to stop and look apprehensively away, much like Kaysen and I were, detained for too long from our journeys. It is a face like the one I wore upon leaving Florence Crittendon, a pale mask, startled, even stunned, but also piercingly perceptive, having seen so much. Kaysen says about the painting: "Interrupted at her music: as my life had been interrupted in the music of being seventeen, as her life had been, snatched and fixed on canvas: one moment made to stand still and to stand for all the other moments, whatever they would be or might have been. What life can recover from that?" (167). Kaysen understands that events can happen to us, events that were meant for our betterment, but from which we do not recover. In writing about her hospitalization, of being "snatched" from the "music of being seventeen," she gives me not only the permission to write about my own exile, but also the allowance to say it was too much to expect me to resume my life as if untouched. I had been forever interrupted.

In the other two Vermeer paintings that hang at the Frick, Kaysen observes the ethereally sublime Vermeer light, a light that does not really exist, though we wish it did. "Most of all," Kaysen asserts, "we wish that everyone we knew could be brightened simply by looking at them," as Vermeer can illuminate the maid holding a letter in one of the paintings and the soldier with a hat in the other. But the interrupted girl is not bathed in that dazzling Vermeer light. "The girl at her music sits in another sort of light, the fitful overcast light of life, by which we see ourselves and others only imperfectly, and seldom" (168). By carefully interrogating a critical episode of her life and a significant delineation of her identity, Kaysen creates a narrative clearing among conflicting discourses on the parameters of mental illness. The light of Kaysen's inquiry does shine through. If we are always destined to see ourselves imperfectly, memoirs such as hers help us see with a greater lucidity.

An Unquiet Mind

> Rational cognition has one critical limit which is its inability to cope with suffering.—Theodor Adorno, Aesthetic Theory

In her memoir, An Unquiet Mind, Kay Redfield Jamison relates her battle with another highly debilitating psychiatric illness, manic depression.[2]

2. An Unquiet Mind has been widely reviewed in both literary and medical journals. In a literary review, Rosemary Dinnage observes that Jamison has written an "outstanding" book that avoids "the dangers of clinical jargon . . . and feel-good optimism"; furthermore, Jamison "throws a good deal of light on why psychiatric patients hate taking drugs," and courageously does "a lot to bridge gaps, and warm those of us who feel, rightly or wrongly, rather shamefully different from the rest of the world" (1996, 13). Anastasia Toufexis finds the memoir "rare and insightful" (1995, 83). In the *International Journal of Social Psychiatry*, Jerome Carson notes that although some professionals ques-

As a professor of psychology at the Johns Hopkins School of Medicine and the coauthor of the standard medical text on manic-depressive illness, she is well aware there will be repercussions for publicly disclosing her heretofore secret and incurable disease. As she puts it:

> I have no idea what the long-term effects of discussing such issues so openly will be on my personal and professional life, but, whatever the consequences, they are bound to be better than continuing to be silent. I am tired of hiding, tired of misspent and knotted energies, tired of the hypocrisy, and tired of acting as though I have something to hide. One is what one is and the dishonesty of hiding behind a degree, or a title, or any manner and collection of words, is still exactly that: dishonest. (1995, 7)

When I read these words, I felt more confirmed than ever to undo my own "knotted energies" of dishonesty, a goal that has taken a long time to realize.

Telling the truth can be quite unpredictable. The solution of one problem can create new ones. By telling their stories, memoirists not only reveal a troubling past, but can also jeopardize uncertain career prospects. The professional hazards of revelation for doctors and teachers who are expected to be credible and trustworthy are real but finally worth the risk.

As a child, Jamison was an eager, adventurous, and independent learner, and in her family, her imaginative precociousness was respected and supported. As an adult, she can better appreciate this support: "An ardent temperament makes one very vulnerable to dreamkillers, and I was more lucky than I knew in having been brought up around enthusiasts, and lovers of enthusiasm" (26). In Jamison's de-

---

tion what can be learned from a single person's account of illness, he must praise Dr. Jamison as a "wounded healer" who provides not only "clinical insights into the nature of manic depressive illness" but also "a beautiful and poetic account of [her] struggle" (1997, 230). Dr. James D. Watson, Nobel laureate, finds it "a riveting portrayal of a courageous brain" (qtd. in Jamison 1996, 53). In *Psychology Today*, Jamison admits that publishing the memoir was costly: You "have more to lose under those circumstances, because you've spent a long time building a certain reputation as a scientist. . . . All of a sudden, your work is subject to questions: 'What was her motivation? Was she objective?' " (qtd. in Paul 1998, 88).

scriptions of her childhood, the nurturing influence of her warmhearted parents is striking. Although she discloses that she probably inherited her propensity for manic depression from her father, she never underestimates the positive influences of her family, who encouraged her medical interests.

Nor does she undervalue the power of her peers. When the family moves from the cloistered, unthreatening world of military bases to California, Jamison must negotiate the wealthy, snobbish, jaded students at Pacific Palisades High School. At first, she is deeply unhappy because she does not fit in, but later, her intellectual world becomes the sustaining part of her existence. Her experience was much like my own when I traveled to Youngstown, began public school, and found that I did not fit in. Unlike Jamison, who was always an excellent student and an aggressive learner, I had not realized my academic potential until I had to fill the lonely time between classes, becoming a permanent fixture in the school library. I was astounded to see each of my tests and essays come back marked A or even A+. Before that sequestered semester, I was unaware that the life of the mind could be more interesting and more gratifying than the reckless, scary excesses of my teenage escapades. This epiphany began an integral shift in who I was and who I would become. My discovery was one of the good life lessons of my year away from the raucous, arrogant, and competitive students of my own California high school where I had relinquished too much out of desperation to belong.

However, just as the ages of sixteen and seventeen revealed my intellectual aptitude, they also sharpened my propensity for depression. Similarly, by the time Jamison is seventeen, she too is beginning to show early signs of what will become a much more debilitating pattern of depression. "After long weeks of flying high and sleeping little, my thinking would take a downward turn toward the really dark and brooding side of life" (35). In her senior year in high school, she has her first manic-depressive episode. She recovers enough to enroll at UCLA, though because of the illness's increasing severity, she feels alienated from her fellow students, agitated, irritable, even hostile.

> I had no idea what was going on, and I felt totally unable to ask anyone for help. It never occurred to me that I was ill; my brain just didn't put it in those terms. Finally, however, after hearing a lecture about de-

pression in my abnormal psychology course, I went to the student health service with the intention of asking to see a psychiatrist. I got as far as the stairwell just outside the clinic but was only able to sit there paralyzed with fear and *shame,* unable to go in and unable to leave. (45; emphasis added)

The key word here is *shame.* Given the remarkable achievements she has already accomplished, what is the source of her shame? It seems to come from self-imposed feelings of failure to live up to her own mania-induced standard of boundless personal vitality, aptitude, and worth. At the heart of her shame and depression is a system of fantasized, grandiose ideals that while in her manic phases she can achieve, but that while depressed she cannot begin to realize. She is ashamed of herself because she cannot ceaselessly measure up to the infeasible standard of her mania.

After several more years of barely managing hyperkinetic mania, decimating depression, and suicidal yearnings, Jamison remarkably completes her undergraduate and graduate degrees only to confront the extremities of her illness, becoming terrifyingly delusional, at one point admitting, "I knew I was insane" (82). Desperate, she finally finds a psychiatrist, is correctly diagnosed, and begins taking lithium and undergoing psychotherapy. The lithium works. It prevents her disastrous highs and diminishes the depressions, but it is the psychotherapy that finally begins to heal her; it provides her a necessary sanctuary where she might "someday begin to contend" with all the complexities of selfhood and mental illness (89).

Despite significant improvement, Jamison resists continuing the lithium because she misses that other grandiose, manic self. She explains: "I compare myself . . . not with others . . . [but] with the best I have been, which is when I have been mildly manic. When I am my present 'normal' self, I am far removed from when I have been my liveliest, most productive, most intense, most outgoing and effervescent. In short, for myself, I am a hard act to follow" (92). The near catastrophic consequences of suspending lithium, however, confirm one of Jamison's objectives for *An Unquiet Mind:* the memoir serves as a warning to those people who might also be tempted to suspend medication. "Unfortunately, this resistance to taking lithium is played out in the lives of tens of thousands of patients every year. Almost always it leads to a recurrence of the illness; not uncommonly it results in tragedy" (105). For Jamison, stopping lithium leads to a profound depression, and although she begins to take the drug again at her psychiatrist's urging, the time off has left her dangerously ill.

When her psychiatrist suggests she go into a psychiatric hospital, it is Jamison's anxiety about secrecy that keeps her from doing so. She attests, "I was concerned that if it became public knowledge that I had been hospitalized, my clinical work and privileges at best would be suspended; at worst, they would be revoked on a permanent basis" (112). This time is not the first that she has been afraid of revealing her illness to others, and not without justification. During her early years at UCLA, she "observed many medical students, clinical psychology interns, and residents denied permission to continue their studies because of psychiatric illness" (130). Her fears of reprisal and the resulting need for secrecy keep her from treatment and health; instead of risking exposure, she resolves to kill herself.

Jamison resorts to suicide because she is profoundly depressed and desperate with shame. She comes close to a "successful suicide" by overdosing on lithium. She survives only because while semicomatose, she instinctively answers the telephone. The caller, her brother, knows something is terribly wrong and calls her psychiatrist.

Again, upon recovering, Jamison has to reconcile that cherished image of herself "as a young girl who had been filled with enthusiasm, high hopes, great expectations, enormous energy, and dreams and love of life, with that of a dreary, crabbed, pained . . . [and sometimes] enraged, utterly insane, and abusive woman who lost access to all control or reason" (121). Her fiercely honest memoir allows intimate readers to live through the specific insidiousness of her mental illness. We experience how manic depression undermines her successes, shattering her best parts.

Perhaps my friend Carol is partially right; I do see Jamison as a victim, but not helpless, because I know now the formidable struggle she faced and the devastating losses she suffered. How would I handle such treacherous loss of self-control? Her willingness to reveal the devastation of her illness leaves me full of respect for her endurance and honesty.

Toward the end of her memoir, Jamison gives us a revealing anecdote about tutoring a blind undergraduate in her office at UCLA. She thought she had some notion of what his life was like, but one day, she entered the blind reading room to meet him:

> I stopped suddenly when I realized with horror that the room was almost totally dark. . . . [N]o lights were on, and yet there were half a dozen students bending over their books. . . . A total chill went down my spine at the eeriness of the scene. . . . It was one of those still, clear moments when you realize that you haven't understood anything at all, that you have had no real comprehension of the other person's world. (168)

Reading Jamison's memoir, I have come to realize that I have never really considered what full-scale derangement might be. How degrading and baffling it must be to lose complete control, to be "physically restrained by terrible, brute force; kicked and pushed to the floor; thrown on my stomach with my hands pinned behind my back; and heavily medicated against my will" (120). Just as the student allowed Jamison to confront endless darkness, Jamison has brought me into the horrifying corridors of manic depression where unpredictability is the only given. Jamison admits that she is "fundamentally and deeply skeptical that anyone who does not have this illness can truly understand it. . . . It is not an illness that lends itself to easy empathy" (174). That her condition does not lend itself to easy empathy is the most important reason for her memoir to be read.

If we are to change attitudes about mental illness, if we are to become better advocates for the mentally ill, we need to know their suffering as intimately as possible. Currently, "the major mental health advocacy groups are made up primarily of patients, family members, and mental health professionals" (183). I would argue that their advocacy comes out of their firsthand experiences. Our culture does not usually allow us firsthand experience with grave mental illness. How can we generate advocacy groups among those people who do not know the agony of this kind of suffering? Who will agitate, badger, and cajole their legislators for increased money for research, social programs, and better understanding of the mentally ill?

If we are going to become informed advocates, we need memoirs like Jamison's that can provide us with those "still, clear moments" when we enter the dark, unfamiliar room of mental illness and realize we do not understand. We need Jamison's and Kaysen's memoirs because they are real. As intimate readers, we come to care about Kay Redfield Jamison and Susanna Kaysen, and in so doing, we become more acutely concerned about others.

Jamison has taken enormous chances in discussing her illness in a memoir. She has betrayed her family's privacy; she has defied the still powerful cultural dictum that "personal matters should be kept personal" (202). In her book *The Vulnerable Observer*, anthropologist Ruth Behar notes that Jamison stretches "the limits of objectivity, . . .exposing [herself] in an academy that continues to feel ambivalent about observers who forsake the mantle of omniscience" (1996, 12). Although we recognize autobiography as a respectable genre in its own right, critics are bothered by "the insertion of personal stories into what we have been taught to think of as the analysis of impersonal social facts" (ibid.). And it is not only anthropology and psychology that expect disinterested observers: "Throughout most of the twentieth century, in scholarly fields ranging from literary criticism to anthropology to law, the reigning paradigms have traditionally called for distance, objectivity, and abstraction. The worst sin was to be 'too personal' " (ibid., 12–13). Jamison has ceded the pretense of academic objectivity and, in so doing, contested a still dominant standard.

Jamison also has more personal concerns about "going public." She worries that friends and colleagues will no longer see her as "zany," "intense," or "a bit volatile," but, like my friend Carol, pigeonhole her as "weak" or, worse yet, "unstable" and "neurotic" (202). But her ultimate fear is one with which I closely identify: "I am deeply wary that by . . . writing about such intensely private aspects of my life, I will return to them one day and find them bleached of meaning and feeling. By putting myself in the position of speaking too freely and too often, I am concerned that the experiences will become remote, inaccessible, and far distant, behind me; I fear that the experiences will become those of someone else rather than my own" (202). Like Jamison, I too am apprehensive about a time when I can talk about Sorrow without my heart racing. I do not want that intensity to be depleted. I want my loss to overwhelm me as always and take me back again to her, forever to her. If I were to become accustomed to telling our story, I would be surrendering what I have of her. Although I know writing about Akron, Florence

Crittendon, and March 20 are healthy ways to renarrate my life, I resist the telling. I do not want Sorrow's loss to become less than the most riveting experience of my life.

Prozac Diary

> There is no way . . . to do the work of therapy, which is . . . the work of relationship, without finding your self in the patient and the patient's self in you. In this way, rifts within and between might be sealed, and the languages of our separate lives might come to share syllables, sentences, whole themes that bind us together.— Lauren Slater, *Welcome to My Country*

One of the most difficult tasks that Jamison has to cope with in learning to live with lithium is revisioning her self. She must renounce her manic self, which was astonishingly gifted and animated, and agree to a medicated self that is more balanced and astute, but less coordinated, less vivacious, and for Jamison, who values her keen intellect so highly, painfully less brilliant. Lithium returns her to a "regular life" of commonplace repetitions devoid of the exhilarating but catastrophic whirlwind of mania.

Lauren Slater's memoir, *Prozac Diary*, extends this challenge of coming to terms with mental illness.[3] After years of living largely incapacitated by anorexia, borderline personality, and obsessive compulsive disorders, Slater is given a remedy: Prozac. Her story is about "the difficulty and compromise of cure, the grief and light of illness passing, the fear as the walls of the hospital wash away and you have before you—

---

3. *Prozac Diary* reviewer D. T. Max finds Slater's memoir "gentle, illuminating," and important because it counteracts the considerable and obdurate backlash that has formed about Prozac and, instead, gives us "the base-line truth": it is not a question of taking a pill if the "natural" self disappoints. "Slater didn't just have the sniffles. She was more like someone with pneumonia waiting for the invention of antibiotics" (1998, 13). Eve Leeman finds the memoir "chatty, sassy, and ultimately deeply moving" in which Slater "grapples with notions of meaning and authenticity, her individual story superimposed on one about neural circuitry" (1999, 155). Slater continues her grappling after the birth of her daughter, Clara. She says: "Wait a minute, Clara. . . . When you dig into your past for explanations, don't forget your papa and me. Don't dismiss me, please. I am not all pill; my influence was greater than that, was it not? . . . [M]ake me into a myth, Clara, and pass me down the line. . . . Story me more than my neurons, your neurons" (1999, 118).

this strange planet, pressing in" (1998, 5). Like Jamison, Slater must let go of her former self when the full force of health hits her. She says: "A new kind of anxiety started to sprout in me. . . . For the world as I had known it my whole life did not seem to exist. Not only had Prozac— thank all the good gods in the world—removed the disabling obsessive symptoms; it seemed, as well, to have tweaked the deeper proclivities of my personality. Who was I? Where was I? Everything seemed less relevant . . . [d]iminished" (29). After beginning Prozac, instead of laboring over her finely calibrated menus that measure each gram of fat and every calorie to be consumed, Slater uncharacteristically goes out for ice cream. She gains some weight, and, surprisingly, the weight gain does not disgust her. More troublesome for Slater is the loss of the intensity of depression and drive that she believed had made her a writer. Even when she was most seriously ill, she always wrote; but early on, her daily dose of Prozac seems to take away her creative abilities. In fact, the drug is taking away her identity, an identity based on being ill. She becomes a different person, "both more and less like me, fulfilling one possibility while swerving from another," and like Jamison, she realizes she is losing something (49).

Nevertheless, Slater gets better and better. She begins her Prozac diary, recording the changes she experiences as she starts to take part in the conventional world: finding a job, setting an alarm clock, buying a chair, going to school. As it did for Jamison and Kaysen, secrecy about her illness becomes an issue. For example, when she starts an internship at a halfway house for alcoholics, she has to agree to drug testing. She is so afraid that Prozac will be detected in her urine that she consults one of her clients, "one junkie to another," about using goldenseal, an herb that will mask her urine screens (106). For Slater, using Prozac is like falling in love, but she remarks, "wonderful as it was, [it] did have its difficulties. . . . The goldenseal issue. The hiddenness" (106).

How to establish a solid self-esteem if one's mental health is first and foremost dependent on a chemical? In order to perform my regular life, I need to sleep at least four or five hours a night; in order to enjoy my regular life, I need seven or eight hours. But in order to accomplish this feat, I often turn to my own necessary medication and take a hypnotic agent, Dalmane. To some extent, both Slater and I depend on drugs in order to cope effectively in our worlds. Having made this intimate connection between her experience and my own, I found Slater's following observation particularly striking: "A plethora of literature . . . proclaimed, with the confidence of a trumpet's note . . . [b]ehind every crooked thought lies a crooked molecule. . . . In light of these findings, the patient's past, the story of self, is no longer relevant. We do not need to explain mental illness in the context of history. We can place it, and its cures, firmly in the context of chemicals" (107–8). If I am to entertain this premise, knowing that part of my mental health is indeed linked to the availability of Dalmane, the axiom on which my thesis rests—that we can benefit from telling our stories and from listening to the stories of others—breaks down. Why tell our stories if swallowing a chemical compound—be it Prozac, lithium, or Dalmane—can make a pestering and distressingly inscrutable past suddenly moot, even insignificant? Why write the memoir? Why read the memoir? If we are no more than chemical concoctions that need to be recalibrated for smoother efficiency, then our life experiences become nothing more than testimony to the balance, imbalance, or insufficiency of those chemicals. Rather than seeking psychotherapy, informal counseling, honest talk with a trusted friend, or writing a memoir, we could place our trust in psychopharmacology, where, notes Slater, "there is no need for intimacy; [where] neither knives nor stories are an essential part of its practice" (11).

For Slater, it is ironically "Prozac poop-out" that allows her to reconceptualize her *self* as more than a chemically recalibrated "beast" and regain her humanness. Falling ill again while taking Prozac obliges her to admit that the tiny green and cream pills with which she has fallen deeply in love will not prove her consummate lover. Finally, chemicals cannot cure. Temporarily returned to the weird complexities of her illness, Slater has to find a part of her self that is more than "crooked molecules" or a "serotonin specific chemical," a part of her self that chooses to live in a space that requires her cultivation and sustenance (126). We can choose our lives, and we do so not as chemically regulated beasts, but as fallible, vulnerable, yet resilient humans. After relapse, Slater comes to understand that she needs her stories, the salubrious potency of language, and the healing comfort of connection. It is by honoring these human needs, aided by efficient connections in the serotonin system, that we are, in fact, made well.

Slater does not entirely resolve her ambivalence about hiding her illness and her past. When a well-meaning friend suggests that she have cosmetic surgery to erase a mesh of small scars running up and down her arms left over from years of self-mutilation, she finds the idea upsetting. "Every day," she observes, she "takes pills whose purpose is to hide her history," but she is reluctant to give up these scars, the "inscriptions" of the truth of her illness (136). Like me, like a lot of people, Slater wants to be known, but she feels like an imposter, a fraud. Her accomplishments are not really hers; she is fooling the people around her. She is nothing more than a woman in disguise, a black stocking pulled over her skull.

I suffered most severely from my own sense of fraudulence as I worked toward my Ph.D. at the University of Washington. For my first two years of study, I believed that I must have been admitted to the program by error. Someone would check and find the administrative mistake as soon as I let down my guard and removed my own "stocking mask." This mask was not the docile "Betty." I fashioned this mask after the articulate, intimidating graduate students whose intellectual prowess dominated our seminars. I resented their acumen but mimicked them just the same to hide my sense of ineptitude that often felt like impenetrable, mute stupidity. Like a trespasser, I zealously delved into the mysteries of postmodernism, only to learn that the self I thought I was hiding was as constructed and contingent as the mask I was assuming. Unfortunately, learning that I had no authentic essence to conceal did nothing to bolster my self-confidence. Nevertheless, I completed my Ph.D., and when I came east for job interviews, I kept that mask firmly in place, adept now at anticipating the expectations of academic communities. It occurred to me after being offered a position in North Carolina that my future colleagues had no idea who they had just hired. I successfully kept all my insecure, ineffectual, unsuitable "selves" hidden throughout my entire campus visit behind my newly fashioned professorial mask.

Slater's husband, Bennett, comes to know all her contingent and constructed, shifting selves, even the ones that are chemically constructed. He sees through her masks, which are, she notes, "so much more permeable, so far less mysterious than ever we think" (145). Within a healing intimacy, she comes to recognize a self: "Lauren. She. Me. So many pieces. Really, it is a way of being rich" (145). Bennett loves what she was before and who she might still be; he cares for her beyond Prozac and before Prozac; he cares for all the people who she is.

Like Bennett, John has seen through my masks, uncovered my hiding places, and watched me unravel the intricate complexities of my past. Before John, those hidden stories all felt indecent, degrading, and shameful—some still do. But John, clear-eyed cultural critic that he is, has helped me gather all my stories and recast them in ways that let me see how cultural and psychological forces pushed me here and there. When John interprets my stories, I am no longer the shameful, disobedient daughter or the unforgivably yielding girl at Florence Crittendon, no longer the unscrupulous adolescent with "hot pants" or the capricious, unreliable wife. John revises my stories with me, making them rich with social significance, windows through which I can more thoughtfully remember, cogently interpret, and judiciously understand the unprecedented decades I grew up in. With his discerning blue eyes, he looks into all my stories—compassionately back at everything I was, lovingly at all I am, and eagerly to who I may be.

In her book *Welcome to My Country*, Slater states, "I believe in a place, somewhere in the air, where my self and your self might meet, merging in what we might learn to call, at least for a moment, love" (1996, xiii). John and I have surely found that place. Slater hopes that therapists and patients might also find that place, at least momentarily, where they can both best serve the healing process. Readers and memoirists can also find that place and take from the transitory meeting of minds and hearts newfound understanding and compassion and sometimes even the ability to transform ourselves.

Jamison concludes her memoir by remarking that when she first conceived of it, she thought it would be about "an illness of moods" in the context of her individual life. But as she wrote, she discovered: "[The book] somehow turned out to be very much a book about love as well: love as sustainer, as renewer, and as protector. After each seeming death within my mind or heart, love has returned to re-create hope and to restore life. . . . It has, inexplicably and savingly, provided not only cloak but lantern for the darker seasons and grimmer weather" (1995, 215). Jamison, Slater, and I are fortunate women to be able to write memoirs that tell not just of sorrow, depression, pain, and defeat, but of ardent love as well.

We do things in our lives that we cannot take back. I abandoned Sorrow; Kathryn Harrison had sex with her father; Claudia Bepko accidentally killed a woman; Kay Redfield Jamison tried to kill herself. Those acts cannot be erased; they will always be ours to confront, to own, even if we do re-create love in our lives. That I found John still impresses me as extraordinary, for I have known no other person who has the unshakable patience and composed strength to shine the constant, benevolent light that can accompany me as I struggle with the dark interludes that my past will always impose.

Slater concludes her *Prozac Diary* without "finding herself" under the many layers of Prozac, illness, health, love, depression, and productivity. She recognizes that given postmodernism, such a search is highly suspect anyway because "the real self as a belief went out in the seventies" (196). Still, like me, Slater will not abandon the exploration. For one thing, it is much too interesting to stop investigating our singular ineffableness. Postmodern sensibility only escalates the allure to mine for the intangible bedrock of the self. The essence is even more beguiling because it is illusive and protean. Whether we arrive at a core or at the brink of an abyss, depth and profundity are intrinsic to both, and our reflective journey will have been meaningful and worthwhile. Steadfastly committed to the quest for a self, Slater sums up: "So. There it is. Here I am. Or here I am not. The difference really matters to me. Probably, despite the trends in our universities, it matters to a lot of people. It could be that many people will continue to believe in bedrock, or better yet, to believe in the importance of the search. The search for the genuine. The gem" (197). The "gem" may be no more than a particular role in a social process, sustained and supported by the social ritual in which we are taking part. Nevertheless, though I may be no more than a myriad of voices from my culture and my history, I harbor hopes, fears, wishes, thoughts, desires, and inspiration. French theorist Julia Kristeva remarks on the effort to balance both the loss of the center and the yearning for stability: "This discovery . . . that I myself at the deepest levels of my wants and desires am unsure, centerless, and divided . . . does not eliminate my capacities for commitment and trust" (1997, 7–8). I seek affirmation and devotion, both to give and to receive. Having come to a better understanding of my past and the events that have kept me from commitment and trust, I am better prepared to fully realize these capacities, and that is a remarkable and wonderful arrival.

What can we learn from memoirs about mental illness and, in particular, the narratives of Kaysen, Jamison, and Slater? Perhaps there is no other test of love as demanding as our encounters with those people who are mentally ill. We are often temperamentally and financially unequipped to provide the dependable care they need. Often, they are sequestered, as was Kaysen. Such isolation, enforced or voluntary, comes at a great cost to those people who are isolated from normal society. The mentally ill can also be left in another kind of solitude, as was Lauren Slater before Prozac. Hers was for the most part self-imposed isolation, but imprisoning nevertheless. Or, like Jamison, they may be accompanied throughout their illness by concerned friends and family, yet, despite their supporters' very best attempts, desperation can lead the afflicted to choose death over life.

These memoirs are not about mentally ill victims, and certainly neither Kaysen, Jamison, nor Slater is asking for our pity. Instead, they are giving us the opportunity to understand. Reading their memoirs helps us recognize that we exist on a continuum, one that extends from reason, lucidity, and sanity to derangement, darkness, and madness. An intimate reading allows us to meet our own obsessions and encourages us to examine our own position on that continuum.

Furthermore, the memoirs let us witness the hopelessness, the loss of control, the disorientation, the obsession, the guilt, and the despair of mental illness. Each in its own unique way gives us a glimpse of what it is like to live on the edge of rationality and beyond. By invoking our empathy, these memoirists help us understand how easily the mentally ill can become victims to institutional hierarchies that pay far too little attention and allocate far too few resources to the emotional and psychological well-being of all of us.

By reading *Girl, Interrupted*, *An Unquiet Mind*, and *Prozac Diary*, we can be better prepared for our own encounters with mental illness if it should surface within our own psyches, within our families, or within our circle of friends and colleagues. We will be more likely to critique our cultural impatience and intolerance for the mentally ill that leave too many sufferers unprotected, poorly cared for, or abandoned. By giving us the opportunity to intimately identify with the overwhelming psychological devastation we call mental illness, we are better informed and better equipped to be advocates for improved care, procurable medication, and increased tolerance. Because of Kaysen's, Jamison's, and Slater's willingness to tell their hard truths about the harrowing journeys each has taken and survived, we are enlightened. We now better understand how such illnesses can invade our lives, how effortlessly they can obliterate the selves we comprehend and trust, how easily they can ravage those selves, causing them to disappear behind transforming veils of depression, confusion, obsession, and loss.

8

OWNING SECRETS
Who Can Tell?

What is important . . . must be spoken, made verbal and shared, even at the risk of having it bruised or misunderstood.—Audre Lorde, *The Cancer Journals*

Memoirs not only reveal the intimate life of the memoirist, but also lay bare the private lives of the memoirist's family, spouses, lovers, and friends. One of the most anxiety-provoking aspects of writing my own memoir is my sense of betrayal for telling my family's secrets. Am I a disloyal daughter? Am I betraying my mother and father by disclosing the long-suppressed stories about my Uncle Richard's tragic family and Sorrow's birth? In *I Could Tell You Stories*, memoirist Patricia Hampl acknowledges that she has lost many people, not to death, but to writing. She recounts some of those people whom she has lost: "The one who accused me of appropriating her life, the one who said he was appalled, the poet miffed by my description of his shoes, the dear elderly priest who said he thought I understood the meaning of a private conversation, this one, that one. Gone, gone. Their fading faces haven't faded at all, just receded, turned abruptly away from me, as is their right. . . . All of them 'used,' one way or another" (1999, 228). In her first book of poetry, Hampl revealed her mother's darkest secret, that she suffered from epilepsy. Although at the time her mother acquiesced to Hampl's request to publish the poem, much later in her life, she admits to Hampl that she has always hated it. Hampl tells us this part of the story as a kind of corrective to the first disclosure. She had tried to justify exposing the secret by presuming it would liberate her mother from the shame of epilepsy. It did not. Of course, Hampl cannot retrieve the secret; all she can do is respectively record her mother's abiding discomfort with its publication,

176

but there will be no assuaging redemption for either her or her mother. I too have painstakingly created intricate justifications for telling secrets, but I cannot assume the outcome of disclosure will be constructive. Who might I lose to writing?

In her book *The Secret Life of Families*, Evan Imber-Black provides guidance for those of us who are puzzled by who owns the past. She maintains, "When you are keeping a secret that *primarily* and *essentially* regards your life, then you are the owner of the secret, and decisions to keep it or open it rightfully belong to you" (1998, 128). Although the consequences of opening the secret of Sorrow may be distressing to others, the secret of her birth belongs to me, her birth mother. It fundamentally concerns my life, and I feel justified in telling this defining intersection of my own self-construction. All my girlhood stories lead up to March 20, 1965; all my other stories lead from it.

But what about Richard? Is his history primary to my life? More than fifty years ago, my family decided to make the murder-suicide a secret. Upon receiving the horrible news, my grandparents eliminated all traces of him and his family from their home. My mother has told me that she was desperate to protect my sisters from the terrible details of what had happened to their uncle, aunt, and cousins, so the Richard Ellerbys were vanquished from my parents' home as well.

My oldest sister recently told me of one clear memory from those traumatic days after the deaths. She recalls lying in my parents' bed with my mother listening to my father on the telephone talking about Richard. From her position next to my mother, she can look out the window and down the street to an intersection. She focuses on the STOP sign there, and she knows intuitively that the sign is telling her not to ask questions, not to say anything. The STOP sign remains a compelling image of her childhood, though she remembers almost nothing about her uncle, aunt, or cousins.

The erasure of Richard and his family from the Ellerby history remained an unexamined agreement, not bitterly guarded, but a shadowy secret nonetheless. Families will conceal suicides, as evidenced in Linda Cutting's *Memory Slips*. Ashamed of their own responsibility for her brother David's despondency and instability, her parents deny his suicide, claiming instead that he died in an auto accident. For them and for many others, acknowledging a family suicide is an occasion for public humiliation rather than private grief (Imber-Black 1998, 57). Cutting's parents were implicated by David's suicide. My parents were in no way responsible for my uncle's crisis; his devastating solution was his own. Nevertheless, the family felt incriminated, undeservedly connected to an act that was for them shamefully unthinkable.

For me the catastrophe of the murder-suicide is agonizing. Even now, as I focus on the details of the deaths, the images I summon are powerful enough to upset me even though it all occurred before my birth. Hoping to find information about the murders and still hesitant to approach my mother again, knowing the anxiety my questions would cause, I had contacted the *Los Angeles Times* research service, but the microfilm that would have told Richard's story is missing from their archives. The Pasadena Public Library did have the microfilm of the *Pasadena Star News* editions that tell of the "double murder-suicide" and kindly sent me copies of the two articles that covered the tragedy even though I have not been a Pasadena resident for years. Ironically, the only pictures of my uncle and his family were found by my own daughter, who located the *Los Angeles Times* stories right here in North Carolina on microfiche in the UNC-Chapel Hill library. She brought the photocopies home on a hot and humid September afternoon: what a jolt! There they were: the faces of Richard, Betty, Richard Jr., and Carolyn Jean. Although I stared at the photos for a long time, I had recognized Richard immediately; he looks so much like my father did as a young man. Then, when I placed a picture of myself at age three next to the picture of three-year-old Carolyn Jean, goose bumps ran up and down my arms despite the sweltering day; the resemblance seems uncanny.

I wish what we all wish—that those people who die so young and so senselessly could be saved, that I could have known them. I feel a palpable connection with Carolyn Jean. Thinking of the inexplicable loneliness I always felt as a child, I wonder if we were meant to have been playmates, girlfriends, confidantes. I think I would have cherished her companionship. I am surprised by the gravity with which I mourn the loss of her place in our lives. In a compelling way, I feel a responsibility to her—this sweet child with her trusting gaze. To keep her secreted away, unknown and unappreciated, seems unfair, yet because of the shame that has undeservedly infected her as well as her father, all I really know about her is that she died almost instantly while sitting on his lap.

More pragmatically, Richard is part of my memoir because of his relevance to the ingrained habit of secrecy in my family. Keeping secrets began for a good reason—to protect us from the shame of an unbearably sad family tragedy. But my own experience with shame and secrets has been so painful and debilitating that I want to put an end to it. As Hampl knows, and I have learned, secrecy finally does not protect us: "We carry our wounds and perhaps even worse, our capacity to wound, forward with us" (33). So I open these secrets to put a stop to the injurious habit of pretending the past can vanish. I open the past in order to serve the future because "our capacity to move forward as developing beings rests on a healthy relation with the past" (ibid.). Keeping shame-laden memories cloaked in secrecy was a consequential mistake for me. Uncovering the painful past allows us to lead more informed, unabridged lives, to make the difficult but more rewarding commitment to deal honestly and openly with all our obstacles as they arise. Although Richard's secret is not mine alone, I open it out of love for my family and with the hope that my sincerity will lead to a deeper, more connected familial bond, an intimate space where we can take risks based on trust and the promise of acceptance.

I proffer this justification for telling my family's secrets because so many literary and social critics have disparaged the kind of memoir that I have written and discussed—the memoir that reveals what has heretofore been secret or unspoken. In his essay "Betrayal Between the Covers," *Washington Post* critic David Streitfeld castigates several recent memoirists for using the memoir as exposé. Streitfeld upbraids Paul Theroux for his memoir about his former friend and mentor V. S. Naipaul, Joyce Maynard for disclosing unflattering details about J. D. Salinger, and Lillian Ross for writing a memoir about "40 years of dalliance" with William Shawn (1998, D1). Streitfeld vilifies these memoirists and others (John Bayley for *Elegy for Iris*, Rosemary Mahoney for *A Likely Story*, and Catherine Texier for *Breakup*) for exploiting the private lives of wives, mentors, ex-husbands, and ex-lovers for the ostensible purpose of "remaining true to their inner selves" (D2). "The only difference," says Streitfeld, "between Paul Theroux and Linda Tripp . . . is that the writer's memory is so good he had no need of a tape recorder" (ibid.). When I read that chilling Streitfeld analogy, I indeed began to worry. Could I unwittingly be in Tripp's egregious camp? My knee-jerk resistance to Streitfeld's comparison reveals my personal insecurity about unlocking the private doors of those people I love.

Here but Not Here: A Love Story

> *The past is radiant. It sheds the light of lived life. One who writes memoir wishes to step into that light, not to see one's own face—that is not possible—but to feel the length of shadow cast by the light.*—Patricia Hampl, *I Could Tell You Stories*

Several critics have "slagged" Lillian Ross for violating William Shawn's confidentiality in her memoir, *Here but Not Here: A Love Story*.[1] Shawn, longtime editor of the *New Yorker*, was indeed a very private man, and his wife, whom he did not divorce and with whom he continued to live throughout the forty years that he was also Ross's companion, is still living. Streitfeld justifiably observes that Ross's memoir is "also the life of Cecille Shawn, who had exposed to the world the claim that her husband was deeply in love with another woman and that her marriage was a fraud" (D2). Ross rebuts Streitfeld: "I wasn't writing about her marriage. . . . I was writing about my love story," and in a sense, she is correct (qtd. in ibid.). Throughout *Here but Not Here*, Ross has very little to say about Cecille other than to comment respectfully on Cecille's unwavering commitment to Shawn. Otherwise, Ross offers no more than heartfelt concern for Cecille's unavoidable unhappiness given what must have been a very bitter reality, for Shawn made no attempt to hide his relationship with Ross from Cecille.

We have, then, what cultural critic Alan Sinfield calls "a contest of stories" between Ross and her critics (1998, 805). One critic maintains that she has tried to cast herself heroically as "the figure behind one of

---

1. Michiko Kakutani finds Lillian Ross "in keeping with the tell-all confessional climate of the 90s," and maintains, "the resulting book is a tasteless, self-dramatizing memoir that presents itself as a valentine . . . even as it undermines the very qualities of discretion and taste its subject championed in life." Kakutani not only admonishes Ross but anyone who might enjoy her "unseemly" memoir (like me), because it "appeals only to the reader's baser impulse to read about an eminent man's adulterous affair" (1998c, E46). Susan Shapiro is equally repelled by the memoir, branding it as "overhyped" and Ross as deluded for never realizing that her forty-year love affair with Shawn "probably remained so passionate because he kept going home to his wife Cecille, not despite that" (1998, 157). Jean Hanff Korelitz observes that even if Ross's memoir was motivated "solely by love," it is "a repellent attempt to possess in death what its author could never quite nail down in life" (1999, 32). Clearly, when women decide to tell secrets about past lovers, they take enormous chances of being pilloried no matter what their motivations, literary reputations, or the possible merits of their work.

the century's great editors"; another says that the memoir serves her interests by making "her out to be the savior of [the *New Yorker*]" (qtd. in Streitfeld 1998, D2). Another, who asks to remain nameless, suggests that the relationship "was less a love story than a morass that Shawn, who famously had trouble ending things, couldn't get out of" (qtd. in ibid.). According to Streitfeld, "Some old-time New York sources are saying that, with her most enduring work, *Picture*, nearly half a century behind her, she is trying both to account for her long absence and write herself into literary history" (ibid.). Furthermore, her credibility is attacked because of some factual inaccuracies in the memoir, and because she asks readers to take on faith the assertion that Shawn wanted her to write this book.

Here then are more of the substantial risks the memoirist encounters when she decides to call up the past to tell the truths of a lifetime, whether to reveal a pivotal event, a crucial person, or a consequential chapter in a family history. She must be concerned about not only unsympathetic and uncharitable responses, but also whether she will be chided for solipsism and self-aggrandization or excoriated for betraying participants. Perhaps, as in Ross's case, she will not even be believed.

I began Ross's *Here but Not Here* as a suspicious reader. Having read several reviews beforehand, I expected to be put off by a tell-all tale by the "other woman." Our cultural tenets about the hallowed status of long marriages make extended love affairs highly suspect, and I did not initially employ the open-mindedness I try to have when I start a book. But Ross's narrative stance captured my respect quickly. It was to describe Ross's journalistic technique that a critic in the 1940s first used the now common phrase "fly on the wall" reporting (Ross 1998, 103). Indeed, she remains true to the technique she helped define by writing a memoir that contains very little analysis or supposition. She narrates the facts of her life with Shawn with straightforward specificity and includes a chronological photo album so that her readers can watch them age together as they go about their interwoven lives.

Early in the memoir, Ross describes an encounter she had in the early 1960s with Dorothy Parker. Ross passes Parker on Madison Avenue as Parker, with a strong alcoholic odor, hair unkempt, in bedroom slippers and a shabby housecoat, unsteadily walks her tiny dog. Seeing the disheveled Parker serves as a frightful warning, and Ross recalls promising herself: "[It] must never be like *that*, never like *that*. One's personal life and professional life, I told myself, could be in line with each other and on the same plane" (55). Her memoir serves as an example of her ongoing determination to keep her professional writing life and her personal life in harmony. Ross writes respectfully and lovingly about her life as the companion of an extraordinary man. She does not attempt to exploit, rationalize, boast, or defend. Instead, she writes forthrightly about the complexities, the contradictions, and the compromises she faced as a single woman living within an unconventional relationship. She focuses not only on the happiness she shared with Shawn but also on their frustrations, sorrows, and remorse.

Still, the issue of Cecille Shawn nags. Ross readily admits that in trying to sort out the inevitable hurtfulness and disappointment that accompanied the awkward logistical adjustments of living arrangements, "we were unable to solve our problems, although we persisted in asking each other most of the unanswerable questions" (107). She confesses that she became very good at not thinking about Cecille's pain or humiliation: "Cecille—no matter how involved she had to be in deciding the hours and days of our life—was in truth *outside* of us," and Ross keeps her outside of the memoir (107). Although my own misgivings keep me imagining Cecille somewhere always in the background of the narrative, Ross is intent on focusing on the love story she shared with Shawn himself.

Shawn was a man beloved by many people, especially writers. It is striking how many of the writers I have read and written about for this project acknowledge him in their memoirs as their mentor and friend (Jamaica Kincaid and Suzannah Lessard in particular). Because of his extensive influence on contemporary nonfiction, one wants to know this man better. Hence, some of the most engaging though controversial aspects of Ross's memoir are her revelations about Shawn's emotional unsteadiness, although she herself never refers to his mental state as such. But she does tell us that Shawn struggled with a long-standing and debilitating feeling of nonexistence. Throughout the memoir, his cryptic declaration about his marriage and his work—"I am there, but I am not there" (10)—echoes. He required from Ross a vital confirmation of his identity. "Do you know who I am?" he would ask her. "Please do not let me forget my own life" (119). Acutely remote, known as a "mysterious autocrat" and "a shy workaholic" whom "even his staff barely knew" (Streitfeld 1998, D2), he turned to Ross to confirm his most authentic self. "Who am I?" he asked. "Am I really here?" (129). Shawn seemed to feel like a counterfeit, so much so that he would lose track of a focused, dependable self-image if it was not patiently reconfirmed by Ross.

Ross herself maintains a vigorous self-respect, never defining herself as Shawn's *mistress*, a term, she claims, that in no way describes who she was. She remained focused on her profession, unfazed by disparaging interpretations of her status, and, for the most part, lived at peace without a marriage certificate. Nevertheless, despite the enduring connection she and Shawn sustained, she observes that Shawn "seemed beyond help in his overwhelming guilt and pain" (122). His guilt may have emanated from his double life, but it did not stem from deception; according to Ross, "he felt no need for secrecy" (126).

He and Ross enjoyed their long and vigorous relationship, I would argue, because they decided on openness and against secrecy. In her book *Secrets*, Sissela Bok observes, "Jung wrote that the keeping of secrets acts like a psychic poison, alienating their possessor from the community" (1989, 8). Because Ross and Shawn decide not to keep their alliance clandestine, they avoid the "psychic poison" of shame and the negative stereotypes of "the philanderer" and "the other woman" that they so strongly resist. Bok continues: "[G]uilty or deeply embarrassing secrets can corrode from within before outsiders have a chance to respond or to be of help" (25). Instead, because they keep no secrets, Ross and Shawn have the respect and support of friends and colleagues who accept the liaison, never lending it the taint of shame. In 1906, Lord Acton stated that "every thing secret degenerates," but because of their mutual determination to resist what might have looked like the shelter of secrecy, the corrosiveness of deceitfulness never infects the esteem Ross and Shawn hold for one another (qtd. in ibid.).

My initial skepticism about the Ross memoir proved unfounded. This book is not a seedy tell-all, written for self-glory or self-justification. The memoir ends with death as the denouement of a noble love story. Ross can be criticized for only a tinge of sentimentality as she makes the romantic observation that even after his death, Shawn remains with her, "here but not here," for she is "always seeing what Bill would see and how he would see it. . . . [W]e are still together," she believes, "defying death" (240).

I should have trusted the cover of the memoir, which is explicit about Ross's intent. It gives not just the title, *Here but Not Here*, but the added words *A Love Story*. From the start, Ross makes it clear that she is writing about the love of her life, and in so doing she follows Shawn's lead in a letter he wrote to his staff at the *New Yorker* of how good writing is undertaken: "Love has been the controlling emotion, and love is the essential word. We have done our work with honesty and love" (219). Ross has done no less. She maintains that when you write about others, you enter their lives and become their friend. "A friend," she notes, "is not to be used or abandoned" (173). I believe her when she says, "[Bill] would be proud to read this story" (239). She has been motivated by what might prove the crucial controlling emotion if a memoir is to be written with integrity—love.

Ross's memoir, then, becomes not an example of betrayal, but a testimony to the intimate places the memoir allows us to travel, inwardly, self-consciously, lovingly close to the heart. Indeed, she provides an insightful reflection on how good writers can and do go wrong:

> It seems at times that writers who are in trouble with themselves and their writing go on the attack against people. . . . Jealousy and rage then replace creative energy in the writer. If a writer is busily engaging his energies in his own work . . . that writer is not looking for anyone to blame for his miseries; there is nobody and nothing to be jealous of. If one were to make a list of the writers and artists who have been giving their time and attention in the past few years to attacks on other writers or artists, one might well find a list of writers and artists who are in deep trouble with themselves. (168)

Ross's purpose is not to attack (except a brief strike at S. I. Newhouse for his tactless firing of Shawn as editor-in-chief), but the memoirs that are being assailed most stringently today have within them an element of attack and an intent to malign.

Paul Theroux's memoir, *Sir Vidia's Shadow: A Friendship Across Five Continents*, about his friendship with and mentorship under V. S. Naipaul, proves a good example of what can go wrong when a memoirist is motivated by jealousy or rage. Like Streitfeld, Michiko Kakutani also uses Linda Tripp to characterize Theroux in her review of his memoir: "Mr. Theroux demonstrates almost as few scruples as Linda Tripp in regaling the reader with voyeuristic tidbits about Mr. Naipaul's life" (1998a, D7). In the *New York Times Book Review*, critic Sara Kerr maintains that although Theroux's picture of a perversely mean Naipaul may be accurate, the memoir comes to us as "one half of a real-life cat fight," a "mix of gossip and righteousness." Kerr continues: "What we have here is a man who claims to be recalling a friendship when obviously he's seeking revenge. The disconnect is monstrous. . . . Theroux is out to prove he's the rejecter, not the rejectee. All he's done is write a memoir that feels less like a memoir than an onslaught of sticks and stones" (1998, 7). According to his critics, Theroux has done what Ross warns against by letting his own troubled ego, overwhelmed by Naipaul's rejection and ill will, focus his energy on maligning Naipaul.

Writing defensively about memory and invention in his own "Book-end" piece in the *New York Times Book Review,* Theroux dismisses the label of betrayer as "laughable." Using the lived experience of one's life, he says, is inevitable whether we write memoirs or fiction: "Re-creating our nearest and dearest, and our secrets, as imaginative subjects . . . is what writers do." He admits to some "revisionism," but, he maintains, it is inescapable given "the towering vantage point of passing time." His memoir, he insists, gives us the kind of truth that "helps us to understand the world": "The best writers are the most fanatical; so the truest portrait of a writer can never be a study of virtue. The hagiographer is a belittler. Any book that shrinks from the enchantments of this fanaticism and invites the reader to see its subject as simple and loveable is a confidence trick" (1998a, 39). Given Theroux's conditions for what makes for the best writers, we might be tempted to dismiss Ross's memoir as inferior because her devoted portrait of Shawn is repeatedly a study of his virtues.

Nevertheless, the Shawn she describes is neither simple nor saintly. Although he treats Ross with love and respect for decades, we learn from her that he is a fallible man who chooses a double life, a lover, and a marriage. He enjoys his sports car, and relishes fine food, fine suits, and sex. Rather than a flat character of uncomplicated uprightness, the William Shawn that Ross portrays is psychologically complex and often emotionally troubled. That Ross tells us about him lovingly hardly makes her memoir "a confidence trick," as Theroux would have us believe.

At Home in the World

> To "spill" too many secrets is to be like a sieve that lets too much through. Some have lost—and others never learned—the sense for how to select and make distinctions in what they say and to whom they speak. Their instant familiarity all too often

breeds but instant contempt.—Sissela Bok, Secrets: On the Ethics of Conceal-
ment and Revelation

Another memoir that has received much attention and mixed reviews is Joyce Maynard's *At Home in the World.*[2] Like Ross, Maynard is criticized for revealing secrets about one of our most reclusive American authors, J. D. Salinger, with whom she lived for nine months when she was eighteen and he was fifty-three. Although Kakutani finds the memoir emotionally candid, she also applies the now repetitive descriptives for memoirs in general: "self-serving," "solipsistic," and "too beholden to the confessional tenets of the therapeutic movement to be a first-rate memoir" (1998b, B6).

Like Theroux, Maynard seems to use her memoir to settle scores against those people who have rejected or harmed her, particularly Salinger, but also her mother, father, and ex-husband. Streitfeld finds Maynard's revelations about Salinger especially offensive, particularly when she suggests that Salinger was "a little too fond of children" (qtd. in Streitfeld 1998, D1). In fact, Maynard's motives are transparent when she takes an unnecessary detour from her narrative denouement in order to be able to quote Salinger's neighbor Dan as saying that his daughters did not think much of Salinger because "he was always kissing them" (1998, 338). Maynard moves, says Streitfeld, "from being famous for her narcissism to being notorious for her perfidy" (D3).

Rather than attempting to respond to the conflicts between what is and is not intrusive or to ponder the moral questions about the boundaries of privacy, Maynard ignores all calls for discretion. She moves, says Streitfeld, "From a childhood where everything was a secret, . . .to believing there shouldn't be any at all" (ibid.). However, the revelation of secrets is not what bothers me about Maynard's memoir; instead, I am exasperated by Maynard's motives and by the memoir's want of social purpose. Whether intentional, Maynard's book commits what Hampl

2. Korelitz's review of *At Home in the World* is much more forgiving of Maynard than of Ross because, she maintains, Maynard seems well aware of the fact that Salinger will find the memoir appalling and proceeds, nevertheless, enthusiastically "to disclose the deep anger she still feels towards him." Korelitz concludes: "Both memoirs . . . are nasty little books, but Joyce Maynard's, at least, comes by its nastiness honestly" (1999, 32). The acrimony of the reviewers toward Ross and Maynard not just as writers but as individuals is both startling and disturbing.

calls the lowest sin of the memoir: "To make a mean little case against the past (aka, mother and father)" (203), or, in Maynard's case, J. D. Salinger, and she does so for no civic purpose that I can discern.

At Home in the World also exacerbates the degree of sexual disclosure the memoir will tolerate. For example, Maynard describes a nightly ritual she performed for Salinger while she was living with him: "His hands reach for my shoulders. He strokes my hair. He takes hold of my head then, with surprising firmness, and guides me under the covers. Under the sheets, with their smell of laundry detergent, I close my eyes. Tears are streaming down my cheeks. Still, I don't stop. So long as I keep doing this, I know he will love me" (155). What does Maynard accomplish by way of these details other than suggesting that Salinger is a lecherous middle-aged man who uses his aura of superiority to get a young girl to service him sexually? Serious memoirists must consider not only what to tell but also why are they telling it. Maynard could argue that she revealed this sexual ritual to warn readers about the vulnerability of young, impressionable girls when they become enchanted by older, powerful men, but that impression is not the one discerned when reading this passage. Instead, she seems to want to make Salinger pay in a way that she knows will be especially painful for him and does so by depicting this intimate sexual practice as coercive. But does she succeed? From the responses of reviewers, it appears that our culture is more tolerant of exploitive middle-aged men than self-righteous tattletales.

Memoirs traverse precarious terrain. They allow us to explore, empathize, and achieve an unusual amount of intimacy with the memoirist. But memoirs such as Joyce Maynard's, Mia Farrow's, and Lillian Ross's also confront us with one of the most compelling issues of our contemporary society—how much privacy can we rightfully claim? In his book *Integrity*, Stephen Carter observes that our concern over privacy has been heightened because we have forfeited the empirical separation between public and private: "Our very homes are becoming so wired to so many others that it is harder and harder to speak of even that most sacrosanct of spaces as *private*" (1996, 236). Maynard has happily taken advantage of this forfeiture by building her own Web site and an active Web-site community with whom she shares her coffee every day (xi). Her maxim remains, "Whatever happens in my life, I can look at it as *material*" (41).

This sense of entitlement jibes with Dinitia Smith's assertion in her essay "Writers as Plunderers": "Writing often involves an invasion, a theft, an exposure of something private, and the issue of a writer's right to use the lives of real people in his work has always been debated" (1998, A19). In fact, each of the memoirs discussed in this book has revealed the private lives not only of its author, but also of her family, friends, and adversaries. Each has raised the issue of disclosure versus secrecy, narration versus confidentiality. Most have opened secrets with a finely tuned sense of the distinction between what should and should not be said. Effective memoirists understand how to be the "sieve" that lets just the right amount of detail through in order to build intimacy rather than contempt.

My Brother

> I only now understand why it is that people lie about their past, why they say they are one thing other than the thing they really are, why they invent a self that bears no resemblance to who they really are, why anyone would want to feel as if he or she belongs to nothing, comes from no one, just fell out of the sky.—Jamaica Kincaid

A compelling memoir that also confronts the dilemma of who can tell and how much can be told is Jamaica Kincaid's My Brother.[3] Kincaid, who wrote for William Shawn at the New Yorker and is also his daughter-in-law, examines her brother's life and his final struggle with AIDS as well as her vexed relationship with their mother, her own experiences with motherhood, and even the death of Shawn, her "perfect reader" (1997, 198). Her telling is significant because she reveals immediately what her brother, Devon, was unwilling to disclose throughout his illness: rather than admit that he had AIDS, he told his mother he had lung cancer and others that he had bronchial asthma (23).

Coming from Vermont to visit her dying brother, Kincaid does not share the overwhelming shame the disease produces in Antigua. Instead, for her own peace of mind and in order to make it real, she tells people that her brother has AIDS (30). But revealing a secret does not just ease

---

3. Although Jamaica Kincaid also tells a secret that some might claim was not hers to tell, she receives none of the severity that Ross and Maynard come by. This nonreaction may be because she is "telling on" her brother rather than her ex-lover, or it may be that her book is that much better crafted, or both. Nevertheless, Kincaid tells in "angry and unsparing detail . . . the story of her brother's blighted life" and has been thoroughly praised for doing so (Frank 1997, 64).

the mind; it also enables others to help us treat what the secret hides. By telling the manageress of the hotel where she is staying that her brother is dying of AIDS, she learns from her of a doctor in Antigua who will treat him rather than surrendering to a putative, automatic death sentence. Telling the truth gives her unexpected help; this doctor will administer to her brother the AZT that she can provide from the United States, and with AZT, Devon's health improves remarkably.

Unlike Maynard, Kincaid has not been maligned by critics for betraying her brother's confidence and revealing his disease. In fact, she has been praised for achieving a more lucid, assertive voice that is "less angry here, and more reflective" than in earlier books such as *A Small Place* and *Lucy* (Wachman 1997, 43). She is commended for her candid chronicling of "her hate-filled, unprincipled family," and for making the "aesthetics of death and darkness . . . luminous" (Pela 1997, 82; McDowell 1998, 1). In contrast, I found only one negative review: in the *New York Amsterdam News*, Kwame Okoampa-Ahoofe Jr. criticizes Kincaid not for revealing secrets but for "her thoroughgoing Americanization" and "blisteringly negative attitude towards her native-country" (1998, 21). What can account for the differences in critical reception between Maynard's and Kincaid's memoirs given that both writers reveal the secrets of those people who had chosen privacy and concealment?

Although Kincaid writes lovingly and compassionately about Devon as a boy and as a man, she does not forgo imparting the negative aspects of his subsequent behavior after his temporary recuperation. For instance, she reveals that he refuses to accept that he is still HIV-positive and insists on having unprotected sex with a girl from Guiana. When confronted, he maintains that he simply cannot go without sex for more than two weeks. Clearly, Kincaid is angry with her brother for his unwillingness to curtail his promiscuity; however, there is an important distinction to be made between Kincaid's disclosures about her brother's sexual promiscuity and Maynard's disclosures about her sex life with Salinger. Unlike Maynard, who details the obligatory oral sex she performed on Salinger in order to expose him as heartlessly lascivious and demanding, Kincaid uses Devon's selfish insistence on frequent sexual gratification to examine men in general: "It must have been a person like this, men like this, men who are only urges to be satisfied, men who say they cannot help themselves, men who cannot save themselves, men who only know how to die, not at all how to live—it must have been such a man that my mother knew of when she communicated to me the grave danger to myself should I allow such a person to know me too well" (69). Kincaid takes the step away from the particularity of Devon's flawed rationalizations to a more general cultural critique of the social construction of men who believe it is rational to have sex regularly even if it means putting their sexual partners at grave risk.

While Devon is dying, Kincaid assumes he has contracted HIV by intravenous drug use or unprotected heterosexual intercourse. It is only after his death that she learns he kept his bisexuality hidden. Kincaid reveals his sexual orientation not out of spite or anger but out of sadness, regret, and a desire to change the necessity for such secrets even within the bonds of the family: "[H]e had died without ever understanding or knowing, or being able to let the world in which he lived know, who he was; that who he really was—not a single sense of identity but all the complexities of who he was—he could not express fully: his fear of being laughed at, his fear of meeting with the scorn of the people he knew best were overwhelming and he could not live with all of it openly" (162). So, Kincaid "outs" her dead brother. A cruel, needless thing to do? Not at all. Instead, it is an opportunity for her to critique a world in which the people who ought to love us best cannot or will not accept, acknowledge, and *name* our life experiences, whether they be homosexuality, infidelity, rape, alcoholism, suicide, or teenage pregnancy. With compassion and sorrow, Kincaid finally understands the doubleness of her brother's existence, the complicated sham he worked so hard at by pursuing women he did not want, and the shadows of duplicity that finally overtook his life's brightness "so that in the end anyone wanting to know him would have to rely on that, shadows . . . of secrets in his life" (176).

Kincaid's memoir is so much more than a sophisticated, lyrical "outing." It is an intimate glimpse at her grieving soul, at the irrevocability of death, and the regret we too will feel if we are not permitted to fully know those people we love. By lovingly revealing her brother's secrets, she reminds us of the need to build our families in ways that allow us to know one another in all our complexity and difference.

At the core of the popularity of the memoir is a hunger for a connection with other people that springs from a particularly modern lack of intimacy. Hampl suggests: "Maybe a reader's love of memoir is less an intrusive lust for confession than a hankering for the intimacy of this first-person voice, the deeply satisfying sense of being spoken to privately. More than a story, we want a voice speaking softly, urgently, in our ear. Which is to say, to our heart" (19). We crave intimacy, yet too often we are denied it in the place where we most desire it, in the circle of our families. Like Kincaid's brother, we dread exile, especially from those ties we hope will unconditionally connect us.

Given the popularity of the memoir, we can surmise that many readers now turn to the intimate voice of the memoirist as a substitute for the intimate language of the heart that we so long to hear and speak. Certainly, one impetus for reading memoirs and writing my memoir has been my hunger for such intimate connection, but unlike Kincaid's brother, I am also motivated to uncover a more valid rendition of myself, to approach the ultimately unattainable destination—the "genuine" self. Like Kay Redfield Jamison and Dorothy Allison, I want my truer stories to be known; like Mia Farrow, I want the shame of the concealed past to fall away. William Shawn lived his life feeling "here but not here." I know that feeling; I want to read and write past it.

9

THE MEMOIR AT WORK

Moving from silence into speech is for the oppressed, the colonized, the exploited, and those who stand and struggle side by side a gesture of defiance that heals, that makes new life and new growth possible. It is that act of speech, of "talking back," that is no mere gesture of empty words, that is the expression of our movement from object to subject—the liberated voice.—bell hooks, *Talking Back: Thinking Feminist, Thinking Black*

For most of my life, I have spoken from a cautious place, a rehearsal room where, alert to exposure, I edit and curtail my speech. Because sincerity and honesty have rarely felt like options, I have also used this "rehearsal room" to prepare my needed prevarications and masks. My duplicity and diffidence have been compounded by the cultural codes that suppress the female speech regardless of any secret pasts they might be trying to conceal. Consequently, although I am an English professor and make my living by way of language, I have difficulty easing into speech. Instead of coming across as articulate and forthright, my voice often betrays an anxious, uncomfortable urgency that makes my listeners ill at ease as well. Furthermore, my efforts at self-editing can prove unsuccessful. Occasionally, propelled by emotion, I will impulsively erupt into overwrought discourse only then to retreat, full of regret and shame. For me, spontaneity is a trap and candor a perilous opportunity I usually bungle. With pen and paper or, better yet, a word processor, I fare better, but clearly, my discomfort with the spoken word often works against my best intentions.

At bedrock, contends Adrienne Rich, language is power: "Those who suffer from injustice most are the least able to articulate their suffering" (1979, 67). Secrecy made memoirists such as Suzannah Lessard, Kathryn Harrison, Nancy Raine, and Linda Cutting unable to articulate the violations they had suffered for too long. They were given cues to suppress their experiences rather than to aim for honesty, not only by their molesters but also by their well-meaning friends and family who asked them to keep silent. In so doing, they did them an injustice, shamed them, betrayed them. Although emotional and psychological wounds irrevocably harm some individuals, these women were able to acquire from their suffering the "opportunity to grow, to move forward rather than backward in the process of self-realization" (hooks 1989, 7). Those people who can take the opportunity to move toward self-realization often begin by writing, and the memoir becomes a functional and salvational vehicle for that process. Rich continues, "The silent majority, if released into language, would not be content with a perpetuation of the conditions which have betrayed them," and in the language the memoir encourages, we can hear the end of secrecy, the beginning of protest, and the appeal for social change (67).

In *Talking Back*, hooks recalls being disciplined as a child for what her parents called her "crazy talk." As they punished her, they told her they had to break her spirit, but their efforts were counterproductive. Instead of retreating into modest reticence, hooks learned how to stand her ground and protect her spirit. Eventually, she claimed her legacy—the sharp tongue of the first Bell Hooks, her great-grandmother, who spoke her mind and was not afraid to talk back. Today, of course, hooks is a leading African American scholar and a respected memoirist. Hooks's writing has encouraged me to reclaim "that part of myself I . . . long ago rejected [and] left uncared for"; to join the fragmented memories of a secret year that held " 'the bits and pieces of my heart' "; to make my "narrative whole again" (159). Released into language, I became not only a woman who reads and writes about the books of others, but also a writer with my own story to tell. Writing the memoir became a means for "talking back," for untangling a long-maintained and ineffective gap in my life, and, more important, for revealing and critiquing social practices that betrayed me.

Although, like me, hooks dreaded being the traitor and breaking the bonds of secrecy and silence that held her family together, she understood that she could "not grow inside the atmosphere of secrecy that had pervaded [their] lives" until she began the process of writing her autobiography (156). When memoirists move from silence into speech, they make new life and new growth possible for themselves and their readers. By unbinding the secrets that entangle, by articulating the assumptions that confine, by pressing toward self-awareness, the memoirist locates the fresh air of change.

In her famous essay "When We Dead Awaken," Rich argues that we need to know about the past, not because we want to pass on tradition, but because we want to be able to break its hold on us: "For writers, and at this moment for women writers in particular, there is the challenge and promise of a whole new psychic geography to be explored. But there is also a difficulty and dangerous walking on the ice, as we try to find language and images for a consciousness we are just coming into, and with little in the past to support us" (1979, 35). Memoirists step carefully from one emotionally charged fragment to another as they explore the psychic geographies of their pasts: the persecutors, the traumas, the betrayals, the secrets, and the shame, but also, thankfully, the love. Challenge and promise beckon in the revitalized, cohesive psychic panorama we can glimpse by venturing out onto the thin ice of personal examination and revelation.

One of the most psychologically problematic aspects of my exile was not just the demand for silence and secrecy about my pregnancy, but also the need for a written counternarrative to explain my disappearance. It became my responsibility to create a plausible counterlife for myself while I was away. Rather than being punished like bell hooks for "crazy talk," I was encouraged to "talk crazy," to fictionalize my life. Because no one back home did discover my pregnancy, the outcome of my outrageous narrative flights was positive, or so I thought at the time. In retrospect, it is not surprising that since then, my ability to tell the truth has been complicated and compromised. The stories I concocted during my year in Ohio grew into a confabulation of stories to hide behind in the years that followed. Remarkably, I was recently given the opportunity to look back at some of the tales I concocted in order to renarrate the shameful realities of my year away.

Letters, 1965

> *Unwed mothers at that time . . . were a specific group; they fell somewhere between criminals and patients and, like criminals and patients, they were prescribed an exact and fortifying treatment; they were made to disappear.*—Alice McDermott, *That Night*

Karen, my best friend since I was ten, recently gave me an astounding gift—through many moves and her own personal upheaval, she had saved for thirty years all the letters I had written her when I was sixteen and living in Youngstown, Akron, and Des Moines, and she returned them to me when I told her I was writing a memoir. What a treasure! What a fright! How often can we step back in our lives and meet ourselves again? When I brought the letters home, I tucked them away unread, apprehensive about the underlying feelings they masked and unsettled by the shame I still feel about that year in my life, compounded by the additional shame of lying so brazenly to my friend. The day I finally read them was both difficult and illuminating.

Because Youngstown was the location for the story I was to tell, they are all postmarked Youngstown except for one postcard from Washington, D.C. I make up marvelous stories for Karen in these letters, fantasizing a teenage dream world in stark contrast to the burgeoning reality of my pregnancy.

The first letter, dated September 25, 1964, lays out the foundations of the fabricated counterlife that was meant to deliver me unscathed from my ignominy:

Dear Karen,
I guess you're probably curious why I was sent here. Well, the week before school started, I got into some trouble down at the beach. . . . My mom found out what happened and decided she didn't want to send me back to San Marino High School. I left Sunday morning for Youngstown. . . . I'm not really sad at all. . . . I have picked my own friends. . . . Tonight I'm going to see *Hamlet* . . . with Nada, my best friend back here. She is so sweet and cute and she makes me feel so much a part of school and the social life. Saturday we doubled to downtown Youngstown. . . . My date, Don, is the co-captain of varsity cross country. . . . I've already been riding 3 times. . . . We ride English and I even got a pair of jodhpurs.

The stories in this first letter lay out some of the parameters of my invented world, peopling it with some plausible characters. But how hastily I have created this new world! I have been in Youngstown for only two weeks, yet already I claim to have a best friend within a circle of chosen friends, a "popular" boy to date, and a classy hobby.

In reality, I am so shy and withdrawn when I enter high school that I make no friends; there is no double date with Don and no Nada to introduce me to the social scene. Do I unconsciously give my "sweet and cute" imaginary best friend the name "Nada" because it means "nothing" in Spanish? Although I do eventually go horseback riding with my cousins, there are no sleek, tight-fitting jodhpurs. Instead, I wear a baggy sweatshirt that hides the waistline of my Levis; I already cannot fasten the top button. But given the license to create the perfect teenage life in my letters home, I proceed without scruples to invent the kind of gregarious adolescence with the lighthearted friends and the chic accoutrements I had so often daydreamed about but had never known.

On October 8, I write Karen about an imaginary date to the homecoming dance, but I do not elaborate other than to say it was "really fun." In this letter I seem more introspective in telling her about a letter I received from Alec, my baby's father, though I have not yet conceptualized the idea "my baby" and how it relates to me. "I can't help but let it phase me a little bit because I still love him. I guess I probably always will in a certain way. I won't be seeing him for so long though. Maybe my heart will straighten out by the next time we meet." Although these comments about Alec are honest, they will prove as naïve as my school-life fantasies. My "heart" will take years to "straighten out," if by this statement I mean to arrive at a modicum of emotional and psychological equilibrium. Though my "love" for Alec will eventually and conclusively end, it will take not just years but decades for me to recognize that my devotion to him was, in fact, a delusional and damaging fixation.

On October 17, I write to tell Karen about going to a "semi-formal dance" and to a "real fun" party after a rainy football game: all makebelieve. I also tell her about falling in love with a horse named Gwen, who does, in fact, exist. Yet, Gwen, a gentle but worn-out stable horse, is finally only one more extension of my groundless daydreams. I spend hours fantasizing about buying her and taking her back to California with me, imagining myself riding with her in a special train car and feeding her sweet grass and apples all across the country. This aspiration is hopeless, even ludicrous; my parents would never consent to my owning a horse, much less shipping Gwen from Ohio to California. Now, in hindsight, I find it bittersweet that even in my dreams, I could return home with only a horse, not a baby.

On November 15, I write to Karen about another new make-believe girlfriend and all we do together. My imaginary leaps are becoming more and more extravagant: "Betsy Bridges was over and she loves the Beatles as much as I do. Betsy is really darling and she works as a model downtown. She is the new Miss Youngstown for Miss Teenage America. It's too bad she didn't win." I must realize I cannot make my imaginary friends too remarkable. Betsy Bridges can be Miss Youngstown, but she cannot have won the statewide competition to become Miss Ohio because Karen might watch the televised Miss Teenage America pageant, and there will be no trim and pretty Betsy Bridges on the runway.

One truthful and constant subject throughout the letters is my enchantment with and longing for snow. In a letter dated December 16, my desire for snowfall is irrepressible. I exclaim, "Guess what the high is going to be tomorrow? Ten degrees!! It snowed all last night and a little today and this weekend I'll probably try my hand at skiing again." I never actually ski while I am in Youngstown, though I make up several elaborate stories about my clumsy attempts and funny falls for Karen. Because I will not return to California with any skiing skills, I create a kind of cute but klutzy character for myself in anticipation of my ineptitude should I ever actually ski.

In another letter, I describe in great detail an imaginary dress I will be wearing to an assembly ball at my aunt and uncle's country club: "It's green silk and I'm going to wear a little necklace with a Christmas tree on it. It's real simple but it's beautiful." The boy I create to escort me is even more remarkable: "I'm going with a boy who looks exactly like Paul Peterson on the *Donna Reed Show.* He's so-o-o good looking." I also add: "Back here, I've become the kind of girl I want to be." The ironic poignancy of this affirmation was lost on me then, but today it stops me cold.

As I reread these adolescent illusions, I am struck by how young I was. Not only are my extraordinary flights of fancy evidence of my naïveté, but my superficial concerns also show how close to girlhood I still was. For example, in almost every letter, I ask Karen about Hildy, her dog, and I often close my letters by sending Hildy hugs and kisses. I am also young enough to be still experimenting with my handwriting; in some letters my words slant to the right, in others to the left. When I tell Karen what I miss most, it is my dad's pancakes.

In a letter dated January 28, 1965, I am writing to Karen from the Florence Crittendon Home, because I do not return to high school after Christmas break. My aunt has brought me to Akron on New Year's Day to wait out my pregnancy at the Florence Crittendon Home. My letter is still postmarked Youngstown, however, because I scrupulously abide by all the maneuvers to ensure the secret. I give my letters to my aunt on her weekly visits to Florence Crittendon, and she mails them from Youngstown. My imagination is still cut free from all the restraints of the ordinary, and I continue the stories of Betsy and my ball gowns, fabricating details with abandon, though I am also making some errors: "Betsy Bridges, my best friend, got the girl lead in our Junior class play, *Teahouse of the August Moon,* and she is Lotus Blossom. . . . I decided not to try out because I'm already too busy. . . . The Assembly Ball was so much fun. . . . I wore a green *velvet* dress. . . . It really was a 'Cinderella ball,' and I'll never forget it." In my December letter, I had told Karen my dress was green silk. By the time I write the January letter, I correctly remember the imaginary dress's color, but have mixed up its material. Now it is velvet rather than silk—a small detail, but representative of the difficulty of sustaining consistency in make-believe lives. Karen does not catch my slip. In fact, she says she never once doubted the faraway Ohio life I was creating for her. To her my "crazy talk" was entirely plausible.

On February 23 when I am beginning my ninth month of pregnancy, I write to Karen about a planned ski trip, but I no longer have the imaginary fervor to dream up details such as a fashionable parka, a comical spill, or a princely rescuer. I end up telling her that the imaginary ski trip had to be canceled for want of snow. I follow this disappointment with a lackluster report of a downtown shopping expedition with unnamed girlfriends, concluding that I found nothing to buy. My tone is very different from the earlier letters, very subdued. The colorful audacity of my heretofore animated imaginary life is tempered now by the actual gray textures of winter in Akron and the heavy reality of my pregnancy. I also tell her about the real death of my grandfather on New Year's Eve, poignantly exposing my lonely feelings of faraway seclusion and conspicuous unsuitability: "I wanted to come home so much then, but I guess it's better that I stayed back here and didn't add to all the confusion and tears." I do not write Karen again for six weeks.

On April 1, I write a letter apologizing: "I'm really sorry I've taken so long in answering your letter. But you can't imagine how busy I've been with testing and everything." I am pretending to refer to school tests, but in fact, ten nights earlier I have been through the most grueling test of my life, Sorrow's birth. The "and everything" are the only words I can employ, apparently, to account for the acute depression and insomnia I have been suffering since giving birth. In this letter I dutifully make up a perfunctory report of decorating for a St. Patrick's Day dance, but I include nothing about attending the dance itself and demonstrate none of my past flare for details.

I do add briefly that I am going on a school trip to Washington, D.C. In fact, this stratagem is one my aunt had worked out earlier that enabled us to have postcards of the Jefferson Memorial at cherry blossom time sent off to my California friends at about the time I was expected to deliver. In case Alec had told his friends that he had sex with me in late June and they have been counting the months, these postcards were meant to silence any remaining conjectures about my abrupt disappearance. I could not possibly be having a baby because here was proof—I was a tourist in Washington, D.C. My aunt had gotten the cards somehow, and I had conscientiously written them out weeks before. On March 20, Sorrow is born, but because I am not supposed to deliver until April 1 and the postcard ruse is already under way, she has them mailed from D.C. by a willing friend as planned. Karen's card is postmarked April 4, and reads: "Dear Karen, Isn't this beautiful? Having a wonderful time. Just got back from seeing the White House. It is really gorgeous. Saw Kennedy's grave too. See you soon—Janet." In actuality, I will not visit Washington, D.C., for another six years, and I have yet to see the cherry trees in bloom, visit the White House, or see Kennedy's grave. Nevertheless, it is fitting and revealing that I mention visiting a huge, old house, for when I dutifully write out this postcard, I myself am buried behind the thick, though finally unprotective, walls of Florence Crittendon. That of all the other places to visit in D.C. I choose Kennedy's grave, where I know he lies buried with the baby that he and Jackie lost, is also telling, for I am soon to lose my own baby, a withholding that will always feel like death to me.

My letters continue, written on my Aunt Jo's Youngstown stationery, though I have left Akron and am now writing from my Aunt May's house in Des Moines. I send them to my Aunt Jo in Youngstown, and she then mails them from there so that they will have the necessary postmark. I am still making up a lot, but no longer pregnant, I actually do get invited to proms, so I can describe truthfully my real gown and my real dates, though my proclivity to embellish will not now be bridled. For example, it is not enough for me to go to a prom; I also have to say that "Claudia Slocoam and the boy she's going with, Jim Martin, both friends of mine, were crowned king and queen." In reality, Claudia and Jim have no clue I even exist. Having been encouraged to embellish a rich, colorful life instead of the bleak realities of absence, trauma, and loss, now I cannot resist.

In the years that follow, I continue to offer revised versions of many of the twists and turns of my life, and my inventions give me a veneer of protection from disapproval, although I rarely feel genuine, legitimate approval either because I am constructing a self on sand. I remain vigilant and apart, concocting the explanations I think people want, wearing my masks, avoiding situations that might reveal my duplicities, working assiduously to maintain a chimera of legitimacy, dressing up the truths of my life. For the next thirty years, no one who knows of my actual whereabouts that year will ask me about the night of Sorrow's birth, but even if they had, I would not have told them the real story. I would have been ashamed to let them know just how desperately that night turned out. And then, with an abruptness that still surprises me, a page turned, and I realized I had to go back to that night in order to heal, in order to grow, in order to change. I began to write my memoir.

Now, as a reader trained in psychoanalytic criticism, I am intrigued by the psychological ramifications of the letters. Interpreting them like dreams, I play with the symbolism of the imaginary world I concocted. I write several descriptions for Karen about the beauty of the snow; I repeatedly express how much I am hoping for more and more snow. I seem to believe in the chastity of the snow, as if it could cover the bare ground of my real life with a clean, sparkling mantle. But I am not content with one layer; I want the cover to be thick and heavy. When I tell a sledding story, it is about the sled flipping over, and I portray myself as an ungraceful ice skater. Why make these narrative choices? Because all these snow stories are fabricated, I could just as easily have painted myself as lithe and quick. Instead, the snow stories are weird, proleptic metaphors; rather than protect me, the massive snowfall on the night I go into labor will be the cause of downright terror. I am amazed by the letter I write from Florence Crittendon shortly before I am to give birth, for I give my secret away so easily when I tell Karen about the canceled ski trip and the shopping trip where there is nothing to buy.

As a cultural critic, I marvel at how written I was by the ideological scripts of my time. The letters are in their own way personalized repetitions of the master narrative for adolescent girls—pretty teenager is befriended by other pretty girls and wooed by many handsome young men; she wears beautiful dresses to Cinderella-like balls and rides a splendid horse. That the narrative has no historical basis in my own adolescence does not lesson its authority. My invented year is as telling for the cultural critic as is the actual year I spent in shadows that grew so deep, and from which I have only just begun to emerge. But I am not alone in living a life partially obscured by shadows. There are many of us who out of shame and a wish to escape the bleak reality of an unchosen life fabricate another.

The Shadow Man

> We think we remember, we want to remember, and we try. What we can't help doing, though, is connecting the pieces from then that we have housed inside us with the feelings we have about them now. Representing others has everything to do with representing ourselves—over time.—Nancy K. Miller, Bequest and Betrayal: Memoirs of a Parent's Death

Although our culture still claims to want the confidentiality once routinely granted in the private sphere, in fact, that space seems to have been irrevocably breached. Now we recognize more than ever the merit of honesty and integrity and the harm that can come from self-serving dissembling. However, when we decide to raid the secrets of others in a spirit of revenge, or out of a need to discredit or degrade, or for attention, or, worse yet, for money or fame, we are guilty of exploiting the truths we have pursued and violating the ethics of revelation. Only when we pursue truth in the spirit of love and the wish to honor can we ethically disclose what has heretofore been hidden.

In *The Shadow Man*, Mary Gordon lovingly opens her family secrets and tells the truth about her father's hidden past.[1] She does so knowing

---

1. Despite her exceptional reputation, Mary Gordon does not escape condemnation for revealing her father's secrets. Furthermore, the disagreement among her reviewers demonstrates the clear evidence that contemporary chroniclers of both literary and

that exploring this psychic geography will come at some cost. To see him under a more revealing light will force her to reevaluate her cherished connection to him. Furthermore, she will be obliged to forgo a core component of her own identity—the loyal daughter of a great man.

Gordon is not as sure of her revelatory mission as is Lillian Ross, who claims that William Shawn would have wanted her to reveal their tacit relationship, or as is Joyce Maynard, who counts all of her relationships as raw material for her craft. Much more uncertain, Gordon asks, "Would [my father] have liked it if he'd known I'd be writing about him? What would he think of my writing this book?" (1996, xix). She knows she may face reproach for opening her father's secrets, and she refrains from assuaging her guilt by creating self-righteous, dubious justifications. Instead, she candidly records her doubts: "I don't know whether it's a fault of character or a fault of the age, this need to explain myself. . . . Perhaps

---

popular culture are still not sure how to deal with writers who tell family secrets. Elizabeth Powers compares Gordon to "East German children who revealed to the secret police their parents' reading habits." With flagrant exaggeration, Powers accuses Gordon of "trumping-up evidence" that indicts her father "for the Holocaust and the crimes of Hitler" (1997, 38). Sara Maitland finds *The Shadow Man* "quite simply a bad book . . . ill conceived, . . .badly structured, sloppily written, and deplorably self-indulgent." Like Powers, Maitland also feels the need to critique not just the book, but Gordon herself, remarking that "the whole [writing enterprise] seems to have rotted Gordon's writerly intelligence" (1996, 17). William H. Pritchard finds Gordon's writing "oppressively up close and personal . . . her sentences seethe and are, if not fevered, . . .overheated" (1996, 5). Pritchard seems to be reacting to the very kind of "fertile" writing that Virginia Woolf calls for in *A Room of One's Own* when she urges women to defy masculine paragons and to resist writing for "some professor with a measuring-rod up his sleeve" (1981, 106). Suzanne Ruta finds the book "underinformed and overwrought" and Gordon herself full of "unavowed anger, a high-mindedness." Ruta closes with a weird presumption: Gordon needed a Jewish mother to help her master the "philosophic shrug, the ironic acceptance of half-loaves and paradoxes, the classic line 'So who's perfect?' " (1996, 26). In a favorable review, Kakutani finds Gordon's memoir not just a "devastating portrait of a father and his daughter," but, more important, "a subtle meditation on the uses of storytelling as a means of containing and redeeming the past." For Kakutani, Gordon manages (unlike Ross or Maynard) to write a book that "somehow amazingly reconciles . . . love and horror, guilt and forgiveness, and transforms them into art" (1996, C29). John Leonard finds *The Shadow Man* "wounding, refulgent and redemptive," and first compares Gordon's art to Sartre, to Nabokov, to Roth, to Germaine Greer (1996, 24). He advances to hyperbole, however, when he places Gordon herself in the same category of Simone Weil, Antigone, and even Joan of Arc because of her courageous resistance to authority.

anyone writing about herself at such length must fight the impulse to apologize. . . . So I approach you, the reader, in a way I wouldn't ordinarily, asking indulgence and attention. But is it you, really, whose indulgence I ask? Or is it my father, whom I lost, and found again?" (xxiii-xxiv). Gordon's humility and apprehension make Ross's and Maynard's avowals sound uncomfortably close to hubris. In search of her father's understanding, Gordon repeats the Jewish prayer said each year at Rosh Hashanah: "May you be inscribed in the book of life" (xxiv). She explains: "This is what I've tried to do. To place or re-place both my father and myself in the book of life. The book of the living" (xxiv). It is in this spirit that I ask for my family's forbearance and indulgence for relocating Richard and his family back into the narrative life of our vibrant family. My uncle was terribly disturbed, but nonetheless, he and his family were loved. We still grieve their loss from our lives. I have also reinscribed Sorrow in the book of my life. Having lost her once and denied her a thousand times, I now claim her forever.

Although Gordon's father died when she was only seven, she grew up defining herself as his beloved daughter; she "lived," she asserts, "at the center of the heart of a passionate man" (xvii). However, to safeguard that ardent center she had to memorialize him, constructing a kind of mausoleum made up "of desire and need, snippets of events or reports of events, lyrics of songs, lines from stories, . . .forgetfulness, refusal of evidence, misplacing of crucial things or precious information, denial of facts" (xvii). In other words, in order to maintain the ideal father who could emotionally support her as she grew, she had to creatively reconstruct him, picking and choosing from the evidence he left behind.

Although my sisters and I have had no forbidding reasons to keep our Uncle Richard a secret, we have done so for our parents, honoring their desire and need that he be forgotten. We have known not to ask question about those "snippets" that slipped out in stories. Out of a reluctance to add to the emotional tension of their lives, we have sustained the denial, loyally abandoning enticing clues. Gordon too has taken significant detours around unsavory hints about her father: "My adult life with my father has been marked by reversals and undoings, moments of frozen incomprehension, shutting my eyes, turning away, finding and then hiding the evidence that says my childhood image is not one I can live by now" (xvi). Gordon re-created the father she needed in order to construct herself as her father's daughter—beloved and full of promise.

My parents excised Richard and his family in order to raise a healthy, vigorous family in the dynamic world of postwar Los Angeles.

Looking back at the pious history she invented for her father, Gordon understands that this transformation allowed her to recast the sad realities of a lonely childhood: "What I was doing was telling myself stories. They were richer, more colorful, and more enjoyable than the texture of my daily life, which was marked by wrongness and loss" (10). Just as I transformed my sixteenth year in collusion with my Aunt Jo, Gordon collaborated with her father, who began the transformation, to create a more culturally appropriate narrative for his life. However, like me, Gordon comes to need the truer story, the one that exists behind the fictions she invented for consolation and identity, the one behind the fabrications her father concocted for deliverance from an identity he was ashamed of.

Nevertheless, as Gordon uncovers her father's unexpected past, it is so discomforting that she resists continuing, even giving up temporarily and returning to her customary life and her uncontested relationship with the past. "I try to live as if I didn't have to write all this. As if I could be not a person marked by my father's death but someone who can think of him or not, whatever she likes. . . . Someone who has forgotten him" (92). But like other memoirists who finally have to confront the inaccuracies of the admissible past, Gordon cannot sustain the pretense of "as if it never happened." Hampl observes that for such memoirists, " 'something' has happened to them," and their memoirs become "the necessary literature of witness" (1999, 223). Though Gordon would like to retreat from the strange and sometimes offensive new father she unearths, she remains marked by his death; she cannot stop thinking about him, and she cannot choose to forget or even to diminish his import.

The following are some of the facts she discovers: Rather than 1899, David Gordon was born in 1894. Rather than Lorain, Ohio, he was born in Vilna, Russia. Rather than David, he was named Israel. Rather than English, his native tongue was Yiddish. Rather than born a Catholic, he was born a Jew. Rather than an only child, he had three sisters, one of whom had died in a mental hospital after being institutionalized for seventy-seven years. He was never an American citizen. He quit high school to work as a stenographer for the railroad. He never traveled in Europe. He had been married before to a free-spirited flapper. He had abandoned his mother, who died in a charity home. He published a pornographic comic book called *Hot Dog*. He was a friend of Joe Mc-Carthy. He thought the Rosenbergs deserved to die. He once wrote, "I myself think that Mussolini's Italy is today the best governed large nation in the world" (Mary Gordon 1996, 83).

Gordon had known of her father's anti-Semitism, but she had concocted her own explanation by blaming this shortcoming on his fellow college students, those contemptuous "Harvard boys, so unbearable he absorbed [their anti-Semitism] to be free of it" (28). However, once she turns detective, that story will not work anymore because her father never actually attended Harvard. She acknowledges, "Facts nose their way into what I thought was the past like a dog sticking his nose under a lady's skirts. How I resent the insidious, relentless, somehow filthy nudging of these facts. Yet I cannot ban them" (125). As her sleuthing yields more, each piece of new information cancels out the invented father and brings "the shadow man" into the light. As a memoirist, Gordon is reluctantly held to veracity: "The detective in love with her client usually ends up murdering or murdered. Both have happened to me. I am both the perpetrator and the victim of a crime. I would have avoided both if I could. But I can't, because I am no longer capable of that love that silences questions with a kiss or a sigh" (162). Unable to turn away, she researches, exposes, and finally reinvents her father. She also discovers the confining circumstances of his early poverty and humiliation that help her understand why he built a new self almost entirely on falsehoods.

The memoir becomes both a dismantling and a construction, testimony of his incontrovertible duplicity and her unflagging affection for him. Neither cancels out the other; both can coexist. She asks in a poem:

> Who is my father?
> The origin and my source.
> My shame and my delight.
> The figure behind every story.
> The stranger on the road.
> The double, feared and prized, approaching from the distance.
>
> (202)

Gordon relinquishes the iconic father for an extraordinary but deeply flawed man and finds she loves him no less passionately. Some may argue that she has dishonored him by writing the memoir and disclosing his secrets. She herself is saddened by all she has uncovered and longs to demonstrate that he still has her respect. But how to commemorate the truer man she has unearthed?

Gordon finds a way to revise the past in a symbolic and profound way. Her father was interred forty years before in his wife's Catholic family plot under a common gravestone marked Gagliano. Observing that "no one would guess there is a Jew there," Gordon decides to have her father reburied (246). Some in her family think her fanatical, others macabre, but she is steadfast: "He is the father who loved me. He is the father whom I loved. He is the father whose bones I am about to move" (254).

David Gordon's reburial is a Catholic ceremony because he was, in fact, a devout convert to Catholicism, and Gordon requests the traditional rituals of faith even though she herself does not know what to believe about the fate of her father's soul. Nevertheless, the form itself serves her purposes, and she finds it "deeply precious, irreplaceable . . . contain[ing] more than most forms and . . . therefore conducive to more beauty, more truthfulness" (269). Although she is speaking here of Catholic liturgy, her insight into the value of form is germane. In the *Four Quartets*, T. S. Eliot opines:

> Only by the form, the pattern,
> Can words or music reach
> The stillness, as a Chinese jar still
> Moves perpetually in its stillness.
> (1971, 121)

Eliot knows that words are but "shabby equipment always deteriorating / In the general mess of imprecision of feeling" (128). But a form will structure our words and allow a vision, such as Keats's Grecian urn, an otherwise unattainable permanence, an impression of harmony and truthfulness.

Whether by way of ritual, motif, or genre, form permits a more lasting mode of commemoration. The protean yet enduring form of the memoir has provided a pattern for writers from Augustine to Anne Frank, from Frederick Douglass to Mary Gordon to undertake what Hampl calls "the necessary literature of witness. Historic truth rests on such testimony" (223). By way of the memoir, Gordon finds the courage to confront the enormity of her father's misrepresentations and to replace his deceit with the benevolent grace of truthful prose informed by understanding, empathy, and love.

At the reburial, touching the wooden box that holds her father's remains, Gordon weeps, "because," she says, "I understand fully for the first time how much of my life I've lived without him. How little of our lives we've shared" (271). Despite his vital and ongoing significance to her writing, marriages, parenting, spirituality, and, finally, her very identity, ultimately she lost her father when she was only seven. That tragedy endures.

Later, as she sits with her son, David, she realizes her sorrow has alleviated. "What I have taken from the cemetery," she determines, "is a sentence that keeps running through my mind like music: Love is stronger than death" (274). Thus she concludes her memoir with equanimity and resolution, having reached a place where all of us who relinquish our secrets and reveal our pasts hope to arrive—a quiet center of peaceful acceptance.

As I ruminate over memoirists such as Mary Gordon and myself, those of us who risk condemnation and rejection for bearing testimony to the heretofore concealed truths of our lives and, more important, the lives of those people we love, I find some comfort in words that Mary Karr includes in *The Liar's Club*, a poem fragment by Zbigniew Herbert, "The Envoy of Mr. Cogito":

> . . . you have little time you must give testimony
> be courageous when the mind deceives you be courageous
> in the final account only this is important.
>
> (1995a, 274)

But as all memoirists come to know, to give testimony is an uncertain enterprise, especially for women.

In his intensely personal film *Sunday's Children*, director Daniel Bergman (Ingmar's son) depicts his father's disquieting relationship with his own authoritarian father. In the film's conclusion, the elderly patriarch finds the diaries of his dead wife, Karin. He is devastated to learn that throughout the fifty years of their marriage, she has called it a failure—a "fiasco"—in the diaries. She had never revealed her discontent to him, and he had assumed their marriage had given them both a measure of contentment. Like Bergman's Karin, I learned early on to speak with what Susan Lanser calls the "double voice," the use of alternate voices made necessary by diverse situations (1986, 349). One of the layers of voice is addressed to those people in power, to those people on whom our well-being rests. This voice dissembles and complies; it refrains from revealing sorrow, frustration, resentment, acrimony; most important, it is a conscious dispossession of the more authentic self. With this voice, Karin addressed her husband. With this unauthentic voice, I wrote my letters to my friend Karen. With an assortment of artificial voices I continued to speak to my extended family, to my colleagues and superiors, to my husbands, even to my friends. Intimate disclosure and the potential for ensuing consolation seemed unavailable to me.

The other layer is the private voice—the one Karin reserved for her diaries. This voice is more legitimate and full of conviction but necessarily clandestine because of the diminished and marginalized status of the speaker. The wife of a rigid and harsh man, Karin's public use of such a voice would have involved tremendous emotional and physical risk, so much so that she could not reveal the secrets of her heart except in her diaries. Dale Spender observes: "The dichotomy of male/female, public/private is maintained by permitting women to write . . . for themselves (for example, diaries) and for each other in the form of letters. . . . There is no contradiction in patriarchal order while women write for women and therefore remain within the limits of the private sphere; the contradiction arises only when women write for men" (1980, 192). While she lives, Karin's private voice does not disturb the patriarchal rendering of her as an outwardly contented wife. But she does not destroy the diaries; she leaves them to be found. When she can no longer suffer the consequences, she dares to let her more honest voice be heard, and her posthumous revelations become her most significant act.

Unfortunately, it is not just in the movies that we see the need for the double voice. The shame of my past silenced my more legitimate voice for years. I can now hold forth in comfortable settings with my husband, children, friends, and students; however, to speak up with earnest confidence in a public forum beyond the classroom or among my extended family is always rather terrifying and still to be avoided. And I am not alone. Although talk show hosts may encourage women to shed the double voice, in our professional and familial domains, most of which remain regulated by patriarchal discourse, women's candid expressiveness is often heard as overly emotional, strident, or silly, and is met with dismissive amusement, defensiveness, or downright hostility.

Besides the difficulty we face in finding or seizing the opportunity to speak with honesty and to be heard with respect, the insights of post-modernism make honesty itself problematic and finally not wholly achievable. Nevertheless, there are truer renditions to be told. Mary Gordon discovered a more valid version of her father's life and did not turn away. I achieved a level of self-confidence that allowed me to tell a more legitimate account of my life. Memoirists today convey publicly what Karin dared impart only in her diaries. They resist the double voice and attempt instead public candor. To claim that the memoirist tells THE TRUTH seems naïve and wrong. Instead, the memoirist approaches a more honest rendition of a past by identifying and disentangling the braided strands of truths and lies, the intersecting and overlapping voices of public and private discourse. Memoirists attempt the ethical. Honesty is the goal, but honesty and integrity are complex endeavors.

Stephen Carter observes: "Integrity . . . requires three steps: (1) *discerning* what is right and what is wrong; (2) *acting* on what you have discerned, even at personal cost; and (3) *saying openly* that you are acting on your understanding of right and wrong" (1996, 7). I use Carter's three steps to illustrate that the criteria for ethical honesty is more than telling one's version of the truth. For example, Joyce Maynard and Paul Theroux try to tell the truth about past private relationships. They are, we might say, using a public forum to "talk back" to J. D. Salinger and V. S. Naipaul, respectively, and some may think the merit of their grievances is sufficient. However, in neither memoir is there evidence that Maynard or Theroux has considered what might be wrong with her or his highly personal attacks on the disappointing mentors. Unless a measure of un-certainty and moral reflectiveness informs the writing process, honesty can exist in an ethical vacuum.

What is deemed fitting or invasive exposure is tied to our evolving cultural mores. Given our current cultural situation, memoirists such as Kathryn Harrison, Mia Farrow, Suzannah Lessard, and Jamaica Kincaid have been judged by many critics as thoughtfully lucid, deeply sincere, and courageously candid, but they have also been branded as negative, solipsistic, whiny, self-aggrandizing, and vindictive. Clearly, with such bitter social and aesthetic criticism awaiting the next memoir, a concept of integrity must serve to move memoirists beyond the response of, for example, Maynard when she justifies lacerating Salinger by claiming, "If you're telling a story to get to a central truth about who you are as a human being . . . then I say you get to tell it" (qtd. in Streitfeld 1998, D2). Getting to the truth of "who you are" is insufficient when it comes to incriminating others in that attempt. Neither self-exploration nor soul-searching grants a writer permission to flat-out implicate others, at least not within the current, dominant cultural conscience that evidently continues to respect Salinger's privacy more than Maynard's need to get to the truth of who she is.

If there is a larger social purpose to be served by way of the memoir's revelations and accusations, the memoir stops being solely one individual's quest for self-actualization and becomes a testimony to the betterment of a particular social ill. The individual memoirist serves then as a metonym for a larger social enterprise, and the memoir achieves a more culturally emblematic and ethical dimension. We consent to the invasion of Woody Allen's privacy because Mia Farrow's unique story drops away and the narrative comes to stand as an illustration of how it is that women, even privileged women, can become willing pawns to the manipulations of persuasive, forceful men to the point that they will even put their children's well-being at risk. The greatest memoirs, says Hampl, "*seem* to be about an individual self, but it is revealed as a minion of memory which belongs not only to the personal world but to the public realm" (205).

Although memoirs are about unique and diverse lives, they can serve a social function for the future. Although my memoir has revealed my struggle to come to terms with an irreparable loss and a legacy of shame, I hope that it will also reveal the psychological liabilities that will continue to exist as long as adoption records remain secret. I hope my persistent psychological denial of my pregnancy will help those people who rush to damn unfortunate adolescent girls to understand why these desperate girls hide their pregnancies from their families, their boyfriends, and themselves, and, in so doing, unintentionally put the fetuses at risk. Perhaps my recounting of the terror-filled night of Sorrow's birth will help others understand how a panicked and forsaken girl in unimaginable pain might hysterically abandon the newborn she has steadfastly denied, whether she gives birth in a delivery room or a high school bathroom. Perhaps my memoir will help our culture understand that we have not yet solved the physical and psychological obstacles that adolescent girls must brave when faced with unwanted pregnancies.

Perhaps my memoir will help our culture understand that adoption is both a joyful and a heartbreaking venture.

Memoirists who make a commitment to the concept of integrity and risk of disclosure are working against isolation. The memoirist says her voice can be trusted, and her example can work as a kind of alchemy, bestowing the potential for frankness in others. Despite the offensiveness of her willful and gratuitous attack on Salinger, Maynard can be commended for her desire to tell her own life—"the story of a real woman with all her flaws"—so that "others might feel less ashamed of their own unmentionable failings and secrets" (1998, 3). A candid storyteller can make us feel less ashamed, can inspire us to tell our own stories, our own interpretations, our more genuine truths.

Hence, the memoir gives us access to each other—a necessary link that goes deeper than the cursory, often frivolous disseminators of today's pop culture. Toni Morrison maintains:

> The resources available to us . . . for vaulting the mere blue air that separates us, are few but powerful. . . . Language (saying, listening, reading) can encourage, even mandate, surrender, the breach of distances among us, whether they are continental or on the same pillow, whether they are distances of culture or the distinctions and indistinctions of age or gender, whether they are the consequences of social invention or biology. (1998, 69–70)

At the close of a century that has witnessed the Holocaust, the Gulag, My Lai, the Killing Fields, ethnic cleansing, and in the United States the dramatic rise in popularity of hate groups such as the Skinheads and the Aryan Nations Church, it is imperative that we find ways to establish empathy, seek truth, discover compassion. One way is to listen carefully to each other's tentative, groping sentences, the details of our lives, the stories that "refuse to stay buried, that demand habitation" (Hampl 1999, 224). As we listen, we thwart dehumanization, we foster intimacy, and we extend the possibility for peaceful coexistence among us.

Memoirists have taught me that we need not be outsiders because of our shame and our secrets. By reading and trusting the heartfelt candidness of memoirists, I have joined a community where there are no strangers. By writing my memoir, I have surrendered the concealment that kept me a stranger; you know me now. But mine is not a unique story; it joins a common narrative, the shared and sorrowful stories that other birth mothers will tell when they can. Someday, we who gave away too much may find ourselves situated in a world where our shame is vanquished, where secret files are opened, understanding is proffered, and reunion is possible. Until then, we can reclaim one part of ourselves by telling others with honesty and love: "When I was still a child, I was sent away from home. While I was gone, I gave birth to Sorrow."

CODA
The Traveler

> . . . this thing is sure,
> That time is no healer: . . .
> Fast forward, travellers! not escaping from the past
> Into different lives, or into any future;
> You are not the same people who left that station
> Or who will arrive at any terminus, . . .
> You shall not think, "the past is finished."
> —T. S. Eliot, "The Dry Salvages"

In the late summer of 1965 after returning from my exile in the Midwest, I go backpacking with my parents in the High Sierra above Yosemite Valley. I still have a snapshot—I am standing with a fishing pole my father has given me. I am smiling broadly, trying hard to be his cheerful girl again. The wild beauty that surrounds us is restorative; my smile is not insincere. I smile so hard, wanting desperately to please them, to make us all forget what I have done. The hiking trip renews my relationship with my parents. I feel they have forgiven me, and I love them even more intensely for doing so. But my penetrating sorrow propels me up and down the mountains and leaves me lying awake late into the cool nights despite my weary body. I hide my sadness; my relationship with my parents is so crucial to me that I will not let them see one tear, not one.

The next pilgrimage is in 1977, twelve years later. I go with my husband, Ricardo, and my children, Todd and Helen. I am pregnant with our third child. I have been very depressed, and my insomnia is agonizing; my marriage is disintegrating. Will the same wild beauty restore me again and help me find a way back to my husband the way it led me back to my

213

parents? Again I smile brightly for Ricardo's camera, hopeful and inspired, but this pilgrimage fails. Nothing is restored; Ricardo leaves us; Sorrow haunts me; I will find my solace in my beautiful new baby, Kezia.

I return again this summer, 1999, just as I am nearing the completion of this manuscript. I go with John; my emotional health seems better than I can ever recall; my insomnia persists, but it seems to be under control. This time I will find the key. Here I will find the chapter's end. The past will finally abate, and the possibility for a whole and pure happiness will be restored. But it is not to be. Sorrow is with me. On this wilderness pilgrimage, I wrap her all about me and carry her on.

Summer 2000: I give "Bearing Sorrow" to my daughters' friend, Debbie, who has been searching fruitlessly for her birth mother, so that she might know how much she means to the woman who had to give her away.

November 2000: My daughters approach me with stunning news. By way of an Internet adoption group and a kind, resourceful stranger in Mississippi, Debbie has been given a name for Sorrow. Merideth. Kezia and Helen have located her married name. From there, I easily find her address.

December 2000: After excruciating preparation, I write to Merideth. A few days pass; the telephone rings and my heart leaps. It is my first daughter, and she is happy to be found. Sorrow subsides as Merideth is born into my life.

January 2001: Once again, on a snowy morning, I meet my daughter. We have traveled to Merideth's home to be greeted by my granddaughter's sign: "Welcome Janet and John." I have a new word to describe my life: miraculous.

Easter, 2001: Merideth, her husband, and my grandchildren are here to visit. As they sleep in the next rooms, I lie awake amazed and thankful for the restorative power of disclosure. I began this memoir with so much trepidation, but now on this warm April night, I can rewrite the ending with the narrative closure I did not dare imagine: Finally and forever, my daughter has come home.

WORKS CITED
INDEX

WORKS CITED

Adorno, Theodor. 1984. *Aesthetic Theory*. Translated by C. Lenhardt. London: Routledge.

Allison, Dorothy. 1996. *Two or Three Things I Know for Sure*. New York: Plume.

Alther, Lisa. 1997. "Blaming the Victim." Review of *The Kiss: A Memoir*, by Kathryn Harrison. *Women's Review of Books* (July): 33–34.

Andersen, Christopher. 1988. *Young Kate*. New York: Henry Holt.

Atlas, James. 1996. "The Age of the Literary Memoir Is Now." *New York Times Magazine* (May 12): 25–27.

Bauman, Zygmunt. 1993. *Postmodern Ethics*. Cambridge, Mass.: Blackwell.

Behar, Ruth. 1996. *The Vulnerable Observer: Anthropology That Breaks Your Heart*. Boston: Beacon.

Bepko, Claudia. 1996. *The Heart's Progress: A Memoir*. New York: Penguin.

Beram, Nell. 1997. "Villain or Victim?" Review of *What Falls Away: A Memoir*, by Mia Farrow. *Women's Review of Books* (Oct.): 25.

Bergland, Betty. 1994. "Postmodernism and the Autobiographical Subject: Reconstructing the 'Other.'" In *Autobiography and Postmodernism*, edited by Kathleen Asheley, Leigh Gilmore, and Gerald Peters, 160–66. Amherst: Univ. of Massachusetts Press.

Bernstein, Richard. 1998. Review of *Shame*, by Annie Ernaux. *New York Times* (Aug. 12): E8.

Birch, Carol. 1999. "Escape from Hades." Review of *After Silence: Rape and My Journey Back*, by Nancy Venable Raine. *Times Literary Supplement* (May 28): 31.

Bok, Sissela. 1989. *Secrets: On the Ethics of Concealment and Revelation*. New York: Vintage.

Botton, Alain de. 1997. *How Proust Can Change Your Life*. New York: Pantheon Books.

Bowman, Catherine. 1995. Review of *The Liar's Club*, by Mary Karr. *Village Voice Literary Supplement* (June 6): 6.

Boxer, Sarah. 1998. "Giving Memory Its Due in an Age of License." *New York Times* (Oct. 27): B1+, B6, national edition.

Brooke, Alan. 1997. "Devouring Love." Review of *The Kiss: A Memoir,* by Kathryn Harrison; *The Shadow Man,* by Mary Gordon; and *Architect of Desire: Beauty and Danger in the Stanford White Family,* by Suzannah Lessard. *New Criterion* (May): 64–70.

Buechner, Frederick. 1991. *Telling Secrets.* San Francisco: Harper Collins.

Carson, Jerome. 1997. Review of *An Unquiet Mind,* by Kay Redfield Jamison. *International Journal of Social Psychiatry* 43, no. 3: 230.

Carter, Stephen L. 1996. *Integrity.* New York: Basic Books.

Casey, Edward S. 1987. *Remember: A Phenomenological Study.* Bloomington: Indiana Univ. Press.

Cheever, Susan. 1993. "A Designated Crazy." Review of *Girl, Interrupted,* by Susanna Kaysen. *New York Times Book Review* (June 20): 1–3.

———. 1997. "Innocence Betrayed." Review of *The Kiss: A Memoir,* by Kathryn Harrison. *New York Times Book Review* (Mar. 30): 11.

———. 1999. *Note Found in a Bottle: My Life as a Drinker.* New York: Simon and Schuster.

Cohen, Paula Marantz. 1996. *The Daughter as Reader: Encounters Between Literature and Life.* Ann Arbor: Univ. of Michigan Press.

Cole, Diane. 1998. "Wake-Up Call." Review of *Slow Motion: A True Story,* by Dani Shapiro. *New York Times Book Review* (Aug. 23): 8.

Conniff, Ruth. 1997. Review of *The Architect of Desire: Beauty and Danger in the Stanford White Family,* by Suzannah Lessard. *Progressive* (Jan.): 31–35.

Conroy, Pat. 1986. *The Prince of Tides.* New York: Bantam.

Culler, Jonathan. 1982. *On Deconstruction: Theory and Criticism after Structuralism.* Ithaca: Cornell Univ. Press.

Cunningham, Mark. 1999. "I Drink, Therefore . . ." Review of *Drinking: A Love Story,* by Carolyn Knapp. *National Review* (Feb. 22): 52–53.

Cutting, Linda Katherine. 1997. *Memory Slips.* New York: Harper Collins.

Daly, Brenda. 1998. *Authoring a Life: A Woman's Survival in and Through Literary Studies.* Albany: SUNY Univ. Press.

Daly, Mary Ann. 1995. "Roses Grown for Their Thorns." Review of *Two or Three Things I Know for Sure,* by Dorothy Allison. *Lambda Book Report* 4, no. 12 (Sept./Oct.): 25–26.

Davidoff, Robert. 1989. "Memorial Day 1988." In *Personal Dispatches: Writers Confront AIDS,* edited by John Preston, 176–78. New York: St. Martin's Press.

De Salvo, Louise. 1996. *Vertigo: A Memoir.* New York: Dutton.

———. 1999. *Writing as a Way of Healing: How Telling Our Stories Transforms Our Lives.* San Francisco: Harper.

DiBernard, Barbara. 1995. "Being an I-Witness: My Life as a Lesbian Teacher." In *Private Voices, Public Lives: Women Speak on the Literary Life,* edited by Nancy Owen Nelson, 99–110. Denton: Univ. of North Texas Press.

Dinnage, Rosemary. 1996. "Why Not Say What Happened?" Review of *An Unquiet Mind*, by Kay Redfield Jamison. *Times Literary Supplement* (Aug. 2): 13.

Dowd, Maureen. 1998. "Of Frogs and Newts." *New York Times* (Nov. 11): A31, national edition.

Drake, David. 1995. "Life Lines." Review of *Two or Three Things I Know for Sure*, by Dorothy Allison. *Advocate* (Sept. 5): 63–64.

Elbow, Peter. 1994. "Closing My Eyes as I Speak: An Argument for Ignoring Audience." In *The Writing Teacher's Sourcebook*, edited by Gary Tate et al., 258–76. 3d ed. New York: Oxford Univ. Press.

Eliot, T. S. 1971. *The Complete Poems and Plays, 1909–1950*. New York: Harcourt Brace Jovanovich.

Ellerby, Janet. 1989. "Repetition and Redemption." Ph.D. diss., Univ. of Washington.

Ernaux, Annie. 1998. *Shame*. Translated by Tanya Leslie. New York: Seven Stories Press.

Farrow, Mia. 1997. *What Falls Away: A Memoir*. New York: Doubleday, 1997.

"Father Kills Two Children, Self; Critically Wounds Wife in Car at Rose Bowl." 1946. *Pasadena Star News* (Nov. 15): sec. 2, p. 13.

Feinstein, David, and Stanley Krippner. 1988. *Personal Mythology: The Psychology of Evolving Self—Using Ritual, Dreams, and Imagination to Discover Your Inner Story*. Los Angeles: Jeremy Tarcher.

Felman, Shoshana, and Dori Laub, M.D. 1992. *Testimony: Crises of Witnessing in Literature, Psychoanalysis, and History*. New York: Routledge.

Fitzgerald, F. Scott. 1995. *The Great Gatsby*. New York: Scribner.

Foucault, Michel. 1980. *The History of Sexuality*. Translated by Robert Hurley. Vol. 1. New York: Vintage.

Frank, Elizabeth. 1997. "Family Matters." Review of *My Brother*, by Jamaica Kincaid. *Mirabella* (Nov.-Dec.): 64.

Franklin, Nancy. 1998. "Show and Tell: When Did Privacy Go Public?" *New Yorker* (Aug. 24–31): 11–12.

Freedman, Diane P., Olivia Frey, and Frances Murphy Zauhar, eds. 1993. *The Intimate Critique: Autobiographical Literary Criticism*. Durham: Duke Univ. Press.

Gergen, Kenneth. 1991. *The Saturated Self: Dilemmas of Identity in Contemporary Life*. New York: Basic Books.

Giles, Jeff. 1997. "A Father. A Daughter. A Kiss Wasn't Just a Kiss." Review of *The Kiss: A Memoir*, by Kathryn Harrison. *Newsweek* (Feb. 2): 62.

Gilligan, Carol. 1997. "The Hollow Man." Review of *I Don't Want to Talk About It: Overcoming the Secret Legacy of Male Depression*, by Terrence Real. *New York Times Book Review* (Feb. 6): 24.

Goldberg, Natalie. 1991a. *Wild Mind: Living the Writer's Life*. New York: Quality Paperback Book Club.

————. 1991b. *Writing Down the Bones: Freeing the Writer Within*. New York: Quality Paperback Book Club.

Goldberger, Paul. 1996. "The Monster Builder." Review of *The Architect of Desire: Beauty and Danger in the Stanford White Family*, by Suzannah Lessard. *New York Times Book Review* (Nov. 3): 7.

Goleman, Daniel. 1997. *Emotional Intelligence*. New York: Bantam.

Gordon, Mary. 1996. *The Shadow Man*. New York: Random House.

————. 1997. "Sex with Daddy." Review of *The Kiss: A Memoir*, by Kathryn Harrison. *Harpers Bazaar* (Apr.): 136–37.

Gordon, Meryl. 1996. "Hitting Bottom." Review of *Drinking: A Love Story*, by Carolyn Knapp. *New York Times Book Review* (June 2): 34.

Gracia, Jorge. 1996. *Texts: Ontological Status, Identity, Author, Audience*. Albany: SUNY Univ. Press.

Graulich, Melody. 1995. "Speaking Across Boundaries and Sharing the Loss of a Child." In *Private Voices, Public Lives: Women Speak on the Literary Life*, edited by Nancy Owen Nelson, 163–82. Denton: Univ. of North Texas Press.

Hampl, Patricia. 1999. *I Could Tell You Stories: Sojourns in the Land of Memory*. New York: Norton.

Harris, Judith Rich. 1998. *The Nurture Assumption: Why Children Turn Out the Way They Do*. New York: Free Press.

Harrison, Colin. 1997. "Sins of the Father." *Vogue* (Apr.): 328–29.

Harrison, Kathryn. 1991. *Thicker than Water*. New York: Avon.

————. 1993. *Exposure*. New York: Warner.

————. 1997a. "Intimate Strangers." Review of *What Falls Away: A Memoir*, by Mia Farrow. *New York Times Book Review* (Feb. 23): 9.

————. 1997b. *The Kiss: A Memoir*. New York: Random House.

Henke, Suzette. 1998. *Shattered Subjects: Trauma and Testimony in Women's Life-Writing*. New York: St. Martin's Press.

Hepburn, Katharine. 1991. *Me: Stories of My Life*. New York: Alfred A. Knopf.

Herman, Judith. 1992. *Trauma and Recovery*. New York: Basic Books.

Hochmann, Andee. 1995. Review of *Two or Three Things I Know for Sure*, by Dorothy Allison. *New York Times* (Aug. 13): 16.

hooks, bell. 1989. *Talking Back: Thinking Feminist, Thinking Black*. Boston: South End Press.

————. 1994. *Outlaw Culture: Resisting Representations*. New York: Routledge.

————. 1997. *Wounds of Passion: A Writing Life*. New York: Henry Holt, 1997.

Imber-Black, Evan. 1998. *The Secret Life of Families: Truth-Telling, Privacy, and Reconciliation in a Tell-All Society*. New York: Bantam.

Ivins, Molly. 1995. "Ezra Pound in East Texas." Review of *The Liar's Club*, by Mary Karr. *Nation* (July 3): 21.

Jackson, Marni. 1997. "Mia the Mistreated." Review of *What Falls Away: A Memoir*, by Mia Farrow. *Maclean's* (Apr. 7): 88.

Jacoby, Mario. 1994. *Shame and the Origins of Self-Esteem: A Jungian Approach.* Translated by Douglas Whitcher. New York: Routledge.

Jamison, Kay Redfield. 1995. *An Unquiet Mind.* New York: Vintage.

———. 1996. "Flights of Mind." *Saturday Evening Post* (Apr.): 53–54.

Jones, Malcolm, Jr. 1998. "It's Better to Tell All Than to Tell It Well." Review of *Slow Motion: A True Story*, by Dani Shapiro. *Newsweek* (July 27): 59.

Joughin, Sheena. 1999. Review of *Slow Motion: A True Story*, by Dani Shapiro. *Times Literary Supplement* (Jan. 22): 32.

Juhasz, Suzanne. 1994. *Reading from the Heart: Women, Literature, and the Search for True Love.* New York: Viking.

Kakutani, Michiko. 1996. "How Could He Have Been Her Wonderful Father?" Review of *The Shadow Man*, by Mary Gordon. *New York Times* (May 3): C29.

———. 1998a. "How to Lose Friends and Influence Readers." Review of *Sir Vidia's Shadow: A Friendship Across Five Continents*, by Paul Theroux. *New York Times* (Sept. 23): D7.

———. 1998b. "More of Her Life, and Love, to Look Back On." Review of *At Home in the World*, by Joyce Maynard. *New York Times* (Sept. 8): B6.

———. 1998c. "A Reluctant Editor but Ardent Lover." Review of *Here but Not Here: A Love Story*, by Lillian Ross. *New York Times* (May 29): E46.

Kaplan, Alice. 1993. *French Lessons: A Memoir.* Chicago: Univ. of Chicago Press.

Karen, Robert. 1992. "Shame." *Atlantic Monthly* (Feb.): 40–70.

Karr, Mary. 1995a. *The Liar's Club.* New York: Penguin.

———. 1995b. "Tell-All Tales." *Harpers Bazaar* (June): 78–79.

———. 1996. "Dysfunctional Nation." *New York Times Magazine* (May 12): 70.

Kaysen, Susanna. 1993. *Girl, Interrupted.* New York: Vintage.

Keene, Sam. 1991. *Fire in the Belly: On Being a Man.* New York: Bantam.

Kerr, Sarah. 1998. "The Writer's Writer." Review of *Sir Vidia's Shadow: A Friendship Across Five Continents*, by Paul Theroux. *New York Times Book Review* (Sept. 27): 7.

Kincaid, Jamaica. 1997. *My Brother.* New York: Farrar, Straus, Giroux.

Kingston, Maxine Hong. 1977. *The Woman Warrior: Memoirs of a Girlhood among Ghosts.* New York: Random House.

Knapp, Caroline. 1996. *Drinking: A Love Story.* New York: Delta.

———. 1998. *Pack of Two: The Intricate Bond Between People and Dogs.* New York: Dial Press.

Korelitz, Jean Hanff. 1999. "Strangers in the Mailbox." Review of *Here but Not Here: A Love Story*, by Lillian Ross; and *At Home in the World*, by Joyce Maynard. *Times Literary Supplement* (Jan. 1): 32.

Kristeva, Julia. 1997. *In the Beginning Was Love*. New York: Columbia Univ. Press.

Lanser, Susan Sniader. 1986. "Toward a Feminist Narratology." *Style* 20, no. 33 (fall): 341–63.

———. 1996. "Toward a Feminist Poetics of Narrative Voice." In *Narrative/Theory*, edited by David H. Richter, 182–94. White Plains, N.Y.: Longman.

Lear, Jonathan. 1998. *Open-Minded: Working Out the Logic of the Soul*. Cambridge: Harvard Univ. Press.

Leeman, Eve. 1999. "Answering Back to Prozac." Review of *Prozac Diary*, by Lauren Slater. *Lancet* (Jan. 9): 155–56.

Lehmann-Haupt, Christopher. 1996a. "Stanford White, as Voracious in Art as in Life." Review of *The Architect of Desire: Beauty and Danger in the Stanford White Family*, by Suzannah Lessard. *New York Times* (Oct. 28): C19.

———. 1996b. "Two Lives, One Lost to Alcoholism and the Other Surviving It." Review of *Drinking: A Love Story*, by Carolyn Knapp. *New York Times* (June 13): C18.

Leonard, John. 1996. "She Lost Her Father." Review of *The Shadow Man*, by Mary Gordon. *Nation* (May 6): 24–28.

Lessard, Suzannah. 1996. *The Architect of Desire: Beauty and Danger in the Stanford White Family*. New York: Delta.

Lieberman, Rhonda. 1997. "Double Exposure." Review of *The Kiss: A Memoir*, by Kathryn Harrison. *Village Voice Literary Supplement* (Apr. 1): 10–11.

Loizeaux, William. 1993. *Anna: A Daughter's Life*. New York: Arcade.

Lorde, Audre. 1980. *The Cancer Journals*. New York: Spinsters Ink.

———. 1984. *Sister Outsider*. Trumansberg, N.Y.: Crossing Press.

Maitland, Sara. 1996. "Final Payment." Review of *The Shadow Man*, by Mary Gordon. *Commonweal* (May 17): 17–18.

"Man Shoots Wife, Kills Two Children and Self." 1946. *Los Angeles Times* (Nov. 15): sec. 1, p. 1.

Marlan, Dawn. 1996. Review of *Girl, Interrupted*, by Susanna Kaysen. *Chicago Review* 41, no. 1: 93–103.

Max, D. T. 1998. "The Big Mac of Medicine." Review of *Prozac Diary*, by Lauren Slater. *New York Times Book Review* (Nov. 15): 13.

Maynard, Joyce. 1998. *At Home in the World*. New York: Picador.

McDermott, Alice. 1987. *That Night*. New York: Delta.

McDowell, Deborah E. 1998. "Darkness Visible." Review of *My Brother*, by Jamaica Kincaid. *Women's Review of Books* (Jan.): 1–3.

McLaughlin, Thomas. 1996. *Street Smarts and Critical Theory: Listening to the Vernacular*. Madison: Univ. of Wisconsin Press.

Merkin, Daphne. 1998. Review of *At Home in the World*, by Joyce Maynard. *New Yorker* (Aug. 24–31): 154.

Merleau-Ponty, Maurice. 1973. *The Phenomenology of Perception.* Translated by Colin Wilson. New York: Humanities Press.

Messud, Claire. 1998. "A Family Apart." Review of *Shame*, by Annie Ernaux. *New York Times Book Review* (Sept. 13): 16.

Michener, Charles, and Andrea Sachs. 1995. "They've Got a Secret." *Time* 23 (Oct. 23): 94–95.

Miller, Alice. 1994. *Drama of the Gifted Child: The Search for the True Self.* Translated by Ruth Ward. New York: Basic Books.

Miller, Nancy K. 1996. *Bequest and Betrayal: Memoirs of a Parent's Death.* New York: Oxford Univ. Press.

————. 1999. "Ethnographers of the Self." Review of *Shame*, by Annie Ernaux. *Women's Review of Books* (July): 35–36.

Moore, Suzanne. 1997. "How Was It for Me?" Review of *The Kiss: A Memoir*, by Kathryn Harrison. *New Statesman* (Aug. 15): 44–45.

Moorman, Margaret. 1997. "Fugue State." Review of *Memory Slips*, by Linda Katherine Cutting. *New York Times Book Review* (Feb. 9): 18.

Morrison, Andrew P., M.D. 1996. *The Culture of Shame.* New York: Ballantine.

Morrison, Toni. 1987. *Song of Solomon.* New York: Plume.

————. 1998. "Strangers." *New Yorker* (Oct. 12): 69–70.

"Murder-Suicide Probe Closed." 1946. *Pasadena Star News* (Nov. 18): sec. 2, p. 9.

"Mystery Woman Linked to Suicide-Murder Case." 1946. *Los Angeles Times* (Nov. 16): sec. 1, p. 1.

Nathanson, Donald. 1999. Foreword to *Scenes of Shame: Psychoanalysis, Shame, and Writing*, edited by Joseph Adamson and Hilary Clark. Albany: SUNY Univ. Press.

Okoampa-Ahoofe, Kwame, Jr. 1998. "Kincaid's *My Brother* Is a Harrowing Read." Review of *My Brother*, by Jamaica Kincaid. *New York Amsterdam News* (Jan. 1): 21.

P. P. R. 1996. Review of *Two or Three Things I Know for Sure*, by Dorothy Allison. *Times Literary Supplement* (Feb. 23): 32.

Paul, Annie Murphy. 1998. "Two Years Later, a Quieter Mind." *Psychology Today* 31, no. 1: 88.

Pela, Robert L. 1997. "Death Watch." Review of *My Brother*, by Jamaica Kincaid. *Advocate* (Dec. 9): 82.

Pipher, Mary. 1994. *Reviving Ophelia: Saving the Selves of Adolescent Girls.* New York: Ballantine.

Plummer, Ken. 1995. *Telling Sexual Stories: Power, Change, and Social Worlds.* New York: Routledge.

Powers, Elizabeth. 1997. "Doing Daddy Down." Review of *The Kiss: A Memoir*, by Kathryn Harrison; and *The Shadow Man*, by Mary Gordon. *Commentary* (June): 38–42.

Pritchard, William H. 1996. "The Cave of Memory." Review of *The Shadow Man*, by Mary Gordon. *New York Times Book Review* (May 26): 5.

Raine, Nancy Venable. 1994. "Returns of the Day." *New York Times Magazine* (Oct. 2): 34.

————. 1998. *After Silence: Rape and My Journey Back*. New York: Crown.

Rich, Adrienne. 1979. *On Lies, Secrets, and Silence*. New York: Norton.

Roemer, Michael. 1995. *Telling Stories: Postmodernism and the Invalidation of Traditional Narrative*. Lanham, Md.: Rowman and Littlefield.

Rogers, Susan Fox. 1997. "Open Heart Surgery." Review of *The Heart's Progress: A Memoir*, by Claudia Bepko. *Lambda Book Report* (May): 12–13.

Roiphe, Katie. 1993. *The Morning After: Sex, Fear, and Feminism on Campus*. New York: Little, Brown.

Rorty, Richard. 1989. *Contingency, Irony, and Solidarity*. New York: Cambridge Univ. Press.

————. 1998. *Achieving Our Country*. Cambridge: Harvard Univ. Press.

Rosenblatt, Louise M. 1994. *The Reader, the Text, the Poem: The Transactional Theory of the Literary Work*. Carbondale: Southern Illinois Univ. Press.

Ross, Lillian. 1998. *Here but Not Here: A Love Story*. New York: Random House.

Ruta, Suzanne. 1996. "Feet of Clay." Review of *The Shadow Man*, by Mary Gordon. *Women's Review of Books* (July): 26–27.

Sachs, Andrea. 1994. "The Unconfessional Confessionalist." Review of *Girl, Interrupted*, by Susanna Kaysen. *Time* (July 11): 60.

Sarton, May. 1980. *Recovering: A Journal, 1978–1979*. New York: Norton.

Scheff, Thomas J., and Suzanne M. Retzinger. 1991. *Emotions and Violence: Shame and Rage in Destructive Conflicts*. Lexington, Mass.: Lexington Books.

Schoemer, Karen. 1995. Review of *The Liar's Club*, by Mary Karr. *Newsweek* (Aug. 7): 61.

Shapiro, Dani. 1997. *Picturing the Wreck*. New York: Plume.

————. 1998a. "The Secret Wife." *New Yorker* (Aug. 24–31): 80–88.

————. 1998b. *Slow Motion: A True Story*. New York: Random House.

Shapiro, Susan. 1998. "Literary Affairs." Review of *Here but Not Here: A Love Story*, by Lillian Ross. *Village Voice* (June 9): 157.

Shengold, Leonard. 1989. *Soul Murder: The Effects of Childhood Abuse and Deprivation*. New Haven: Yale Univ. Press.

Shnayerson, Michael. 1997. "Women Behaving Badly." *Vanity Fair* (Feb.): 54–60.

Shweder, Richard A. 1998. "To Speak of the Unspeakable." Review of *After Silence: Rape and My Journey Back*, by Nancy Venable Raine. *New York Times Book Review* (Sept. 20): 13.

Silverman, Sue William. 1996. *Because I Remember Terror, Father, I Remember You*. Athens: Univ. of Georgia Press.

Sinfield, Alan. 1998. "Cultural Materialism, *Othello*, and the Politics of Plausibility." In *Literary Theory: An Anthology*, edited by Julie Rivkin and Michael Ryan, 804–26. Malden, Mass.: Blackwell.

Slater, Lauren. 1996. *Welcome to My Country*. New York: Doubleday.

———. 1998. *Prozac Diary*. New York: Random House.

———. 1999. "Prozac Mother and Child." *New York Times Magazine* (Oct. 17): 115–18.

Smith, Dinitia. 1998. "Writers as Plunderers." *New York Times* (Oct. 24): A19, A21.

Smith, Janna Malamud. 1997. *Private Matters: In Defense of the Personal Life*. Reading, Mass.: Addison-Wesley.

Spender, Dale. 1980. *Man Made Language*. London: Routledge and Kegan Paul.

Streitfeld, David. 1998. "Betrayal Between the Covers." *Washington Post* (Oct. 27): D1-D3.

Sunday's Children. 1994. Script by Ingmar Bergman. Directed by Peter Bergman. First Run Features.

Swift, Graham. 1983. *Waterland*. New York: Vintage.

Theroux, Paul. 1998a. "Memory and Invention." *New York Times Book Review* (Nov. 1): 39.

———. 1998b. *Sir Vidia's Shadow: A Friendship Across Five Continents*. Boston: Houghton Mifflin.

Tompkins, Jane. 1993. "Me and My Shadow." In *The Intimate Critique: Autobiographical Literary Criticism*, edited by Diane P. Freedman, Olivia Frey, and Frances Murphy Zauhar, 23–40. Durham: Duke Univ. Press.

———. 1995. Foreword to *Private Voices, Public Lives: Women Speak on the Literary Life*, edited by Nancy Owen Nelson, xiii-xv. Denton: Univ. of North Texas Press.

———. 1996. *Life in School: What the Teacher Learned*. Reading, Mass.: Addison-Wesley.

Toufexis, Anastasia. 1995. "Sliding Past Saturn." Review of *An Unquiet Mind*, by Kay Redfield Jamison. *Time* (Sept. 11): 83.

Udovitch, Mim. 1997. "The Evil Dads." Review of *The Kiss: A Memoir*, by Kathryn Harrison; and *What Falls Away: A Memoir*, by Mia Farrow. *New York* (Mar. 17): 57–58.

Wachman, Gay. 1997. "Dying in Antigua." Review of *My Brother*, by Jamaica Kincaid. *Nation* (Nov. 3): 43–44.

Weedon, Chris. 1987. *Feminist Practice and Poststructuralist Theory*. Oxford: Basil Blackwell.

Wells, Susan. 1996. "Rogue Cops and Health Care: What Do We Want from Public Writing?" *College Composition and Communication* 47 (Oct.): 325–41.

Williams, Linda M. 1999. "Damage Control." Review of *After Silence: Rape and My Journey Back,* by Nancy Venable Raine. *Women's Review of Books* (Apr.): 21–22.

Winnicott, D. W. 1971. *Playing and Reality.* New York: Tavistock.

Wisechild, Louise. 1988. *The Obsidian Mirror: An Adult Healing from Incest.* Seattle: Seal Press.

Wolf, Naomi. 1993. *Fire with Fire: The New Female Power and How It Will Change the Twenty-first Century.* New York: Random House.

Wolff, Tobias. 1997. "Literary Conceits." *New York Times* (Apr. 6): 19E.

Woolf, Virginia. 1981. *A Room of One's Own.* New York: Harcourt Brace.

Wurmser, Leon. 1981. *The Mask of Shame.* Baltimore: Johns Hopkins Univ. Press.

INDEX

CREDITS

WRITING AMERICAN WOMEN
Carol A. Kolmerten, ed.

Titles in this series include: